Black Legislators in Louisiana
During Reconstruction

CHARLES VINCENT

Black Legislators in Louisiana During Reconstruction

LOUISIANA STATE UNIVERSITY PRESS·Baton Rouge

ISBN 0–8071–0089–7
Library of Congress Catalog Card Number 74–77328
Copyright © 1976 by Louisiana State University Press
Manufactured in the United States of America

*To my parents
and to my daughter,
Shari Delise*

Contents

Illustrations and Maps

Acknowledgments

I should like to express my appreciation to the staffs of the following archives and libraries: the National Archives, Library of Congress, Moorland–Spingarn Research Center at Howard University, New Orleans Public Library, Louisiana State Archives and Records, Howard–Tilton Library at Tulane University, Louisiana State University Department of Archives and Manuscripts, Southern University Library, and Amistad Research Center at Dillard University. Special thanks are due Evangeline Lynch and her staff at the Louisiana Room, Louisiana State University Library, for making materials available.

I appreciate the aid, critical comments, suggestions, and encouragement of many other persons, including Thomas Holt, Howard University; Marcus B. Christian and Joseph Logsdon, University of New Orleans; John W. Blassingame, Yale University; Shirley M. Jackson, Bowling Green State University, Bowling Green, Ohio; E. Russ Williams, Jr., Northeast Louisiana University; Mark T. Carleton, Louisiana State University; James Lewis, Master Mason, Baton Rouge; Joseph A. Cardozo, Southern University; and Simuel M. Austin photographer, Southern University. The staff at the Louisiana State University Press, especially my editor, Martha L. Hall, have been of invaluable aid in the final preparation of the manuscript.

I am deeply grateful to my major professor, T. Harry Williams, for the patient and helpful guidance he gave as I prepared the study as a dissertation. I received financial aid from the Southern Fellowship Fund of Atlanta, Georgia, over a three-year period during my graduate career, a support I sincerely appreciate. Above all, I thank the members of my family, especially my wife, Deloris, whose help in good times and bad went a long way toward helping complete this work.

Introduction

The performance and numerical strength of blacks in state legislatures during Reconstruction have been a source of much historical debate. Most earlier writers observe that blacks dominated the legislatures and local offices. These studies characterize the number of blacks in positions of political power as a vicious ruling majority. Their incompetence, the story goes, contributed to an end of honest government.

The origins and abilities of black leadership were often distorted by contemporary newspapers. According to many papers, a majority of the new black officials were illiterate field hands, who had little political knowledge. Although it is true that most were never trained to hold elective offices and were newcomers to political positions, black leadership had been tested on the battlefields of the Civil War, and many blacks had organized battalions and regiments for the Union cause. P. B. S. Pinchback, an officeholder during Reconstruction, spoke of black participation for the Union: "These men had made many sacrifices to get the positions they held, many of them had given up lucrative situations, quit remunerative business, spent all or nearly all they possessed in organizing their companies, subsisting the men for a time out of their own means." Such subsequent leaders as James H. Ingraham, Emile Detiege, Caesar and Felix Antoine, Robert H. Isabelle, Jean B. Jourdain, Jacques A. Gla, William Barrett, and Pinchback himself were a few of the many who, despite the indignities they endured, prepared themselves for leadership roles in Reconstruction politics. Historically, New Orleans already had a large, wealthy, well-educated, articulate free black population, paying taxes on more than $15 million worth of property in 1860. In addition, former slaves fought as soldiers and attended regimental night schools in preparation for freedom and leadership. Other elements providing training and aid to the emerging black leaders were the black churches, black family, urban setting, Freedmen's Bureau, jobs in the Customhouse, native shrewdness, and skills and education acquired before emancipation. Blacks were generally elected from parishes containing a black majority. Typical of these were parishes along the Mississippi and Red rivers and in South Louisiana.

In addition to their service as soldiers, blacks, as officials, urged a broad range of progressive legislation to benefit the entire citizenry. Even before blacks obtained the franchise and while the South was under Presidential Reconstruction, the black press in New Orleans opposed the Black Codes and segregation. They opposed unfair labor contracts because such practices and laws debased blacks and whites, and they opposed the Democratic state legislature's effort to pass the "quadroon" bill, which was designed to permit persons with a certain percentage of white blood to vote. Blacks also expressed unity in terms of support for teaching and organizing the freedmen, "our dormant partners." The Reconstruction acts of 1867, which were passed under congressional leadership, quickened the pace of black participation. Black delegates in the Constitutional Convention of 1867–1868 urged statewide public education, civil rights, universal suffrage, an extensive bill of rights, liberal homestead laws, and an excise tax on liquor, as well as opposition to the stringent disfranchisement clause. Their legislative programs and demands were singularly lacking in vindictiveness; often their programs were designed to finance internal improvements, education, and relief and to establish social reforms. Black members never received appointive positions in proportion to their numbers and were seldom assigned to important committees.

Thus, I have concentrated more especially on black legislators than on the economic and social progress of blacks. Although a deeper look at their economic and social progress would make a more extensive study, I was hindered by the short supply of primary sources on the general subject. Therefore, I am almost limited to the legislators themselves, giving all available information on their educational backgrounds, social statuses, wealth, age, and more important, their committee assignments, legislative demands, programs, and how they voted.

In examining black political participation, I found little evidence to substantiate the traditionalist view that these leaders were vengeful or ignorant or that they promoted all, or any great portion, of unsound or corrupt legislation. Indeed, most of their programs were intended to benefit citizens of both races in Louisiana.

Black Legislators in Louisiana
During Reconstruction

CHAPTER I

Black Leadership During the Civil War

Part of the drama of the Civil War experience for southern blacks was their own participation in the fight for their freedom. For the first time in Louisiana's history, blacks served in large numbers as soldiers, and in serving they helped to preserve the Union. The war was also an experience in political education for blacks. Many who would later serve as leaders in Reconstruction emerged during the war.

At the outbreak of the war the white population of Louisiana was apprehensive about the presence in their midst of a large black population, slave and free. Whites naturally wondered if blacks, especially the free blacks in New Orleans, would be docile during the conflict or attempt to sabotage the war efforts.

Initially, free blacks expressed a sentiment to fight for the Confederate cause. As early as January 20, 1861, a small group of them petitioned Governor Thomas O. Moore, offering their service to the state. The petition affirmed their faithfulness to the government and asserted that they "formed part of our best population" and had "attained the highest position in art, commerce and science." They recalled their ancestors' service with General Andrew Jackson in 1814–1815 as the Battalion of Free Men of Color. According to newspaper reports, these free Negroes held a meeting to discuss possible participation in the Confederate war effort on April 22, 1861. Their announced purpose was to organize military companies and to volunteer for state service in case of any enemy attack.[1]

In late April, 1861, Jordan Noble and approximately fifteen hundred men of the creole free Negro class assembled at this downtown meeting. On May 12, 1861, the governor issued a proclamation providing for the enrollment of as many free Negroes as were necessary to form a regiment, staffed by black officers; this unit was to aid in protecting New Orleans in the event of Union attack. Immediately, in early 1862, these companies were organized. They were called the Native Guards, Louisiana Militia, Confederate States. Most companies armed and uniformed themselves at their own expense, and captains' commissions were given to the black organizers. These units were soon making appearances at local ceremonial parades because the commanding general of Confederate forces, Major General Mansfield Lovell, was reluctant to recognize them in other capacities and refused to issue them arms and supplies.[2]

When the Union capture of New Orleans ended in the retreat of the Confederate forces on April 28, 1862, the Native Guards refused to leave the city. They did not desire to leave their homes to fight with the Confederate forces elsewhere, and it is doubtful that they had wanted to join the Confederate service in the first place.

1. "Appeal in Behalf of the Colored People of N[ew] O[rleans] & Offering Their Services," January 20, 1861, in Rebel Archives, Record Division, War Department, Louisiana State Archives, Baton Rouge; Roland C. McConnell, *Negro Troops of Antebellum Louisiana: A History of the Battalion of Free Men of Color* (Baton Rouge: Louisiana State University Press, 1968), 52–53; New Orleans *True Delta*, April 23, 1861, cited in Mary F. Berry, "Negro Troops in Blue and Gray: The Louisiana Native Guards, 1861–1863," *Louisiana History*, VIII (Spring, 1967), 167; Donald E. Everett, "Ben Butler and the Louisiana Native Guards, 1861–1862," *Journal of Southern History*, XXIV (May, 1958), 202. See also David C. Rankin, "The Origins of Black Leadership in New Orleans During Reconstruction," *Journal of Southern History*, XL (August, 1974), 433–34.

2. Noble owned real estate valued at $1,500 and personal property worth $500. U. S. Census Reports, cited in Donald E. Everett, "Demands of New Orleans Free Colored Population for Political Equality, 1862–1865," *Louisiana Historical Quarterly*, XXXVIII (April, 1955), 48; Alice Dunbar-Nelson, "People of Color in Louisiana, Part II," *Journal of Negro History*, II (January, 1917), 67. *The War of the Rebellion: A Compilation of the Official Records of the Union and Confederate Armies* (Washington, D. C.: Government Printing Office, 1880–1901), Ser. I, Vol. XV, 556, hereinafter cited as *Official Records*; Everett, "Ben Butler," 204–205; Berry, "Negro Troops," 167.

Their complex motives are difficult to appraise. Apparently, many free men of color had been forced to join the Confederate cause, and this brief show of sympathy, for most of them, was simply an effort to save their lives and property. Testimony given to the Select Commission on the New Orleans Riot of 1866 lends support to this conclusion. Charles W. Gibbons, an educated free black man who had lived his entire life in New Orleans, testified that at the outbreak of the war, white leadership urged all free blacks to aid the seceding states. "A majority of the population of the city of New Orleans," Gibbons contended, "had to do the same thing [join] in order to save themselves"; but they had not gone "with the intention of fighting for the rebels." These soldiers had planned to "drop their arms" the moment they saw the Union flag. Gibbons himself had been warned by a policeman that he had a choice of either entering the Confederate service or being lynched. After this warning, he joined the Negro company organized by Captain Jourdain but resigned after serving two weeks. In reply to other questions, Gibbons stated that some of the free black men in the city refused to join the Confederate army despite threats to life and property.[3] Other reasons could be their historically demonstrated loyalty to New Orleans and the *de facto* government, be it Spanish, French, or American. Others were owners of considerable property, including slaves, which would be lost if the South were defeated. Evidence is lacking, however, to substantiate the conclusion that a free Negro and Confederate alliance was based on their common interest in slaveholding.

When General Benjamin Butler learned of this organization in New Orleans, and after he was petitioned by the blacks, he sent for several of the most prominent black men of the city and inquired why they had accepted service "under the confederate

3. *House Reports*, 39th Cong., 2nd Sess., No. 16, pp. 124–26; Although this testimony was possibly influenced by the race riots and setting of the late 1860s, it provides perhaps the only statements we have about the free black activities during the early occupation; Rodolphe Lucien Desdunes, *Our People and Our History*, trans. and ed. Sister Dorothea Olga McCants (Baton Rouge: Louisiana State University Press, 1973), 118, 120–25; Berry, "Negro Troops," 172–73.

Government which was set up for the purpose of holding their brethren . . . in eternal slavery." They told of threats to their lives and property. Others thought that their service in the Confederacy would advance them closer to white acceptance, though they claimed that they had longed, and still wished, to throw the weight of their class behind the Union cause. Pickney Benton Stewart Pinchback, later lieutenant governor, indicated that these men had made "many sacrifices," to fight for the Union, subsisting for a time "out of their own means."[4]

General Butler was cautious about their offer. He was not convinced that free blacks would fight. However, one of his subordinates, Brigadier General John W. Phelps, a volunteer officer, believed that the South had missed an opportunity by not employing blacks, even slaves, in its armies. He believed so firmly in using black soldiers that he was accused of enticing them away from the plantations.[5] In a letter to General Butler on July 30, 1862, Phelps said: "I would raise the three regiments proposed in a short time without holding out any inducements or offering any reward. I have now upward of three hundred Africans organized into five companies, who are willing and ready to show their devotion to our cause in any way that it may be put to the test. *They are willing to submit to anything than to slavery.*"

In reply, Butler, who had earlier surrendered slaves to masters loyal to the Union, suggested that the "contraband" should be used only to cut down trees and build fortifications in the camps. Phelps indignantly refused to serve as a "slave driver" and handed in his resignation. Butler rejected the resignation because

4. Charles Wesley, "The Employment of Negroes as Soldiers in the Confederate Army," in *Journal of Negro History*, IV (July, 1919), 243–44; See also Benjamin F. Butler, *Autobiography* (Boston: A. M. Thayer Co., 1892), 505 (commonly referred to as *Butler's Book*); undated draft of speech, "On the Negro in the Civil War," in P. B. S. Pinchback Papers, Box 2, Manuscript Division, Moorland-Spingarn Research Center, Howard University, Washington, D.C.

5. Howard P. Johnson, "New Orleans under General Butler," *Louisiana Historical Quarterly*, XXIV (April, 1941), 88; Richard S. West, *Lincoln's Scapegoat General: A Life of Benjamin Butler* (Boston: Houghton Mifflin Co., 1965), 176; Louis S. Gertis, "From Contraband to Freedman: Federal Policy toward Southern Blacks, 1861–1865" (Ph.D. dissertation, University of Wisconsin, 1969), 142–48, 150–152.

President Lincoln had not indicated his policy on using black troops. In these exchanges Phelps informed Butler of the recent visit he had had from the "free colored men of New Orleans" who proposed to raise several regiments of volunteers. When they visited Butler himself in mid-August he seemed more willing to accept their offer and was impressed by their desire to wear the uniform of the United States Army. He described the darkest as being about the complexion of "the late Daniel Webster." With assurance from the black officers that the erstwhile Confederate Native Guards could be re-formed if they were armed. Butler prepared to issue an order for the enlistment of free black men in the military service of the United States.[6] Several weeks later, he informed the secretary of war of his intentions to muster Negro regiments formerly recognized by the Confederacy.

In General Order No. 63, issued August 22, 1862, Butler stressed the precedent of the Native Guards as a legally organized part of the state militia. His order was of a verbatim reiteration of the commission issued to black officers and troops and Governor Moore's order of March 24, 1861, that had legalized Louisiana's Confederate Negro troops. Butler's order stated: "A large portion of his militia force of the State of Louisiana are willing to take service in the volunteer forces of the United States and be enrolled and organized to 'defend their homes from ruthless invaders,' to protect their wives and children and kindred from wrong and outrage, to shield their property from being seized by bad men, and to defend the flag of their native country as their father did under Jackson at Chalmette against Pakenham and his myrmidons, carrying the black flag of 'Beauty

6. New Orleans *Daily Picayune*, August 27, 1862, May 29, 1863; Dudley T. Cornish, *The Sable Arm: Negro Troops in the Union Army, 1861–1865* (New York: W. W. Norton Co., 1956), 58–63; *Private and Official Correspondence of General Benjamin F. Butler, During the Period of the Civil War* (Mass.: The Plimton Press, 1917), II, 142–48, (Hereinafter cited as *Butler Correspondence*). An act of Congress on March 13, 1862, had prohibited army and navy officers from employing any of these forces "for the purpose of returning fugitives from service or labor who may have escaped from any persons to whom such service or labor is claimed to due." West, *Lincoln's Scapegoat General*, 180–82; Gertis, "From Contraband," 149. Secretary of War Edwin M. Stanton had told General Butler to use his own discretion.

and Booty.'" Butler did not stop here. He expressed appreciation of their motives, and praised their "well-known loyalty and patriotism." He then ordered that all members of the Native Guard and other free blacks recognized by the late governor be organized; officers were to be appointed, paid, given rations, arms and equipment similar to "other volunteer troops of the United States, subject to the approval of the President of the United States." Finally, the order required that all such persons should "report themselves at the Touro Charity building, Front Levee Street, New Orleans, where proper officers will muster them into the service of the United States."[7]

Free blacks responded favorably, and a large crowd gathered the following day in the designated building. More than five thousand free black men were enlisted during the first week, and in fourteen days a regiment was organized. This order provided the stairway on which much black leadership ascended and eventually emerged as a factor in Louisiana politics. The black press, in the form of *L' Union*, was born in late September, 1862. It declared *liberty* to be the objective of the war.[8]

Black men assisted in recruiting and enlisting the units. They were anxious to see the war as one of liberation. Charles H. Hughes, a thirty-four-year-old free black resident of New Orleans since 1849, testified that he recruited the first company of black soldiers for the Federal army under General Butler. Although he did not join the army because of his physical disabilities, he lived in the city during the occupation. He was a baker, and for a short while he cooked for a captain of the Thirteenth Connecticut Regiment. In addition, he recruited both officers and enlisted men for the Second and Fourteenth regiments.

7. Butler to Halleck, August 22, 1862, Butler to Stanton, August 16, 1862, in *Official Records*, Ser. I, Vol. XV, 549, 557.

8. Joseph T. Wilson, *Black Phalanx: A History of the Negro Soldier of the United States in the Wars of 1775–1812, 1861–1865* (Hartford: American Publishing Co., 1888), 179. See also Cornish, *Sable Arm*, 66–67; Donald Everett, "Free People of Color in New Orleans, 1803–1865" (Ph.D. dissertation, Tulane University, 1952), 278–79; New Orleans *L'Union*, September 27, 1862. See Chap. II herein; "New Orleans Riot: Report of the Select Committee," 102–103, 105, 208–209.

Another active recruiter was Jean B. Jourdain, a thirty-year-old cigar maker and free black man who was born in New Orleans. He received a commission in the Federal army and helped raise a company in which he served briefly as a lieutenant. Although Jourdain, a future legislator, lost "over $6,000 during the war," he had "property still left amounting to about $5,000" in 1866. This consisted of real estate as well as personal property. [9]

In other areas of the state, blacks sought to participate. Caesar C. Antoine, free born, who became later lieutenant governor during 1872–1876, also joined the Union army as soon as the opportunity presented itself. When the Confederate general Richard Taylor moved on Baton Rouge in the winter of 1862, Antoine, a barber, put up his shutters and immediately exchanged his scissors and comb for sword and revolver. Thus equipped, he sought black soldiers, and in forty-eight hours he raised a company of sixty-day men, who were mustered in as Company I, Seventh Regiment, Louisiana Militia, with Antoine as captain. At their head, he served in the Brashear City area where Union Brigadier General Godfrey Weitzel had built an entrenchment to block Confederate entry to Baton Rouge or New Orleans.[10]

James Lewis, a native of Woodville, Mississippi, who later became prominent in Reconstruction politics as administrator of public improvements in New Orleans, received a commission for raising two companies of black infantry. When the war broke out, Lewis was a steward on board the Confederate transport steamer *Desoto* and served on this vessel in the fighting around New Madrid. During this time, the first news of emancipation reached him. Gladdened by the hope of liberation of his race, knowing that the freedom fight needed all its friends, Lewis made his way to New Orleans, then under the control of Union forces. Along with other black men, he petitioned the commanding officer of the Department of the Gulf for permission to raise

9. *House Reports*, 39th Cong., 2nd Sess., No. 16, pp. 208–209.

10. The Honorable C. C. Antoine Scrapbook, Black Heritage Room, Southern University Library, Baton Rouge; Civil War Pension Files, Records of the Veterans Administration, RG 15, NA.

regiments of black troops. He received the authority and served as captain of Company K, one of the two black infantry companies he raised and mustered into service in September, 1862.[11]

The other companies had equally qualified black leaders and officers. James H. Ingraham, state senator during Reconstruction, organized a company of troops and was later promoted to captain. A native of Mississippi and a carpenter, Ingraham was enlisted in September, 1862, and assumed command of Company E, First Infantry Corps d'Afrique in August, 1863, after his heroic fighting at the Port Hudson campaign. He later became a colonel in the Third Regiment, Louisiana State Militia.[12] He was forced to resign in March, 1864, under pressure to remove black officers.

Robert H. Isabelle had been one of the first blacks to be commissioned in October, 1862. Although he had joined the army "with the sole object of laboring for the good of the Union," he found that racial prejudice had not ceased as it had during the War of 1812. This prejudice prevented the "cordial harmony among officers which is indispensable for the success of the army." He resigned in March, 1863, but reenlisted in July, 1863. He would later serve as a delegate to the constitutional convention and as a legislator.[13]

Another black man, William B. Barrett, recruited a battalion of free men of color in August, 1862. In October he was mustered and he resigned the next year, July, 1863. Northern-born, Barrett would serve as a legislator and customhouse official during Reconstruction.[14]

Pinchback, the son of a white Mississippi planter and slave mother, was a recruiter and officer. Born May 10, 1837, near Macon, Georgia, while his mother was in transit from Virginia to Mississippi, Pinchback was educated in Ohio, attending the

11. William Simmons, *Men of Mark: Eminent, Progressive and Rising* (Cleveland: Geo. M. Rewell Co., 1887), 954–55.

12. Carded Military Service Record, RG 94, NA.

13. *Ibid.*; Civil War Pension Files, Records of the Veteran Administration, RG 15, NA.

14. Civil War Pension Files, Records of the Veteran Administration, RG 15, NA.

Gilmore High School until his father died. While still a youth, Pinchback secured a job working on the Miami Canal, running from Cincinnati to Toledo, Ohio. Later, from 1854 to 1861, he worked for steamboats on the Red, Missouri, and Mississippi lines, and reached the highest position attainable by a black, that of a steward. On May 10, 1862, in Yazoo City, Mississippi, he abandoned the steamer *Alonzo Child*, on which he served as a steward, and ran the Confederate blockade and arrived in New Orleans two days later and enlisted in the First Louisiana Infantry, a white regiment of the Union army. Although he was a private, Pinchback attracted the attention of his commanding officers; when it was discovered that he had Negro blood, he was detailed for more important service.[15]

When General Butler issued his order on August 22, 1862, calling upon the free black men of Louisiana to aid the Union, Pinchback, who had recently been released from a two-month jail term because of a fight with his brother-in-law, immediately applied for duty and was assigned by the following authority:

New Orleans, August 27, 1862

By authority vested in me by Major General B. F. Butler, Pickney Pinchback is hereby authorized to recruit a company of Louisiana Volunteers for the United States Army.
S. H. Stafford,
Superintendent Recruiting
Arrangement.[16]

Pinchback opened an office for recruiting black soldiers on the corner of Bienville and Villeré streets in New Orleans, and by

15. Simmons, *Men of Mark*, 775, 760–61; Louisiana State University Purchasing Department to James Campfield, February 24, 1923, in P. B. S. Pinchback Papers, Howard-Tilton Memorial Library, Tulane University, New Orleans; New Orleans *Times*, March 11, 1872; *House Miscellaneous Documents*, 41st Cong., 2nd Sess., No. 154, p. 286; Biographical Sketch of P. B. S. Pinchback in New Orleans *Semi-Weekly Louisianian*, July 6, 1871; James Haskins, *Pickney Benton Stewart Pinchback* (New York: Macmillan Co., 1973), 24–26.

16. Quoted in Agnes S. Grosz, "The Political Career of Pickney Benton Stewart Pinchback," in *Louisiana Historical Quarterly*, XXVII (April, 1944), 6.

September 6, 1862, he had organized Company A, Second Louisiana Native Guards. He was commissioned as its captain on October 12 and served in this position until September 11, 1863.

Because of the treatment received by the black officers at the hands of white Union officers, Pinchback left the army with a feeling of injured self-respect, as he indicated in his letter of resignation:

> FORT PIKE, Louisiana, September 10, 1863.
> General: In the organization of the regiment I am attached to (Twentieth Corps d'Afrique) I find nearly all the officers inimical to me, and I can forsee nothing but dissatisfaction and discontent, which will make my position very disagreeable indeed. I would therefore, respectfully tender my resignation, as I am confident by so doing I best serve the interest of the regiment.
> I have the honor to be, sir, very respectfully, your obedient servant.
>
> > P. B. S. Pinchback,
> > Captain Second Louisiana
> > National Guard[17]

Shortly thereafter, Pinchback was reinstated in his position and was given special authorization by General Nathaniel P. Banks to recruit a company of black cavalry. Banks, who replaced Butler in December, 1862, inaugurated a new scheme in May by which all black troops were placed in a unit designated *Corps d'Afrique*. Then he applied for a commission as captain in another effort to be mustered into the Union army. This request was disapproved by Banks, because no authority existed for the employment of black people in any capacity except as noncommissioned officers and privates.[18]

Many white officers, influenced by racial prejudice, contended that blacks would not fight. But ample evidence exists to demonstrate that blacks welcomed the opportunity to prove themselves. The black officer James H. Ingraham echoed the feelings

17. Biographical sketch in New Orleans *Semi-Weekly Louisianian*, July 6, 1871.
18. Grosz, "P. B. S. Pinchback," 7.

of most when he asserted in late 1862 before they had met the
enemy: "We are still anxious, as we have ever been, to show the
world that the latent courage of the Africans is aroused, and that
while fighting under the American flag, we are and will be a wall of
fire and death to the enemies of this country, our birthplace."[19]

Not only were the free blacks willing to serve, but the slaves
demonstrated a desire to participate actively in Union work.
Many slaves who were given time off for Christmas in December,
1862, decided to extend it to a permanent vacation. When the
Emancipation Proclamation freed more slaves in the areas, they
entered Union camps to enlist. The tendency to leave work
accelerated when Union forces invaded a plantation. One writer
described what happened on the Elmwood plantation, just below
Alexandria, as Banks's army approached up the Red River: "The
arrival of the advance of the yankee alone turned the negroes
crazy. They became utterly demoralized at once . . . restraint
was at an end. All business was suspended . . . no work was done
and the place swarmed with negroes from other places." By 1863
slaves were admitted to the military.[20]

They flocked into the Union camps. Most brought their
families. These new glimpses of freedom brought many advantages to blacks. They were jubilant to be away from the daily toil
and the whip. Almost immediately they began to improve
themselves—many learned the forbidden alphabet and numbers.
General Nathaniel P. Banks inaugurated a system of education to
teach reading and writing to blacks. At one camp the men were
"drilled four hours a day and had one hour in school."[21] Henry

19. New York *National Anti-Slavery Standard*, November 20, 1862, quoted in
John W. Blassingame, "A Social and Economic Study of the Negro in New Orleans,
1860–1880" (Ph.D. dissertation, Yale University, 1971), 100.

20. John D. Winters, *The Civil War in Louisiana* (Baton Rouge: Louisiana State
University Press, 1963), 238; Jefferson D. Bragg, *Louisiana in the Confederacy* (Baton
Rouge: Louisiana State University Press, 1941), 211; Joe Gray Taylor, "Slavery in Civil
War Louisiana," *Louisiana History*, VIII (Winter, 1967), 28–29; Bell I. Wiley, *Southern
Negroes, 1861–1865* (New Haven: Yale University Press, 1938), 44–62.

21. Kenneth E. Shewmaker and Andrew K. Prinz (eds.), "A Yankee in Louisiana:
Selections from the Diary and Correspondence of Henry R. Gardner, 1862–1866," in

Demas, later a political leader of St. John the Baptist Parish, Cain Sartain of Carroll Parish, Vincent Dickerson of St. James Parish, and Frederick R. Wright of Terrebonne Parish, all learned how to read around campfires.

The sense of dedication felt by black officers was later reflected in their conduct during the war. Outstanding among them were Captain F. Ernest Dumas and Captain André Cailloux, both of whom were free before the war. Dumas served in the Second Regiment and organized and attached a company of his own slaves to this regiment. He was later promoted to the rank of major and commanded two companies at Pascagoula, Mississippi. He received several commendations.[22] N. U. Daniels, colonel of the Second Louisiana Native Guards Volunteers, made the following report after Dumas rescued a company of his men from almost certain annihilation:

> The expedition was a perfect success, accomplished all that was intended; resulting in the repulse of the enemy in every engagement with great loss. . . .
> I would particularly call the attention of the Department to Major F. E. Dumas, Capt. Villeverd, and Lieuts. Jones and Martin, who were constantly in the thickest of the fight, and by their unflinching bravery, and admirable handling of their commands, contributed to the success of the attack, and reflected great honor upon the flag under and for which they so nobly struggled. Repeated instances of individuals bravery among the troops might be mentioned.[23]

Captain Cailloux's identity with his race could never be mistaken, for he prided himself on being the blackest individual in the

Louisiana History, V (Summer, 1964), 278, 287; John W. Blassingame, "Union Army as an Educational Institution for Negroes, 1862–1865," in *Journal of Negro Education*, XXXIV (Spring, 1965), 152–59; Fred Harrington, *Fighting Politican Major General N. P. Banks* (Philadelphia: University of Pennsylvania Press, 1948), 107–10.

22. Wilson, *Black Phalanx*, 176.

23. *Ibid.*, 211. The other officers mentioned are also blacks. Butler said of Dumas: "He has more capability as a Major than I had as a Major General." See, John W. Blassingame, "The Selection of Officers and Non-Commissioned Officers of Negro Troops in the Union Army, 1863–1865," *Negro History Bulletin*, XXX (January, 1967), 11.

Crescent City. Well educated, polished in manner, a splendid horseman, a good boxer, bold, athletic, and daring, he was much admired. When the valor of the black men was put to a severe test at Port Hudson, Captain Cailloux was in the front line and bravely led his men into battle. Although Captain Cailloux was among those killed, "the self-forgetfulness, the undaunted heroism, as exhibited that day," William Wells Brown commented, "created a new chapter in American history for the black man." No Negro-hater, Brown continued, "will ever again care to urge the withholding of our [Negroes] right upon the plea that we will not fight." Banks reported that "they answered every expectation. In many respects their conduct was heroic. No troops could be more determined or more daring. Because of his bravery, Captain Cailloux later became a hero to Union sympathizers in New Orleans. Henry R. Gardner, a New Yorker who served in Louisiana, wrote from Port Hudson to his parents in 1863: "The colored troops have had a trial and from all report have done well." [24]

Regardless of their valiant efforts, black soldiers, and especially black officers, had to endure abuses and racist sneers. Some white officers refused to serve with them. General Banks, upon becoming commander in the Department of the Gulf, began a drive to eliminate Negro officers. With the consent of Secretary of the Army Edwin M. Stanton, Banks dismissed all black officers of the Louisiana Native Guards in early 1863; by mid-1864 he informed officers that it was the government's policy not to have

24. William Wells Brown, *The Black Man: His Antecedents, His Genius, and His Achievements* (Savannah: James Symms Co., 1863), 301–302; Shelby Foote, *The Civil War: A Narrative: Fort Sumter to Perryville* (New York: Random House, 1958), 397; Winters, *Civil War in Louisiana,* 253–54; Thomas Durant to N. P. Banks, January 23, 1864, in N. P. Banks Papers, Box 41, Library of Congress; James M. McPherson, *The Negro's Civil War: How American Negroes Felt and Acted During the War for the Union* (New York: Vintage Books, 1965), 183–86, 169–70, 195–96; Cornish, *Sable Arm,* 144; Harrington, *Fighting Politican,* 120–22. Edward Cunningham, *The Port Hudson Campaign, 1862–1863* (Baton Rouge: Louisiana State University Press, 1963), 53–56, gives the conservative account that blacks exhibited no bravery. Howard C. Wright, *Port Hudson: Its History from an Interior Point of View* (St. Francisville, La.: St. Francisville *Democrat,* 1863), 35–36, takes a similar view. Everett, "Ben Butler," 211.

commissioned black officers.[25] He ordered many officers of the Second Louisiana Native Guards to come before an examining board; wholesale dismissal was the result, making them eligible to be drafted again since many had not spent two years in the service. Banks then appointed whites in their places. With the war drawing to a close in early 1865, and a change occurring in the War Department, Banks reappointed a few blacks.[26]

Just three months after Butler began to recruit free black soldiers, their regiments, including twenty-seven hundred men, were in the field, and several artillery batteries and another infantry regiment were in training. The line officers of the First Regiment, Native Guards, were black and the field officers were white. Those who made up this regiment were not all free blacks; many were slaves who had escaped from plantations and come to New Orleans and represented themselves as "free Negroes." The Second Regiment, Native Guards, like the First, had black line officers; the Third Regiment had both black and white officers. In addition, the noncommissioned officers of all three regiments were blacks.[27]

The occupations of these men varied. "Twenty per cent of the men in the First Regiment," one source stated, "were bricklayers; fifteen per cent, carpenters; two per cent, plasters; six per cent, shoe makers; and the remaining forty per cent laborers." By contrast, the men of the Second and Third regiments were primarily laborers and farmers. They were recruited from the sugar-growing Teche distict of the state.[28]

25. Blassingame, "A Social and Economic Study of the Negro in New Orleans," 103; J. B. Jourdain resigned before he was dismissed. *House Reports*, 39th Cong., 2nd Sess., No. 16, p. 208; Others to resign included Robert H. Isabelle, James H. Ingraham, Emile Detiege, Jacques A. Gla, P. B. S. Pinchback, C. C. Antoine, and Felix Antoine.

26. Blassingame, "Selection of Officers," 9–10. The New Orleans *Tribune*, September 13, 1864, May 14, 1865, has the soldiers' letter of April 25 to General Banks outlining their patriotism and stating injustices.

27. Berry, "Negro Troops," 177; Cornish, *Sable Arm*, 103; Gerald M. Capers, *Occupied City: New Orleans Under the Federals, 1862–1865* (Lexington: University of Kentucky Press, 1965), 21–22; Benjamin Quarles, *The Negro in the Civil War* (Boston: Little, Brown & Co., 1953), 118.

28. Berry, "Negro Troops," 175–77.

According to Wilson's roster of the Negro officers of the Louisiana Native Guards, there were nine captains in the First Regiment and ten lieutenants. The Second Regiment was composed of one major, eleven captains, and sixteen lieutenants. Although the Native Guards served in the Confederate and the Union armies, they performed only parade, drill, and guard duty during their period in the Confederacy; while in the service of the Union, they were utilized for combat and engineer purposes.[29] Collectively, the officers of these black regiments presented the best-trained and most qualified black leadership in the state at the time. Their participation in the war was a major step toward political careers during Reconstruction.

29. Wilson, *Black Phalanx*, 176; Dunbar-Nelson, "People of Color," 68–69.

CHAPTER II

Political Activities
of Blacks,
1862–1867

Before the war a large and prosperous community of free blacks, numbering 10,939 persons, had existed in New Orleans. The presence of Federal authorities in the city after April, 1862, emboldened the leaders to press for political rights for themselves and for their brothers in bondage. Preeminent among them was Doctor Louis Charles Roudanez who had completed his medical training in Paris with honor. He believed that it was vital for blacks to bring their case before the general public. Consequently, he and his brother, Jean Baptiste, and some of their friends launched the first black newspaper in the state, *L'Union*, a militant Republican journal that appeared triweekly in French and was printed less frequently in English. The editor was Paul Trévigne, a well-educated man, who spoke several languages and who had taught for forty years at the Institution on Catholique des Orphelins Indigents in New Orleans.[1]

L'Union represented the first attempt to mold the energies of the black race into a political force. Initially the newspaper advocated the abolition of slavery and economic and civil equality—including suffrage—for the black population. In the first issue, published on September 27, 1862, editor Trévigne launched what

1. Edward Tinker, *Creole City: Its Past and Its People* (New York: Longmans, Green Co., 1953), 106–108; McPherson, *The Negro's Civil War*, 276–77; Charles Barthelemy Rousséve, *The Negro in Louisiana: Aspects of His History and His Literature* (New Orleans: Xavier University Press, 1937), 118–19; Desdunes, *Our People and Our History*, 66.

would be a long drive for Negro rights. He visualized a new era in the history of the South: "The hour has sounded for the fight of great humanitarian principles against a vile and sordid interest which breeds pride, ambition and hypocrisy." Addressing his fellows, he exhorted, "You were born for liberty and happiness! Don't deceive yourselves, and don't deceive your brother."[2]

During November the editor discussed the free Negro's relationship to slaves and former slaves. He noted that freedmen were uneducated and needed proper training to become full citizens. Leadership would have to come from an elite who could teach the newly free that "the word 'liberty' is not the sign of anarchy and of laziness" and that they must be industrious and assume many responsibilities. It further advised unity within the Negro population: "Let us not forget to inculcate in our freed brothers this principle that true liberty is achieved only by practice of all the religious and social virtues." In December, after Lincoln had issued the preliminary Emancipation Proclamation, *L'Union* enthusiastically supported it. However, the measure only added more confusion to the status of blacks in the states. Slaves quickly left plantations and came to New Orleans, creating administrative difficulties. General Banks consented to a policy of arresting some and returning others to the plantations. Free blacks also came under the harsh "curfew" laws and were subject to arrests and discriminatory treatment. A "pass" system was inaugurated to prevent blacks from entering the city. General Banks later consented to permit blacks to be drafted in Union-held parishes.[3]

Meanwhile, Congress was debating the readmission of south Louisiana, and the recognition of its representative was a pressing

2. New Orleans *L'Union*, September 27, 1862. These translations were done by Roger Des Forges for James M. McPherson of Princeton University who permitted the writer to use them. F. Patrick Leavens, "*L'Union* and the New Orleans *Tribune* and Louisiana Reconstruction" (M.A. thesis, Louisiana State University, 1966), 40–42; McPherson, *The Negro's Civil War*, 276.

3. New Orleans *L'Union*, November 15, December 30, 1862. See commemoration celebration two years later as described by the New Orleans *Tribune*, January 19, 1865. New York *National Anti-Slavery Standard*, February 21, 1863; John W. Blassingame, *Black New Orleans, 1860–1880* (Chicago: University of Chicago Press, 1973), 31–33.

question. The Committee on Elections had recently rejected claims from other southern districts because a substantial proportion of the antebellum electorate had not participated. But since Louisiana's provisional military governor, George F. Shepley, had ordered the election and two representatives were elected, both congressmen-elect from southern Louisiana were seated. One, Benjamin F. Flanders, was a native of New Hampshire and a graduate of Dartmouth College. He was a lawyer by profession and had come to New Orleans in 1845. The other representative, Michael Hahn, was born in Bavaria but came to New Orleans as a child and was educated in the public school and at the University of Louisiana before being admitted to the bar in 1851.[4] Both men served from February 3 to March 3, 1863 in the Thirty-seventh Congress.

One man who saw new hope for Unionists in Congress' decision to seat the representatives was lawyer Thomas J. Durant, the main force behind the radical movement. A native of Philadelphia, Durant was educated at the University of Pennsylvania, and came to the city as a young man in the 1830s. He began outlining a plan to reestablish civil government through the election of delegates to a constitutional convention, under the leadership of the newly formed Union Association.[5]

In May the various Unionist clubs assembled in Lyceum Hall to create a permanent Free State Organization. This organization supported the election of delegates to a convention to draw up a new constitution. The voters were to consist of loyal whites who could take a special oath of allegiance. No public endorsement of black suffrage was forthcoming at this time. The military governor, General Sheply, tentatively approved the plan of a constitu-

4. James P. McCrary, "Moderation in a Revolutionary World: Lincoln and the Failure of Reconstruction in Louisiana" (Ph.D. dissertation, Princeton University, 1972), 70–77. N. F. Berry to Benjamin F. Butler, March 25, 1862, in Benjamin F. Flanders Papers, Folder 3, Department of Archives and Manuscripts, Louisiana State University, Baton Rouge; Amos Simpson and Vaughan Baker, "Michael Hahn: Steady Patriot," *Louisiana History*, XIII (Summer, 1972), 229.

5. McCrary, "Moderation in a Revolutionary World," 79–81; Thomas J. Durant to N. P. Banks, July 20, 1863, in Nathaniel P. Banks Papers.

tional convention by naming Durant attorney general of the state and also commissioner of registration. When General Banks returned from campaigns against Confederate forces in Bayou Teche and at Port Hudson and was informed of the positive steps taken by the radical movement in the city, he sided with the conciliatory and conservative policy of the planters. Banks's attitude and President Lincoln's announcement of his "ten per cent" program in October drained national support from the Free State Movement. Moreover, the conservative forces in the state were undercutting Durant's program.[6]

The black press continued its drive for voting privileges at "Union meetings." At a mass meeting at Economy Hall in New Orleans, on November 5, 1863, the Durant forces were strongly endorsed by the press and black population. It was reported that both "white Americans and Africans" were present. A white dentist, Dr. A. P. Dostie, who had Radical Republican sympathies, urged the assemblage not to be hasty in their demands for the franchise, but this caution was coldly received. A black speaker, François Boisdore, favored immediate action. He recalled promises received by their forefathers who fought with Jackson in 1815: "They were told that they would be compensated. . . .We have waited long enough." He advised that if the authorities in Louisiana would not heed their demands, they should "go to President Lincoln." He pointed out that illiterate foreigners could vote but literate black men were denied that privilege.[7]

Captain P. B. S. Pinchback was the next speaker on the program. He stated that he had entered the army solely for patriotic reasons, that he had not expected to receive any pay for several months, and that neither he nor his fellow black citizens had any favors to ask of the United States government. They only demanded that they be allowed "the right of suffrage." They were

6. McCrary, "Moderation in a Revolutionary World," 78–93, 175–79, offers a perceptive analysis.

7. New Orleans *Times*, November 6, 1863; Emily Hozen Reed, *Life of A. P. Dostie or the Conflict in New Orleans* (New York: Wm. P. Tomlinson, 1868), Chaps. 9 and 10.

fighting in battles and were willing to fight, he continued. "They did not ask for social equality, and did not expect it," he claimed, "but they demanded political rights—they wanted to become men." He believed that if black people were not citizens, they should be exempted from the draft.[8]

Before concluding the mass meeting, the black population resolved to address Brigadier General George F. Shepley and ask permission to register as voters, a right to which they considered themselves entitled. They informed the military governor that "they are loyal citizens . . . and ardently desire the maintenance of National unity" for which they would sacrifice their lives and fortunes. Since a large portion of the free blacks attending the meeting were owners of real estate and engaged in commerce, industry, and trades, they were fitted to enjoy "the privileges . . . belonging to the condition of citizens of the United States." The resolution further observed that many free blacks were descendants of those men whom Jackson styled "his fellow citizens," in the War of 1812. Notwithstanding their forefathers' service, the petitioners declared that "until the era of the present rebellion," the free blacks had "been estranged and even repulsed, excluded from all rights, from all franchises, even the smallest" Nevertheless, at the call of General Butler, "they hastened to rally under the banner of the Union and they had never ceased to be good citizens, paying their taxes on assessments of more than nine millions of dollars."

The grievances of the petitioners continued with a description of their services in the Civil War and closed with these remarks: "They have no hesitation in speaking what is prompted by their hearts. 'We are men, treat us as such.' General, the petitioners refer to your wisdom the task of deciding whether they, loyal and devoted men . . . are to be deprived of the right to assist in establishing in the new Convention a Civil Government in Louisiana, and also in choosing their representatives both

8. New Orleans *Times*, November 6, 1863.

for the Legislature of the State, and for the Congress of the Nations."[9]

General Shepley apparently referred the petitioners' call for suffrage and equal rights to the higher authority, General Banks, who was not in favor of mass black enfranchisement. Refusing to be discouraged, blacks continued their drive for political rights. On December 15 representatives and delegates from various Union organizations in the state met at Lyceum Hall in New Orleans with a biracial organization, the Louisiana State Convention of the Friends of Freedom. Since the local commander had responded unfavorably to their request for voting rights, the Union Association, one of the two New Orleans Negro organizations admitted to the Convention of the Friends of Freedom, later prepared to send a delegate, Pascal M. Tourne, to place their grievances before President Lincoln.[10]

Nationally, the radical congressional minority, with Edwin M. Stanton as an ally in the War Department, was anxious to set in motion the machinery of wartime reconstruction. Several days after the convention, Secretary Stanton sent James M. McKaye as a special commissioner of the American Freedmen's Inquiry Commission to investigate the petition and complaints of the black population and asked that he report on the best methods to protect and improve them. At a mass meeting in Lyceum Hall, McKaye advised the leaders to depend largely "upon their own labor for their salvation." McKaye and two other commissioners issued reports on their findings, a preliminary report in June, 1863, and a final summation in May, 1864. These reports showed the need for a radical program of Reconstruction in the South— creation of a Bureau of Emancipation, land confiscation and "Civil freedom and rights" for blacks. Sensing a possible change in the national policy, blacks began preparing resolutions stating

9. "Louisiana," *The American Annual Cyclopedia and Register of Important Events of the Year 1863* (New York: Appleton Co., 1865), 591–92.

10. New Orleans *Tribune*, January 20, 1864 quoted in Everett, "Political Demands," 47–48.

the "wishes and feelings" of the black people, and declaring their belief that the war would bring about judicious legislation for the equalization of human rights."[11]

In the gubernatorial election[12] of February 22, 1864, ordered by General Banks, who had taken charge of the situation, the franchise for both free blacks and the freedmen was a paramount issue. Despite, and perhaps because of, the fact that an opponent of black enfranchisement, Michael Hahn, was elected governor, the black leaders sent a delegation from New Orleans to Washington. They were determined to present their grievances to Federal officials. Moreover, in March, 1864, the conservative Banks had ordered a convention to amend the state's 1852 constitution, and the leaders felt that now might be their last opportunity to obtain a settlement of the question of Negro rights. Their petition, which contained over a thousand names, urged suffrage for all black men, both the free and the former slaves.

Although President Lincoln received the delegation, he advised them that he could take no action on their demands. He must have been impressed by their petition, for on the following day he wrote a letter to Governor Hahn. In it he suggested that perhaps the coming convention could define the franchise to include some blacks: "I barely suggest for your private consideration, whether some of the colored people may not be let in—as, for instance, the very intelligent, and especially those who have fought gallantly in our ranks. They would probably help, in some trying time to come, to keep the jewel of liberty within the family of freedom. But this is only a suggestion, not to the public, but to you alone."[13] Although Lincoln showed this significantly favorable attitude

11. John G. Sproat, "Blueprint for Radical Reconstruction," *Journal of Southern History*, XXIII (February, 1957), 33–41; New Orleans *Tribune*, July 26, 1864; Willie M. Caskey, *Secession and Restoration of Louisiana* (Baton Rouge: Louisiana State University Press, 1938), 105; Everett, "Political Demands," 48.

12. This election was between Benjamin F. Flanders and Michael Hahn. *L'Union* supported Flanders, who was "moderate" on Negro suffrage. Nevertheless, Michael Hahn, who opposed Negro suffrage, was elected governor. Caskey, *Secession and Restoration*, 99–107.

13. The delegates sent to Lincoln were Jean-Baptiste Roudanez (the doctor's brother) and Arnold Bertonneau. The former was an engineer and the latter a wine

toward Negro suffrage, Governor Hahn had not the slightest intention of following the president's suggestion. The constitution adopted by the convention did not extend black suffrage, but an act was adopted with General Banks's approval, giving the legislature power to extend suffrage by law.

The new constitution included a few concessions to blacks, and these were the result of determined effort by a small minority of delegates. A provision was included which enabled the legislature to grant suffrage to persons who might be entitled to it because of military service, payment of taxes, or "intellectual fitness." It also provided for public education for blacks and whites. But the provision also stated that the "legislature shall never pass any act authorizing free blacks to vote or to immigrate into this state under any pretense what ever." When the newly elected legislature convened, it rejected black suffrage.[14]

At the same time, *L'Union*, critical of the constitution, launched an attack on segregated public transportation. General Butler had prohibited such practices, especially the streetcars but the car companies won a judgment giving them the right to reinstate segregated cars. General Banks allowed the ruling to stand. The paper criticized the illogic of different streetcars for the two races. It remarked that the most obscene white persons would answer the question, "why colored persons cannot enter all the vehicles without distinction," with the comment "This personage of

merchant who was captain in the first black regiment raised by General Butler. Benjamin Quarles, *Lincoln and the Negro* (New York: Oxford University Press, 1962), 227; Durant who had recently resigned as attorney general, wrote a letter of introduction for the two delegates. McCrary, "Moderation in a Revolutionary World," 252; Caskey, *Secession and Restoration*, 105. McPherson, *The Negro's Civil War*, 278–79, observes that the two delegates were invited to Boston by Republican leaders, and attended complimentary dinners. Abraham Lincoln to Michael Hahn, March 13, 1864, in Roy P. Basler *et al* (eds.), *The Collected Works of Abraham Lincoln* (New Brunswick, N.J., 1953), VII, 243; New Orleans *Tribune*, December 3, 1864 for Durant's criticism of Lincoln's reluctance to act.

14. "Louisiana," *The American Annual Cyclopedia and Register of Important Events of the Year 1864* (New York: Appleton, Co., 1866), 497; Caskey, *Secession and Restoration*, 128–32; McCrary, "Moderation in a Revolutionary World," 298–301; Rousseve, *The Negro in Louisiana*, 100; John R. Ficklen, *History of Reconstruction in Louisiana Through 1868* (Gloucester, Mass.: Peter Smith, 1966), 67–87; New Orleans *Tribune*, December 9, 1864, April 25, 1865.

equivocal cleanliness will answer surely: 'We don't permit *niggers* to sit next to whites.'"[15]

The attack against political discrimination in Louisiana was also increased and intensified. They ceased only when threats were made by vigilantes to kill Trévigne and to burn the printing office. The newspaper was dissolved on July 9, 1864, because of the threats. The creation of a new organ was imperative if the movement for black rights were to continue. Therefore, the bilingual New Orleans *Tribune* was inaugurated by Dr. Roudanez twelve days later, on July 21, 1864. A bilingual publication, it first appeared triweekly, but after October 4, 1864, it became a daily except Mondays—the first black daily in America. It employed essentially the same staff as *L'Union*, including editor Paul Trévigne. Its first crusade was against both the ratification of the constitution and Lincoln's 10 percent plan. The *Tribune's* first editorial was, however, an all out attack on the discriminatory laws in Louisiana. Under the heading, "Is the Black Code Still in Force" the editor remarked: "The black code of Louisiana is as bloody and barbarous as the laws against witchcraft . . . and far behind the spirit of the times." The editor pointed out that the Emancipation Proclamation was the law and observed that the judge who considered the Black Code still in force "must be so tangled up in legal cobwebs as to be quite disabled for all practical purposes; so involved in mental obscurity as to be positively 'inepacitated [*sic*] to act.'"[16]

By August, 1864, the editorials began to emphasize the necessity of uplifting their "dormant partner," the freedmen. The editors observed that the four million freed slaves were free citizens of the United States and were certain to become "active participants" in the state government. To their hands, the paper

15. *L'Union*, May 24, 1864; Roger A. Fischer, "The Post War Segregation Struggle" in Hodding Carter et al (eds.), *The Past as Prelude: New Orleans, 1718–1968* (New Orleans: Tulane University, 1968), 290–91.

16. Charles B. Rousséve, *The Negro in New Orleans* (New Orleans: Archives of Negro History, 1969), 8–9; New York *National Anti-Slavery Standard*, May 11, 1867; New Orleans *Tribune*, July 21, 28, October 4, 1864.

predicted, "political power will soon be entrusted." Their votes will be "solicited by contending parties and these votes 'will be the decisive elements' in the controversy. How important, then, that they should be educated up to the requirements of their new position!" They must be made to understand "the absolute right and wrong of every question before them, that they may know their rights." [17]

In pursuing their goal of political equality, black leaders called numerous political rallies to which "all colored citizens" were invited. The assemblies generally opposed the Louisiana Constitution and its denial of black suffrage. The speakers were almost always military and business men. Apparently the black population concentrated their efforts on suffrage and military service to the national Congress. The *Tribune* considered its primary duty to be that of opposing "all and every constitution which will be founded upon the State Rights principles." [18]

During the fall two new editors were added to the staff, and the editorials became more outspoken. One of the editors was Jean C. Houzeau, a white immigrant from Belgium; the other was a black man, Charles Dallas, a native of Texas. Houzeau, a scientist by training, came to New Orleans in February, 1863, where he met Dr. Roudanez and enlisted in the *Tribune's* crusade for Negro suffrage. [19]

Charles Dallas, like Houzeau, advocated universal suffrage. He had come to New Orleans during the last phases of the Civil War and soon joined the staff of the *Tribune*. He had been forced to leave Texas because of his Unionist attitudes, and he continued to espouse his ideas in Louisiana. According to his testimony before the House committee investigating the New Orleans riot of 1866, his movements were watched, and his life was constantly threatened by vigilantes. [20] With the aid of these men, the paper

17. New Orleans *Tribune*, August 11, 1864.
18. *Ibid.*, September 6, 15, 20, 1864.
19. Leavens, "*L'Union* and the New Orleans *Tribune*," 22–23; Tinker asserts that "Dalloz" and Houzeau were the same. Tinker, *Creole City*, 108–10.
20. *House Reports*, 39th Cong., 2nd Sess., No. 16, pp. 73–74.

made a strong stand for universal suffrage; as a result, circulation rose and correspondence came in from Congress and even Europe. An attack was also launched against General Order Number 12 which attempted to inaugurate a plantation labor system in January, 1863. The major decisions, under this plan, were made by a three-member Sequestration Commission; the members held views unsympathetic toward the freedmen and more favorable toward the planters. The terms of the labor system called for one-year labor contracts, which compelled employers to provide food, clothing, and proper treatment or fixed monthly wages. The alternative to acquiesence was forced labor on the public works. Thus officers were directed to return blacks to their masters. Frederick Douglass, famed abolitionist, observed that the new system "makes the Proclamation of 1863 a mockery and delusion."[21] According to the paper, the government had leased out the large abandoned plantations to "a teeming swarm of avaricious adventurers," who had an uncertain wage schedule for the laborers. Under this system blacks were to work on plantations for long hours with practically no compensation. The editor observed that the former slaves were merely instruments in the hands of these "intermediates and third persons" who exploited black labor for their own profit motives. The editors advocated a more liberal plan:

> The old plantation system should have been summarily abolished; the plantations divided into five acre lots, and partitioned among the tillers of the soil. These should hold directly from the United States, as owners or lessee, at a *nominal price*. They should be armed, equipped and drilled; ready at a moment's warning to subdue insurrections and repeal invasions. They should be educated as fast as possible, and taught to act as free men and loyal citizens; to honor the flag and to hate their former rebel masters as murderers of our common country.[22]

21. Gertis, "From Contraband to Freedman," 157–59; T. Harry Williams, "General Banks and the Radical Republicans in the Civil War," *New England Quarterly*, XII (June, 1939), 272–73; McPherson, *The Negro's Civil War*, 128–29.

22. New Orleans *Tribune*, September 24, 1864. See also letters from New York

The editors saw the Civil War as the "slaveholder's rebellion." When Federal troops arrived, they declared, the entire system—half civilized and half patriarchal—"went up." Since the slaveholders were the chief instruments in bringing on the war, they were guilty of "treason unparalleled in the world's history," hence, their lands were forfeited and their slaves were freed. Nevertheless, the editors observed that the national government had acted imperfectly and hastily in taking charge of this abandoned property. Again, it called for a division of land among those who had helped create the wealth of the South. "The former slaves were no more than serfs; their wages ridiculous and absurd." They were denied freedom to select their own employers, and to pass from place to place within the federal lines. "In physical comfort," the *Tribune* asserted, "they were in a worse condition than before the advent of Farragut." They did not need a superintendent of Negro labor. "Give the men of color an equal chance," the article concluded, "and this is all they ask. Give them up at once to all the dangers of the horrid competitive system of modern commerce and civilization and . . . they will . . . find a happy issue out of all their suffering."[23]

The Federal provost marshal received the special wrath of the *Tribune*. This official was a referee between planters and laborers. His assistants were often inexperienced former soldiers, many of whom were too much influenced by planters' views toward laborers. One source stated that he met one provost marshal who "enters deeply into the feeling of the slave-owners, and secretly connives at the corporal punishment of the black man, which has been abolished by law."[24]

An editorial entitled "Prejudices" appeared on October 6, 1864. The editor warned that the present position of public affairs

Tribune in October 2, 1864. McCrary, "Moderation in a Revolutionary World," 48–50; McPherson, *The Negro's Civil War*, 129–30.

23. New Orleans *Tribune*, September 10, 1864.
24. George H. Hepworth, *The Whip, Hoe and Sword or the Gulf Department in '63*

kept the blacks from having the "slightest confidence in the wisdom, integrity or patriotism of the bogus administration under our new bogus constitution controlling the State." It further cautioned that "our internal enemies are as numerous as our friends. . . .They are either the avowed opponents of the nation or the secret panderers to the slave powers." These prejudices were exhibited by the uneducated and the vulgar, it commented. Political distinction on the basis of black or white in a free republican country, according to the *Tribune,* "is in entire antagonism with every principle or rational liberty."

Distrust of Louisiana's local political leaders extended into national politics. During the presidential election of 1864 the editors continued to caution blacks about political leaders at both levels. Abraham Lincoln has been in office for four years, it wrote, "pretending to be the Head and Executive of a great nation, but very slow and sometimes altogether failing to act." The other candidate, George McClellan, a war Democrat, "has been in the Army for some years, leading it to the most disgraceful defeats, during the Rebellion, in the Peninsular campaigns and to one of the most glorious victories at Antietam." Neither platform of principles, it warned, was worth a straw since the election was merely a scramble for office and political plunder. As for Lincoln, the editor observed several factors that weakened his probability of success. "*He wants to maintain, if he can, union and slavery.*" On the other hand, McClellan would unite all who are committed to the war for the Union, all war Democrats, and all radical antislavery men. In this political ferment, the *Tribune's* sympathies were with neither party. But it felt that McClellan would

(Boston, 1864), 235; New Orleans *Tribune*, October 22, 1864, January 21, 22, 25, 30, 1866. See also, Elvirn C. Williams to W. E. Whiting, July 24, 1867, in American Missionary Association Archives, Amistad Research Center, Louisiana files, Dillard University, New Orleans, hereinafter cited as Amistad Research Center; Howard A. White, *The Freedman's Bureau in Louisiana* (Baton Rouge: Louisiana State University Press, 1970), 102–103; J. Thomas May, "The Freedman's Bureau at the Local Level: A Study of a Louisiana Agent," *Louisiana History*, IX (Winter, 1968), 9–10.

best carry into force the old Jacksonian war cry of the "Union—
It must be preserved."[25]

Since President Lincoln had not indicated his views on Negro
suffrage, the national political picture was still uncertain. The
blacks of Louisiana rallied, however, behind a platform adopted
by the National Convention of Colored Men, held in Syracuse,
New York, in October, 1864. This convention's expressed purpose was to consolidate thought and action of blacks in America.
A National Equal Rights League was established, with state and
local branches to serve as unifying instruments. Most blacks of
the state readily accepted the declaration of "Wrongs and
Rights" included in the platform. After setting forth the grievances of the blacks in America, the declaration asked for consideration of three principles: "First . . . that all men are born
free and equal; that no man or government has the right to
repeal . . . or render inoperative this fundamental principle, except for crime. Second . . . as natives of American soil we claim
the rights to remain upon it. Third . . . as citizens of the Republic we claim the rights of other citizens." In addition, the convention gave praise to the First Louisiana Regiment, Native Guards,
its flag, and its gallant charge at Port Hudson. One of Louisiana's
delegates, Captain James H. Ingraham, of the First Louisiana,
endorsed the resolutions and moved that they be sent to President Lincoln.[26]

On the local level, the convention also prepared the black
community to withstand a severe test during the fall of 1864.
This involved the fight over the "quadroon bill," a measure
which provided that all persons having not more than "one-
fourth Negro blood shall be recognized as white" in Louisiana.
Such a law was absurd, according to the *Tribune*. "O! friends
of Justice and Union," it exclaimed, "can you witness without

25. New Orleans *Tribune*, September 22, 1864, October 11, 1864; McPherson, *The Negro's Civil War*, 302–303, 308.
26. New Orleans *Tribune*, October 25, 1864; McPherson, *The Negro's Civil War*, 286; Elsie M. Lewis, "The Political Mind of the Negro, 1865–1900," *Journal of Southern History*, XXI (May, 1955), 189–90.

indignation this act excluding the black soldier from a share of the sacred rights for which he has fought" Although the bill "is an advantage to some, it is the grossest injustice to others." In this time of turmoil, the *Tribune* felt that the sons of the land should be linked together in "an unbroken column to front the common foe. . . . The friends of progress are expecting something more liberal."

Since the black soldier had proved himself on the battlefield, the paper asked, and since he was intelligent, brave, and patriotic—why should he be treated with contempt? The friends of justice would not be silent at this outrage about to be committed against "the best defenders of our . . . country." The editors concluded with the words of Mirabeau, "privilege will have an end, but the people is eternal." Changing the figure to Patrick Henry, they declared that the black population was determined to risk all and stand the consequences: "give them their rights or give them death."[27]

After the quadroon bill was set aside, the elite blacks in New Orleans became active in forming a local branch of the National Equal Rights League, an all inclusive organization designed to promote interracial harmony and attain equal rights for all blacks. Later, members joined from Port Hudson, Baton Rouge, Morganza, Carrollton and Bernard Parish.[28] The *Tribune* was a potent force in drawing blacks closer together. When a mass meeting was called on December 27 by the league's state committee, Captain Ingraham of the First Regiment, was one of the featured speakers of the evening. He called upon blacks of "refinement and education" to act for the less fortunate ones, and he urged the establishment of a local office where league officers would

27. New Orleans *Tribune*, November 10, 12, 15, 16, 18, 22, 1864. Another scheme offered by the legislature and opposed by the *Tribune* was a literacy qualification for black voters. Even in antebellum Louisiana, the free colored, secretly and outside the law, aided slaves in learning to read and helped educate many. See Nathan Willey, "Education of the Colored Population of Louisiana," *Harper's New Monthly Magazine*, XLIII (1866), 244.

28. New Orleans *Tribune*, December 22, 1864, see "communicated." The league's meetings were held at a place called the School of Liberty.

give counsel to all blacks and channel their complaints to the military authorities. "To attain that result," Ingraham maintained, "we have to set aside all differences and unite in one spirit." The "quadroon bill was a firebrand thrown out to divide us." It was the educated freedmen's duty, he declared, "to do something for the new freedmen, to educate and organize them."

To implement these reforms, the assemblage proposed the calling of a Convention of Colored Men of Louisiana to "get our best men in it—men of intellect and education—" involved in the civil rights movements. Among other activities, they would devise plans to work the government plantations. The basis for representation in the proposed convention was one delegate for every one hundred members of any society represented. The convention was to be composed of every black person without distinction on the basis of sex. Another black speaker, Dr. Robert I. Cromwell of Wisconsin, averred that this type of organization "was the only means to get the rights that they had been deprived of."[29]

When the Convention of Colored Men of Louisiana, comprising over fifty delegates, met in New Orleans in January, 1865, its purpose was to extend support to the National Equal Rights League. In the *Tribune*, Captain Ingraham, president of the state branch of the league, urged the establishment of local district leagues. The convention was, however, concerned with three principal aims: first, the setting up of the league as a permanent

29. New Orleans *Tribune*, December 27, 1864; Lewis, "Political Mind," 196–97. The paper was disturbed over the conference of planters held in November, under the guidance of Benjamin F. Flanders who was superintendent special agent of the Treasury Department. The *Tribune* felt that the workers (freedmen) should also hold a conference in New Orleans to set forth their grievances. The operation of the governments in forming colonies—home and labor—were of great concern. The home colonies were asylums, for helpless persons, under government direction; whereas the labor colonies, consisting of confiscated plantations, were organized by private efforts. The *Tribune* observed that the old free colored class could provide great aid, partnership with freedmen in aiding the labor colonies. In a mass meeting on December 2, the preceedings were opened by declaring that they regarded "all black and colored men as brothers and fellow sufferers." The featured speakers were Dr. J. P. Randolph of New York and Thomas Durant. Oscar Dunn was appointed president. New Orleans *Tribune*, November 24, 30, December 3, 4, 11, 1864.

organization; second, the establishment of a permanent board that would concern itself with the interest of the entire black population; third, the welfare of freedmen. The convention also advocated the organizing of a "board of freedmen, whose members would be taken from among the emancipated slaves." Captain Ingraham was elected president of the convention and endorsed the above proposals.[30]

The constitution and rules established by the convention put the objective of the assemblage in perspective. All members were given the right to speak. Article I of the constitution stated that the object of the state branches of the league was "the promotion of moral development, education, and industry"; Article II established an executive committee to provide necessary regulations to fulfill the constitution. Other articles provided a one-year term for the committee members, a Bureau of Industry in New Orleans and other localities, annual meetings for the election of the league's officers, and a majority basis for amending the constitution.[31]

During the early sessions one black delegate, Captain William B. Barrett, launched an attack against discriminatory practices on the city's street railways and the treatment accorded black soldiers. And Captain Ingraham urged, "We must ask our rights as men." "If we are not citizens," he concluded, "why make soldiers of us?" A. E. Barber expressed dismay over a denial of freedmen's rights to an education.[32]

When the convention ended and the executive committee was finally selected, the *Tribune* remarked that this event "inaugurated a new era." At this assemblage, which represented a heterogenous group of delegates from various parishes, both the rich landowners and merchants and the newly emancipated slaves were "seated side-by-side." The editorial summarized the brilliant manner in which Ingraham conducted the proceed-

30. New Orleans *Tribune*, December 29, 1864, January 4, 8, 1865.
31. *Ibid.*, January 11, 12, 1865.
32. *Ibid.*, January 12, 14, 1865.

ings and described his oratory. The other names listed in the accounts of the convention revealed that army officers, physicians, and preachers were the most active participants in the debates.[33]

More important is the fact that this convention gave blacks an opportunity to search their own ranks for leadership. Delegates were present from the city of Baton Rouge and other country parishes including Jefferson and Terrebonne. The *Tribune* praised the unity of effort by the Negro population. The members of the various committees attempted to implement the work of the convention. Significantly, a large number of positions were filled by free blacks who had some military experience. Oscar J. Dunn was a member of the committee in charge of publication of the convention proceedings. He became one of the leading black politicans in Louisiana Reconstruction, serving as lieutenant governor from 1868 to 1871. Born in New Orleans in 1827, Dunn was the free son of a free black woman who kept a rooming house for white actors and actresses. He did not fail to profit from his environment; during his boyhood he learned the art of elocution from these actors and singers, training that served him well when he entered politics.[34]

Captain Ingraham chaired a committee to procure a building for use by the Bureau of Industry, which aided freedmen in obtaining employment, and other members of this committee included Dunn and Jordan Noble. Also, Ingraham was a member of the committee on ways and means. The latter was concerned with obtaining money from the people of Louisiana in order to carry out the purposes of the convention. C. C. Antoine and Emile

33. *Ibid.*, January 15, 1865.
34. Marcus B. Christian, "The Theory of the Poisoning of Oscar J. Dunn," *Phylon*, VI (Third Quarter, 1945), 254. In his youth, Dunn was apprenticed out to learn painting and plastering with the large contracting firm of Wilson and Patterson. His dislike of these trades provoked him to run away from his employers. See A. E. Perkins, "Oscar James Dunn," *Phylon*, IV (Second Quarter, 1943), 107; *Appleton's Biographical Encyclopedia* (New York: D. Appleton, Co., 1899), VII, 250. Dunn was also a master mason and operated an intelligence (employment) agency. New Orleans *Tribune*, November 26, 1865, February 22, 1866.

Deteige were secretaries; A. E. Barber was vice-president of the First District League; Captains Robert H. Isabelle and Arnold Bertonneau as well as Dr. Robert I. Cromwell, Jordan Noble, Emile Deteige, J. B. Jourdain, E. C. Morphy, and Thomas Isabelle were appointed to various committees, such as the one to visit the orphan asylum on Toulouse Street, and the Comité sur les Règlements.[35]

Land reform was one of the most prominent issues brought to the attention of the black leaders at the convention. The *Tribune* observed that the plantation question and the welfare of the freedmen were closely connected. It advocated the setting up of the plantation under "associate managers," who could be obtained from the old free black population. This would not only elevate the African race, the paper commented, but it brings two great results: "First, it would set an example for others and stimulate the great social revolution through which we are passing, and next, it will give a sufficient proof of our competence." Furthermore, under this plan the laborers would share in the net proceeds; they would be free to feed and clothe themselves, a process that would develop their self-reliance. They would be bound to the plantations by their interest only; and they would not only receive weekly and monthly pay but would share in the profits received from sale of the crops. Such a plan, the paper maintained, would promote the advancement of the freedmen by stimulating them to labor for their own interest.[36]

By May, 1865, the idea of keeping the freedmen engaged in agricultural work had gained wide acceptance throughout the state. This led to the creation of the Freedmen's Aid Association, an organization designed to give such assistance as loans, land, agricultural equipment, and legal counsel. It was largely organized by free-born blacks in the state. The *Tribune* announced

35. New Orleans *Tribune*, January 14, 15, 20, 1865. Benjamin F. Flanders and Thomas Durant attended several sessions and were invited to seats on the platform.
36. *Ibid.*, January 28, 29, February 2, 1865.

this effort as the inauguration of a "new regime." The amount needed to launch the organization financially was listed at $20,000. If this amount could not be attained through partnership efforts, the freedmen would have to pledge their crops, their mules, and their plows. Since many interested parties could not invest a large amount then, the paper asked not for quarterly fees "but for investments of any amount, to be trusted to . . . a Board of Directors." This board would lend money, furnish means of education, and keep the freedmen informed about the association, with the understanding that after the crop was sold the laborers would pay back loans. "Nothing will be compulsory in the agreement," the editors commented, "All will be done by reciprocal good will."[37]

The black soldiers could be, according to the *Tribune's* reasoning, the primary entrepreneurs in such a program. Since the planters "are no longer needed in the character of masters," the black soldiers "will gladly contribute to a fund which will enable their mothers, sisters, and brothers to make a home for themselves." This could be accomplished by making cash advances that would be reimbursed when the crops of the plantation were gathered. The payments would cost the soldiers nothing, since the checks would be drawn on unpaid money still due them. Under this plan, the soldiers would not only help their brethern, but this would be in "accordance with the democratic spirit."[38]

At a large meeting in Economy Hall on March 17, the featured speaker, Captain Ingraham, launched another vigorous attack against the plantation system, General Banks, and the superintendent of the Bureau of Free Labor, Thomas Conway. "No system of gradual elevation is needed to make us men," the captain declared. "The defenders of such a system are not the

37. *Ibid.*, February 24, 1865. See also earlier editorials November 30, December 4, 1864, critical editorials, July 9, 11, 1865; Leaflet of the Officers of the Freedmen's Aid Association, in The American Missionary Association Archives, Box 58, Amistad Research Center, Louisiana files.
38. New Orleans *Tribune,* March 1, 21, 1865.

friends we intend to have." The entire system is set up to "reenslave us—an enslavement on caste and color." Further, he claimed that the laborers were worse under the new system than they were under the old. Under this "disguised slavery" system there had been many reports of brutality, deaths by starvation, and severe beatings. Ingraham advocated the eradication of every stain that General Banks had left in this department.

Resolutions were then adopted to urge the abolition of the new plantation system provided for by Order Number 23.[39] Other resolutions attacked unfair tax policies, discrimination in traveling facilities, and unequal rights. The assemblage then called for the establishment of a Tribunal of Arbitration, composed partly of freedmen, to decide cases of appeal from the decisions of parish provost marshals on matters of labor. This "disguised bondage" had to be denounced, the resolution continued, and since no progress could be expected in the Bureau of Labor under Superin-

---

39. In early March, 1865, the new plan (Order Number 23) for administrating the plantation was initiated. Although it had set salary stipulations, it was still basically unfair. It provided for voluntary contracts between planters and laborers. The laborers were required to work ten hours, between daylight and dark in the summer, and nine hours in the winter of each day except Saturday and Sunday. On the sugar plantations, the workers were required to serve on night-watch duty. Also, the laborers were allowed a certain amount of land, according to class of hand and size of family. The pay schedule ranged as follows:

Male Hands		Female Hands	
1st class,	$10 per month	1st class,	$8 per month
2nd class,	8 per month	2nd class,	6 per month
3rd class,	6 per month	3rd class,	5 per month
Boys under 14 were paid		Girls under 14 were paid	
$3 per month.		$2 per month.	

New Orleans *Tribune*, March 17, 1865. A small faction of blacks praised the work of General Banks. Their organ, the New Orleans *Black Republican* published from mid-April, 1865 till May 20, 1865, was organized by one of Banks's cohorts, Thomas W. Conway. The editor was Dr. S. W. Rogers, with C. C. Antoine and A. J. Gorden as assistants. The publisher was J. B. Noble. Although it praised General Banks, the paper expressed serious doubts concerning the planter's ability to deal fairly with laborers (see especially the April 16, 1865 issue). White, *The Freedmen's Bureau in Louisiana*, 18–19, contends that Conway attempted to have the military authorities suppress the *Tribune* and removed the military subsidy from the paper. See the *Tribune*'s critical editorial on Banks's order, June 10, 1865, issue.

tendent Conway, this post, which was "inconsistent with freedom," was not needed.[40]

When the resolutions were sent to General Stephen A. Hurlbut, who had replaced General Banks in early March, 1865, the new commander gave a rather defensive reply which asserted that the freedman was paid for his labor, that the freedman's family was given free education, and that freedmen could bring suit and serve as witnesses. The *Tribune* violently criticized the general's assertations. The slave's wife and family as well as the freedman's wife and family "are not considered as such by most owners or lessees of plantations," the editorial claimed. For instance, when the laborer died, "the unpaid balance of his wages is obstinately kept from his relatives." As to the question of wages, the *Tribune* remarked that the present salary of the freedmen was "insufficient and precarious." Nevertheless, the paper felt that the general could correct this situation with one order because "prejudices are not founded on reason, and therefore, are not open to suasion and are not liable to progress."[41]

A letter protesting Hurlbut's action appeared in the March 31 issue. Signed "Junius, Not a Rich Creole," it criticized the premise that the free blacks were not assisting the "moral and physical improvement of the freedmen." This statement had very little validity according to Junius. Ever since the Federal occupation in April, 1862, Junius remarked, the free blacks "of this city and state have night and day been working for the interest of the freedmen." Even under General Butler, when slavery was recognized by the authorities of the United States government, "free public schools were opened under the auspices" of the free blacks, "and no distinction was made in regard to the former status of the pupils." He warned that the Negroes needed to work

40. New Orleans *Tribune*, March 18, 1865. The *Tribune* wanted the Freedmen's Bureau to become more active in providing political education for blacks. See John and LaWanda Cox, "General O. O. Howard and the 'Misrepresented Bureau'" *Journal of Southern History*, XIX (November, 1953), 442, 446.
41. New Orleans *Tribune*, March 18, 29, 1865.

in their own way and that those who were really their friends would assist them.

A new effort by free blacks to aid the freedmen in New Orleans began when a branch of the Freedmen's Aid Association was established there. It provided assistance and counsel through financial loans, and promoted cooperative and rudimentary instruction on political issues. Officers and sponsors included Charles Dallas, J. B. Roudanez, and a number of whites. Later, in June, a party of radicals of both races formed the Friends of Universal Suffrage; it designated the *Tribune* as its official organ.[42]

These organizations became more powerful during the summer of 1865. The executive board of the National Equal Rights League called a mass meeting to announce the arrival of Chief Justice Salmon P. Chase during late May. In a speech made before this assemblage, the Chief Justice stated that it was "both natural and right" that black Americans should claim their rights. He advised them to "strive for distinction by economy, by industry . . . by constant improvement of religious instructions, and by constant practice of Christian Virtues." Blacks adherence to these guidelines would eventually bring universal suffrage, Judge Chase predicted.[43]

At the same time, there was strong sentiment from certain black leaders in favor of supporting a recently formed organization, the Union Free State party, a party that, because of its name, led

42. *Ibid.*, April 15, 26, May 16, June 17, December 20, 1865; Broadside in the American Missionary Association Archives, Amistad Research Center, Louisiana files. The officers were: Benjamin F. Flanders, president; J. B. Roudanez, vice-president; James Graham, secretary; Sidney Thezan, treasurer; C. W. Hornor, corresponding secretary. The association solicited and urged assistance and cooperation from similar associations in other states. The free women of color were active from May 25 until June 5, their organization, Orphans' Industrial and Educational Home for the Children of Freedmen, held a "Fair for the Benefit of the Orphans." Some of the officers were Mrs. Roudanez, treasurer, Mrs. Louise De Mortie, president, and Mrs. Mary B. Williams, secretary. Blassingame, *Black New Orleans*, 107–12.

43. "Louisiana," *The American Annual Cyclopedia and Register of Important Events of the Year 1865* (New York: Appleton, Co.,1866),515–16; New Orleans *Tribune*, May 23, 24, June 6, 1865.

many blacks to assume that it favored universal suffrage. "We have to stand our ground," the *Tribune* editorialized, "and defend the rights of our population. We have to watch the political parties in the state, and be cautious as to whom we give our confidence."[44]

The *Tribune's* warning concerning this political party proved to be well founded. Later, the Union Free State party, a group of pro-Confederate sympathizers, actively campaigned for J. Madison Wells for governor and opposed Negro suffrage. The party's official organ, the *True Delta*, urged the party to vote for Wells to "get rid of the colored suffrage." The *Tribune* congratulated itself for not supporting the party.[45]

Apprehension over such groups as the Union Free State party and anxiety for their political rights caused blacks to seek more active goals that would lead to power in Louisiana politics. The grand meeting for universal suffrage, held June 16, 17, 18, 1865, and sponsored by the executive committee of the National Equal Rights League, formed a new organization, the Friends of Universal Suffrage. This organization promoted several long-range and meaningful resolutions. W. R. Crane, a white Unionist, who served as chairman, urged a "voluntary registration of the American citizens who are not recognized as voters." This would occur at the next gubernatorial and congressional elections. In addition, Captain Ingraham submitted a proposal calling for the appointment of agents in the parishes outside of Orleans Parish to assist in this registration. Another speaker urged the importance of watching the former rebels and of putting up a candidate "of our own and see what the colored vote will be." These resolutions were unanimously endorsed by the meeting.[46] The

44. New Orleans *Tribune*, May 19, 1865.
45. *Ibid.*, May 20, 24, 1865.
46. *Ibid.*, June 17, 18, 1865. The urgency for registration increased after the war ended; Lincoln had been assassinated; President Andrew Johnson was granting amnesty to former confederates; and Governor Wells had ordered a new statewide registration. Ingraham was sent to Shreveport (Caddo Parish) as a registrar. New Orleans *Tribune*, October 13, 1865. This accounts for Ingraham later serving as a delegate to the constitution convention of 1868 from Caddo Parish.

appeal from the executive committee of the Friends of Universal Suffrage to Governor Wells was presented by Oscar James Dunn. After reviewing the Declaration of Independence, the appeal stated: "A man is not what his name and his extraction have made him; he is what he makes himself. All discrimination on account of origin is . . . repugnant to the principles of our Government, and to American manners." Injustice went unpunished, it continued, "when the proscribed race has not voice in the legislative hall. . . . Happiness itself . . . cannot be attained without adequate protection and justice to the individual."

When Governor Wells refused to sign the petition ordering a registration of black voters and ignored the appeal, the *Tribune* remarked that his arguments were expected and were "borrowed from the old proslavery school." Thus the executive committee decided to place the matter before the president.[47]

These discouragements did not cool the ardent determination of blacks and their white allies to become a political force. In July the Friends of Universal Suffrage joined forces with an organization formed by the carpetbag former Federal soldiers in New Orleans, the National Republican Association of Louisiana. The latter's platform emphasized that it had national support. It advocated the adoption of a system of universal education, in order that the children of both rich and poor could become enlightened citizens; it pledged to support the principle of universal suffrage as the only true basis of a republican form of government; and it favored distribution of land by the states to heads of families as free homesteads for actual cultivation.[48]

By September political unity within the black population was

47. *Ibid.*, July 8, 12, 14, 21, 1865; McCrary, "Moderation in a Revolutionary World," 393; the *Tribune* was the official organ of the Friends of Universal Suffrage. New Orleans *Tribune*, June 30, 1865; C. W. Stauffen to Warmoth, February 6, 1866, in Warmoth Papers.

48. New Orleans *Tribune*, July 13, 1865; August Meier, "The Negroes in the First and Second Reconstruction of The South," *Civil War History*, XIII (June, 1967), 123–24; Thomas Durant was elected president of the executive committee of the Universal party.

established at the state convention of factions from both groups held in New Orleans. This convention marked the official birth of the Republican party in Louisiana. Organized in Louisiana in 1863 with Thomas Durant, a northern-born white lawyer who had come to New Orleans before the war as chairman, the party was in the hands of the state committee which included both white Unionists and black men.[49] Delegates to the convention, a meeting called by the state executive committee of the Friends of Universal Suffrage, also headed by Thomas Durant, numbered over one hundred, and the majority of the black delegates represented the wealthy and educated group, the same group that had been in the vanguard of the movement for equal rights.

Many blacks were called to serve on the reorganized state committee in preparation for the November election. Among the black leaders who served as honorary vice-presidents and members of the central committee were Arnold Bertonneau, Dr. Louis Charles Roudanez, J. B. D. Bonseigneur, D. B. McCarthy, Paul Trévigne, Pierre Canelle, Oscar J. Dunn, Joseph L. Montieu, Charles Hughes, Gustavo Deslonde, and Antoine Dubuclet. Dunn, who had been one of the first blacks involved in the movements, used personal funds to organize a political machine covering the whole city of New Orleans.[50]

The convention was able to secure the attention of both races, primarily liberal whites and freedmen, and continued to urge reforms previously advocated by the *Tribune*. The delegates, according to the editors, were "men of devotion, faith and tal-

49. New Orleans *Tribune*, August 4, September 8, 1865. Delegates from Orleans included Charles Hughes, R. I. Cromwell, R. H. Isabelle, O. J. Dunn and others. Philip D. Uzee, "The Beginning of the Louisiana Republican Party," *Louisiana History*, XII (Summer, 1971), 199, 206; Henry C. Warmoth, *War Politics, and Reconstruction: Stormy Days in Louisiana* (New York: Macmillan Co., 1930), 43–45; Durant to Banks, July 20, 1863, in Banks Papers, for Durant's early activities.

50. New Orleans *Tribune*, September 2, 27, 28, 1865; Elvirn C. Williams to W. E. Whiting, July 24, 1867, Amistad Research Center. See P. G. Deslonde to Henry C. Warmoth, May 7, 1867, September 18, 1867, in Warmoth Papers. Deslonde was organizing political rallies in Iberville Parish and urged speakers to come.

ent . . . entirely competent to pilot the ship during the coming
storm of public and congressional discussion." Their task was
twofold: "universal liberty and universal suffrage." The paper
further remarked that "wisdom must be united with boldness"
since their demands were "based on justice and justice does not
admit compromise." The president of the convention, Thomas
Durant, declared that attaining universal suffrage was the "noble
end" of the convention.[51] Apparently the other delegates had a
similar attitude. The resolution adopted by the convention, proposed by both whites and blacks, provided that their organization
be called the Republican party of Louisiana; it endorsed the
platform of the national Republican party; it denounced the Ordinance of Secession, reaffirmed the principles of the Declaration of
Independence, and adopted as its fundamental principles, universal suffrage, liberty, and the equality of all men before the law.[52]

Later, although the franchise had not been extended to them
under state law, black men, both freedmen and free-born , were
registered as Republicans by officials of the Freedmen's Bureau
and voted in a special election designated by the Republican
convention on November 6, 1865.[53] This voluntary election was
designated to demonstrate the views of the Union men of
Louisiana to Congress and to show the national party the
support they could expect if universal suffrage were legalized. After Thomas Durant declined to run as a "delegate"

51. New Orleans *Tribune*, September 26, 28, 1865. Some of the delegates were: R. I.
Cromwell, O. J. Dunn, C. Dalloz, A. Marie, A. E. Barber, J. Lewis, R. H. Isabelle, H. C.
Warmoth, L. Boguille, P. Bonseigneur, P. G. Deslonde (Iberville), P. F. Valfroit (Assen-
sion), Thomy Lafon (7th district, Orleans), and Frederick Marie (Terrebonne).

52. Warmoth, *War, Politics, and Reconstruction,* 43–45; New Orleans *Tribune*,
September 27, 28, October 1, 5, 1865; Uzee, "Beginning of Louisiana Republican Party,"
206.

53. The day before the election, General O. O. Howard, head of the Freedmen's
Bureau arrived in New Orleans. This caused great excitement among the radicals, but the
blacks were disappointed when the general did not endorse Henry C. Warmoth's candi-
dacy nor make a statement in favor of Negro suffrage. See William S. McFeely, *Yankee
Stepfather: General O. O. Howard and the Freedmen* (New Haven: Yale University
Press, 1968), 181–83; The New Orleans *Tribune*, July 28, August 11, 1865, tells of the
Friends of Universal Suffrage sending twelve blacks who were refused the franchise by
local authority.

to Congress representing the territory of Louisiana, Henry C. Warmoth was elected. Born in Illinois in 1842, Warmoth was destined for prominence in Louisiana politics. He was a former Union colonel who served under General John McClernand in the Trans-Mississippi region. At the end of the war, he came to New Orleans, established a law practice, and became active in politics.

According to the *Tribune's* analysis, a majority of Warmoth's 21,405 votes in the state came from the black voters—1,000 were from free-born soldiers, 5,000 from other free-born black men, 2,000 from emancipated soldiers, and 8,605 from other freedmen.[54] Warmoth's credentials were signed and sealed by the secretary of state. Warmoth spent several months in Washington during the next session of Congress and was given a seat on the floor of the House of Representatives. On the other hand, his counterparts, the senators and representatives elected by the Johnson-Wells state government, had to take seats in the galleries.

Meanwhile, the feud between Governor Wells (who had succeeded Michael Hahn as governor in January, 1865) and the state's Democratic legislature, composed mostly of former Confederates continued. Now the issue was widened to include the question of Negro suffrage. Wells had won reelection in November, 1865, and was anxious for peace; but his lieutenant governor, Albert Voorhies, was a Democrat, and their policies conflicted. Moreover, the legislature passed labor laws compelling agricultural workers to sign contracts. It appeared to many observers that the laws were designed to return the state government to the 1852 constitution.[55]

54. New Orleans *Tribune*, September 2, December 13, 1865. See also Everett, "Political Demands," 63. Many blacks in New Orleans donated one dollar toward defraying Warmoth's expenses though some planters in the parishes did not permit employees to participate. New Orleans *Tribune*, October 22, 31, November 10, 1865.

55. Walter M. Lowrey, "The Political Career of James Madison Wells," *Louisiana Historical Quarterly*, XXXI (October, 1948), 1042–1076; Simpson and Vaughan, "Michael Hahn: Steady Patriot," 248–49; LaWanda Cox and John H. Cox, *Politics, Principle, and Prejudice, 1865–1866: Dilemma of Reconstruction America* (New York:

Wells had reversed his opinions during the meetings of the antagonistic Democratic legislature. His position had shifted to one of advocating black suffrage, which could best be obtained in a new constitutional convention. The president of the 1864 convention, Judge Durrell, refused to reconvene the convention. Thus, Govenor Wells had only one way of obtaining his convention; he was persuaded to issue a proclamation calling for an election to fill vacant seats within the convention, signed by Justice Rufus K. Howell. The Republicans also favored reconvening the convention and considered such action as the best way to thwart the Democrats. The Convention was to meet on July 30, 1866.[56]

The national political picture was also encouraging to the blacks. Congress was giving consideration to the Fourteenth Amendment and had enacted the Civil Rights Act of (April) 1866 over Johnson's veto. This act extended citizenship to all persons born in the United States without regard to "color . . . or previous condition of slavery or involuntary servitude." These two legislative events greatly encouraged the Republicans in Louisiana. Many blacks, along with white allies, proceeded to the Mechanics Institute Building in New Orleans on July 30 in an effort to reconvene the convention of 1864. After gathering at twelve noon, the delegates took a recess to wait for a quorum to assemble. When a procession of blacks stopped to cheer the assembly, they were attacked by a mob of hecklers, former Confederates, Democrats, and policemen. According to one historian, W. E. B. DuBois, forty-eight persons were killed outright,

Macmillan Co., 1963), 166–67. See New Orleans *Tribune*, July 19, 20, December 22, 1865, for comments on Opelousas' Nine O'clock Rule, vagrancy laws, and labor laws. Meanwhile auxiliary clubs of the Republican party's central executive committee were being established in country parishes to get more blacks involved. New Orleans *Tribune*, January 14, 19, 1865, February 13, 14, 1866; S. Belden to Warmoth, February 20, 1866, in Warmoth Papers.

56. Warmoth, *War, Politics, and Reconstruction*, 47; Ficklen, *Reconstruction in Louisiana*, 158–59; Rembert W. Patrick, *The Reconstruction of the Nation* (New York: Oxford University Press, 1967), 83–84.

sixty-eight were severely wounded, and ninety-eight were slightly wounded.[57] To most northerners the riot was another step back toward slavery and another attempt of the former Confederates to regain political power. However, the national political picture had changed. In the congressional election held during September, October, and November, 1866, the ratio in Congress was tipped strongly in favor of the Radical Republicans. The Senate had 42 Republicans to 11 Democrats, and in the House, Republicans outnumbered Democrats by 149. The Republicans would now enact a Reconstruction plan, and the plan they settled on was embodied in the Reconstruction Acts of 1867.[58]

The Democrats viewed the first Reconstruction act with mixed emotions. Governor Wells accepted them with "satisfaction," and declared that an election should be subject to the new provisions. The acts reduced the South to a conquered territory by dividing it into five military districts governed by military commanders. This pressure and the threat of black voting soon changed the optimism of the Louisiana Democrats, who heretofore had shared Governor Wells' opinion. The state legislature, during the spring of 1867, refused to take steps to implement the acts, or to repeal the election laws for municipal authority, or to establish an effective Board of Levee Commissioners. At that time, General Philip H. Sheridan, military governor of the Louisiana and Texas District, removed the mayor of New Orleans, John T. Monroe; the judge of the First District Court, E. Abell; and attorney general of the state, Andrew S. Herron. At the same time Sheridan appointed to respective offices thus vacated Edward Heath, W. W. Howe, and B. L. Lynch. He also refused to

57. W. E. B. DuBois, *Black Reconstruction in America, 1860–1880* (New York: Harcourt, Brace Co., 1935), 465; "New Orleans Riot: Report of the Select Committee," *passim*; Patrick, *Reconstruction of the Nation*, 84–85; Donald E. Reynolds, "The New Orleans Riot of 1866, Reconsidered," *Louisiana History*, V (Winter, 1964).

58. John Hope Franklin, *Reconstruction: After the Civil War* (Chicago: The University of Chicago Press, 1961), 63–64; W. R. Brock, *An American Crisis: Congress and Reconstruction, 1865–1867* (New York: St. Martin's Press, 1963), Chaps. 4 and 6; James G. Randall and David Donald, *The Civil War and Reconstruction* (Lexington, Mass.: D. C. Heath, 1969), 594–98.

support segregated streetcars. Later, by order in early June, 1867, General Sheridan removed Governor Wells from office because the governor was in Sheridan's words, "unfit to retain the place, since he was availing himself of every opportunity to work political ends beneficial to himself." Benjamin F. Flanders was appointed to replace him, after General Sheridan's first choice, Thomas Durant, had declined. The police force of New Orleans was reorganized and other local officials were also replaced.[59]

The actions of General Sheridan were not acceptable to President Andrew Johnson. The president, who was in the midst of his own impeachment proceedings, wanted to water down the Reconstruction acts. He dismissed General Sheridan as commander of the Louisiana-Texas District and appointed General Winfield S. Hancock. Earlier in August, however, General Sheridan had set in motion the registration of voters that culminated in the election of delegates, on September 27 and 28, to a constitutional convention. One observer, J. Willis Menard wrote that at the registration office, hundreds of blacks were "waiting with joy-lit eyes for their turn to get 'my voting papers.'"[60] The number of registered voters was officially declared to be 127,693. The *Tribune* cautioned black voters to be mindful of two matters. One was the "eligibility" of black delegates voted for, and the other was equal admission to the public schools. "Education," the editor exclaimed, "should be given to all."

The blacks' desire to vote for delegates to the convention was intense, and their confidence in the democratic system was quite moving. The Alexandria *Democrat* described the black voters

59. *Personal Memoirs of P. H. Sheridan, General United States Army* (New York: Charles L. Webster Co., 1888), II, 253–54, 266–67, 274; *Senate Documents*, 40th Cong., 1st Sess., No. 14, pp. 198–205; New Orleans *Tribune*, June 4, 1867; New York *National Anti-Slavery Standard*, May 11, 1867. General Sheridan had also refused to support segregated streetcars, "star cars." See Roger A. Fischer, "A Pioneer Protest: The New Orleans Street Car Controversy of 1867," *Journal of Negro History*, LIII (July, 1968), 228–29.

60. Eric L. McKitrick, *Andrew Johnson and Reconstruction* (Chicago: The University of Chicago Press, 1960), 494–95. Hancock did not assume command until November 29, the temporary appointee being General Charles Griffin, and after his death, General

and members of the Radical Republican clubs of Rapides Parish with these words: "They came from every portion of the parish and none were left home. The lame, the cripple, the blind, the halt; old, young, one-eyed, one legged, no legs, no arms, deformed, diseased, sick, well, dressed, ragged, barefooted all, all were on hand eager and panting from freedom's boon! Oh! it was a grand jubilee for them all!" [61]

Of approximately seventy-five thousand votes cast for the constitution, only four thousand were against it. Of the ninety-eight convention delegates elected, forty-nine were white and forty-nine were blacks; all but two were Republicans. [62] The black delegates consisted of men who had been active in the political struggle throughout the Civil War and under the Wells administration. Many of these leaders were from the elite free group with military experience, and, in most cases, they owned valuable private property and were well educated. A few slaves also emerged. All had gained the confidence, respect, and allegiance of the majority of the black population because of their intelligence, diligence, and earnestness in the struggle.

Joseph A. Mower. See also Michael Les Benedict, *The Impeachment and Trial of Andrew Johnson* (New York: W. W. Norton Co., 1973), 39, 89. See Menard's letter in New York *National Anti-Slavery Standard*, May 11, 1867.

61. Alexandria (La.) *Democrat*, October 2, 1867; Baton Rouge *Tri-Weekly Gazette and Comet*, October 1, 1867; D. F. Boyd to W. L. Sandford, August 6 1867, in David F. Boyd Letters, Fleming Collection, Box 5, Folder 33, Department of Archives and Manuscripts, Louisiana State University, Baton Rouge.

62. To most blacks during Reconstruction, the Republican party was the party of freedom, liberty, and all else "was the sea." Most of them reluctantly remained in the party. Black Democrats were often criticized. New Orleans *Daily Picayune*, June 23, 1868; Thomas B. Waters to R. H. Taliaferro, May 25, 1867, in Taliaferro Papers; New Orleans *Republican*, October 17, 1871, especially the treatment of black Democrat Willis Rollins, July 30, 31, August 4, 1868; Natchitoches *Times* quoted in Bossier *Banner*, October 15, 1870.

CHAPTER III

Black Delegates
and the Constitutional
Convention

The political situation in Louisiana had become extremely tense during the summer of 1867. Throughout the early months the Radical Republicans had held meetings and continuously asked for equality before the law for the black population. Their platform "indorsed the Acts of the thirty-ninth and fortieth Congresses," and pledged to support Reconstruction in Louisiana upon the congressional basis. In addition, it promised to discourage any "attempt on the part of any race to assume political control of any other race or class."[1] Thus, when the constitutional convention was called, blacks had obtained some political experience and were more unified, both economically and politically, than ever before.

Black delegates represented leadership in the black community and probably drew some of their political knowledge of activities from Radical Republicans.[2] Several former slaves of unusual political talent would also emerge. The delegates were to be elected according to congressional districts and wards. Unlike the black delegates in the constitutional convention of Texas, where none of the delegates were native born, approximately half of the

1. New Orleans *Tribune*, June 12, 15, 18, 1867, July–August, 1867, *passim*.
2. My authority for black membership in the constitution convention is A. E. Perkins, "Some Negro Officers and Legislators in Louisiana," *Journal of Negro History*, XIV (October, 1929), 523–28, and Perkins, *Who's Who in Colored Louisiana* (Baton Rouge: Douglas Loan Co., 1930), 53. See also Appendix A, herein, for a more complete list of delegates, compiled from journals and newspapers.

black Louisiana delegates identified were natives. As early as July 31 the *Tribune* had advised voters on the caliber of men to elect. It declared that "they should be men of worthy character, men of good sense and sound judgment, trusty and devoted to the liberal cause." Taking this seriously, the voters elected firm Republican party men who had support from the party and shared many of the same attributes: education, shrewd natural ability, military service, business ownership, and professional careers.[3]

James H. Ingraham was one of the leading black delegates. In addition to his military achievements, the thirty-five-year-old former carpenter held numerous political offices prior to his selection to serve as a delegate from Caddo Parish. He had represented Louisiana's black population at the National Convention of Colored Men held in Syracuse, New York, and as president of both the state branch of the National Equal Rights League and the Convention of Colored Men of Louisiana which met in January, 1865.[4]

Another high army officer elected as a delegate was thirty-year-old Pickney Benton Stewart Pinchback, of Orleans Parish. His father, Major William Pinchback, was a white planter in Holmes County, Mississippi; his mother, Eliza Stewart, was a mulatto.[5]

Caesar C. Antoine, a delegate from Caddo Parish, was fluent in both English and French. His ancestors, according to one source,

3. J. Mason Brewer, *Negro Legislators of Texas* (Dallas: Mathis Publishing Co., 1935), 115. Robert Cruden, *The Negro in Reconstruction* (Englewood Cliffs, N.J.: Prentice-Hall, 1969), 94–95. A shorter version of this chapter appeared in *Louisiana History*, IX (Fall, 1969). The writer acknowledges the permission to reprint a portion of this granted by the journal.

4. Ingraham paid $28 in taxes on $1,400 worth of real and personal property according to the *Register of Taxes*, 1871, City Archives, New Orleans Public Library, New Orleans, hereinafter cited as *Tax Register* with appropriate date; Custom House Nominations, Louisiana: New Orleans, June, 1869–May, 1870, Box 110, Record Group 56, National Archives; New Orleans *Semi-Weekly Louisianian*, November 26, 1871; Rankin, "The Origins of Black Leadership in New Orleans During Reconstruction," 421–22, contends that Ingraham was a slave, freed by his master at age six.

5. Simmons, *Men of Mark*, 759; Haskins, *Pickney Benton Stewart Pinchback*, 2–6; George Sewell. "Hon. P. B. S. Pinchback: Louisiana's Black Governor," *The Black Collegian*, IV (May–June, 1974), 8–10, 58.

"transmitted to him characteristics which are essential to the greatness of individuals."[6] He was born in New Orleans in 1836, the son of a veteran of the War of 1812 who had fought the British at the Battle of New Orleans. Antoine's mother was a native of the West Indies and the daughter of an African chief, whose parents were brought as slaves from Africa. On his father's side, his grandmother, Rose Gorrone Antoine, was also, in her childhood, brought as a slave from Africa. A remarkable woman, she raised herself to prominence as a midwife, purchased her freedom, and eventually accumulated a fortune of approximately $15,000. At her death she had acquired such a large estate that she was able to leave her seven children over twenty thousand dollars each.

Caesar passed his childhood as most black boys in the cities and at the age of ten was sent to the school of one William Mulford. He remained there nine months, and after being graduated he entered into one of the few occupations which, in the days of slavery, was open to an ambitious man of his color—that of barber. After quickly learning his trade, he negotiated a loan of sixty dollars with one of the editors of the New Orleans *Times*. With this aid, Caesar opened a barbershop in New Orleans, located on Perdido Street opposite the Carrollton Railroad depot. He continued to operate his shop until the outbreak of the war.

His success in the Union army and his business endeavors provided a background for his polticial activities. He had served his country as a captain in the famous Seventh Regiment, Louisiana State Militia. At the conclusion of the war, he decided to leave New Orleans and move to Shreveport, where he established himself in the grocery business and operated a commission house. His native shrewdness enabled him to prosper sufficiently and ingratiated him with his customers. The voters of Shreveport elected him, against his protests, to the constitutional convention.[7]

6. Simmons, *Men of Mark*, 1132.
7. C. C. Antoine Scrapbook. When Antoine died in September, 1921, he was very wealthy; he had purchased a small plantation in Caddo Parish and had also purchased some city lots in Shreveport and a $1,300 residence. In addition, he had been part owner,

Qualified black delegates, like Antoine, had entered professional careers and frequently were descendants of wealthy ancestors. Robert I. Cromwell, who represented the Second District, New Orleans, was a doctor of medicine. A thirty-seven-year-old native of Virginia, Dr. Cromwell was perhaps the ablest delegate in the convention. He came to New Orleans in January, 1864, from Wisconsin. He entered politics and was determined not to permit injustice against blacks to continue. During the New Orleans riot of July, 1866, he was inside the Mechanic's Institute Building and was forced to leap out of a window; he was immediately arrested, beaten, and robbed by a policeman. The next spring, Cromwell was determined to bring the policemen guilty of this unprovoked attack before the courts. When he attempted to gather all the names of those who had taken part in the disturbance, one policeman refused to give his name and proceeded to arrest Cromwell for "disorderly" conduct. After his release, Cromwell took the matter to U.S. Commissioner R. H. Shannon. He brought charges against the policeman, who was later indicted and placed under one-thousand-dollar bond in default of which he was jailed.[8]

Jules A. Masicot, who represented Orleans Parish, attended college for four years and served as lieutenant in the First Louisiana Cavalry. He was a resident of New Orleans, living at 78 Piety Street, and was near the Mechanic's Institute Building on July 30 when the riot occurred. Masicot later served in several

---

with Pinchback, of the *Semi-Weekly Louisianian*. George F. Porter (ed.), "Documents," *Journal of Negro History*, VII (January, 1923), 84–87. Register of Signature of Depositors in Branches of the Freedmen's Saving and Trust Co., Shreveport Branch, Records of Veterans Administration, in RG 101, NA.

8. *House Reports*, 39th Cong., 2nd Sess., No, 16, p. 76; Dr. Cromwell later established a newspaper, the *Negro Gazette*, after service in the convention. New Orleans *Semi-Weekly Louisianian*, April 11, May 11, July 6, 1872; Bossier *Banner*, April 11, 1868. Cromwell was later employed in the customhouse as inspector of beef and pork, New Orleans *Daily Picayune*, August 2, 4, 1868. In early 1867, he had addressed a long letter to "The Colored People of Louisiana and the Ten Rebel States" to aid in instructing, and enlightening new voters. Lewis, "Political Mind," 196–97; Rankin, "The Origins of Black Leadership," N. 18; Warren Brown (comp.), *Check List of Negro Newspapers in the United States, 1827–1946* (Jefferson City Mo.: Lincoln University School of Journalism, 1946), 25.

political posts, including recorder for the Third District, criminal sheriff, and state senator.[9]

Many of the delegates were of African-French parentage. Pierre G. Deslonde, a wealthy forty-one-year-old sugar planter and free man of color, was one of these. He was "not very familiar with the English language," but his political honesty earned him numerous friends and, subsequently, several high-ranking positions, including secretary of state from 1872 to 1876. Later he published a newspaper in Plaquemine, Iberville Parish, the *News Pioneer*. L. A. Rodriguez was said to have been "one-fourth African and three-fourths French." He was a native of New Orleans and owned property valued at three thousand dollars. Rodriguez was a forty-year-old former captain of Company K, Louisiana Volunteer Regiment, when the convention was held. When asked by a member of a congressional committee investigating the election of 1868 if he had ever held slaves, Rodriguez answered, "No sir; I never owned a slave in my life." He was "an hereditary freedman" and skilled shoemaker with no slave ancestors. Louis François was also an educated free man of African-French ancestry. A sergeant in Company B, First Regiment, Louisiana Infantry Native Guard, he was approximately twenty-seven at the time of the convention.[10]

J. B. Esnard of St. Mary Parish was also of African-French descent. He was one of the youngest men at the convention, being only twenty-two years old. Although Esnard was born in New

9. *House Executive Documents*, 39th Cong., 2nd Sess., No. 68, pp. 215–16; Carded Military Service Records, Volunteer Organization, Civil War, RG 94, NA; *House Miscellaneous Documents*, 41st Cong., 2nd Sess., No. 154, Pt. 2, p. 220; New Orleans *Times*, April 21, 26, 1868. Masicot was under thirty when he served, and his right to the post of recorder came under heavy criticism. New Orleans *Times*, May 15, 1868; *Edwards' Annual Director of the Inhabitants, Institutions, Incorporated Companies, Manufacturing, Business, Business Firms, etc., etc., in the City of New Orleans for 1870* (St. Louis and New York: Southern Publishing Co., 1870), 755.

10. *House Miscellaneous Documents*, 45th Cong., 3rd Sess., No. 31, p. 1107; Sucession of George Deslonde, Iberville Parish Courthouse, Plaquemine, Louisiana; Iberville *Weekly South*, December 12, 1868; *House Miscellaneous Documents*, 41st Cong., 2nd Sess., No. 154, Pt. 2, pp. 493–95, 634, 636; Custom House Nominations, Louisiana, New Orleans, June, 1875–July, 1877, RG 56, NA; Carded Military Service Records, RG, 94, NA.

Orleans, he had moved to St. Mary Parish shortly before the convention and was elected as a delegate. Esnard, along with his ancestors, was free, but his father had been a slaveowner. Shortly after his service in the convention, he was forced to flee north to save his life because of threats from hostile whites. Nevertheless, he later returned and, as a Republican, represented the parish of St. Mary in the legislature from 1868 to 1870.[11]

Curtis Pollard, of Madison Parish, was a Baptist preacher and was, at fifty-eight, one of the oldest members in the convention. He had moved to Madison Parish in 1864 and started raising cotton, corn, and vegetables on rented land. His success as a farmer earned him the admiration that resulted in his election, first as a delegate and later to an eight-year term as an "independent Republican" state senator. In the late 1870s he was forced to leave the South because of terrorist activities against him in the Kansas Exodus. Another minister who served as a delegate was William Murrell of Lafourche Parish. He had come from New Jersey, and he remained for over twenty years in Louisiana. He was for a time coeditor of the Lafourche *Times*, and he served in the lower House.[12]

Other black delegates were also well qualified. Fortune Riard of Lafayette was a native of Louisiana but had been educated in France, where he served as a naval officer. Riard possessed property in Lafayette and later established a general commission and employment agency in New Orleans. This business, Riard's Employers' and Servant-Intelligence and Claim Agency was one of the largest in the state and possibly the largest in the South. Located at 184 Poydras Street in New Orleans, it claimed to find work for all types of unemployed persons. His advertisement

11. *House Miscellaneous Documents*, 41st Cong., 2nd Sess., No. 154, Pt. 2, p. 698; New Orleans *Daily Picayune*, April 30, 1868.

12. W. L. McMillian to Henry C. Warmoth, October 24, 1870, Frank Morey to Warmoth, October 31, 1870, in Warmoth Papers; Vicksburg *Herald* quoted in New Orleans *Daily Picayune*, April 25, 1868; Bossier *Banner*, October 8, 1870; *Senate Reports*, 46th Cong., 1st–2nd Sess., No. 693, Pt. 2, p. 512, Pt. 3, pp. 47–48; Clara L. Campbell, "The Political Life of Louisiana Negroes, 1865–1890" (Ph.D. dissertation, Tulane University, 1971), 96–97; *Semi-Weekly Louisianan*, November 19, 26, 1871.

appeared in numerous issues of the *Louisianian*: "The under-signed having had many years experience in one of the largest northern cities, in the selection of servants for employers, and believing in the advantages of the public a permanent bureau—where those needing . . . first class cooks, waiters, nurses, stewards (males and females), matrons, housekeepers, seam-stresses, traveling servants. . . . Boys for any occupation and likewise laborers for plantations, white and colored." This Intel-ligence Agency also urged "English, French, American-Germans, and Spanish employers wishing first class help, and those desiring a good situation in the city or country" to take advantage of his services. Planters needing first-class laborers from "the North or any of the Southern states (white or colored) can have their order filled on short notice" by addressing the agency. This could be easily done since it had "agents in each of the Southern states as well as in Northern cities, expressly for the purpose of engaging hands." Riard's agency also offered "liberal compensation" for persons wanting to serve as agents in Alabama, Georgia, Mississippi, and Texas.[13]

Since Riard was a member of the legal fraternity, he was well-read in law and judicial procedure. His agency qualified therefore as a United States Claim Agency. After his service in the convention, Riard served in the lower House and briefly in the Senate. His appointment as deputy internal revenue collec-tor came after the restoration of white supremacy in 1881 as an attempt to unite the declining Republican party in the state.[14]

Several other delegates were leading businessmen. The Isa-belles, Thomas and Robert, were born free and were later offi-cers in the Union army, lieutenant and captain respectively, and leading businessmen in New Orleans. Thomas managed a sewing machine store on Baronne Street and advertised his business establishment in almost every issue of the *Tribune*.

13. *Senate Reports*, 46th Cong., 2nd Sess., No. 693, Pt. 3, p. 150. See also *Weekly Louisianian*, September 30, 1878, November 30, 1878–October 18, 1879
14. *Weekly-Louisianian*, January 17, 1880, August 6, 1881.

Robert H. Isabelle, a forty-one-year-old native of Opelousas, was a property owner, part-time clerk, and was listed as a dyer in the New Orleans business directory. Prior to his election to the convention, he had served as secretary of the Radical Executive Central Committee during the Radical convention in June, 1867. He resigned his position as a corporal on the New Orleans police force to serve as a delegate to the convention.[15]

Other Orleanians included Hy Bonseigneur, proprietor of a cigar store at 142 Camp Street. David Wilson, a free man of color, was a forty-two-year-old native of Kentucky who operated a barbershop at 152 Calliope Street. Ovide C. Blandin, a grocer, was approximately twenty-nine years old. Solomon Moses was a forty-one-year-old builder and later Customhouse official, and twenty-one-year-old Leopold Guichard was listed as a clerk and native Louisianian. Arnold Bertonneau, who represented the Third District, was a wine merchant and a former captain in the First Negro Regiment raised by General Butler.[16]

15. New Orleans *Tribune*, August, 1864–March, 1869, *passim*. Thomas Isabelle's real estate and personal property was listed at $150 in the 1871 *Tax Register*, Orleans Parish. *Gardner's New Orleans Directory, 1867* (New Orleans, 1867), 212. Robert Isabelle worked as a part-time clerk in a large New Orleans cotton factory. New Orleans *Crescent*, October 17, 24, 1867, October 2, 4, 1868. Later he was appointed pension agent for New Orleans by the president. New Orleans *Republican*, February 16, 18, 1871. Robert Isabelle's real estate and personal property was valued at $3,000 in *Tax Register*, 1871, F–K, Orleans Parish. In 1876 Isabelle was graduated from Straight University Law School. See the Reverend E. M. Cravath, D.D., field secretary of the American Missionary Association Class Roll for the Law Department of Straight University, June 1, 1874, in Louisiana files, Box 59, the American Missionary Association Archives, Amistad Research Center, Dillard University; John W. Blassingame, "A Social and Economic Study of the Negro in New Orleans, 1860–1880," 247; Civil War Pension Files, RG 56, NA.

16. *Gardner's New Orleans Directory, 1866* (New Orleans, 1866), 93, 471; Custom House Nominations, Louisiana, New Orleans, June 1869–May, 1870, Box 110, June, 1875–July, 1877, Box 115, in RG 56, NA; Rankin, "The Origins of Black Leadership," n18; *Gardner's and Wharton's New Orleans Directory for the Year 1858: Embracing the City Record, A General Directory of the Citizens and a Business and Firm Directory* (New Orleans, 1858), 227, 324; *Gardner's 1867*, p. 186; Quarles, *Lincoln and the Negro*, 227. Bertonneau later served as assistant internal revenue collector. *Semi-Weekly Louisianian*, November 26, 1871.

Many of the delegates, as far as can be determined, were in their twenties or early thirties. Victor M. Lange, of East Baton Rouge Parish, was twenty-eight years old and a native of Baton Rouge. He was a member of a large family, a property owner, and, along with his brother Robert, served in the 1868–1870 legislature. The parish of Assumption was represented by Robert Poindexter, who was in his early thirties. His enthusiasm for the Republican party declined when he decided that it was not interested in establishing schools. He then became a lukewarm Democrat, after serving as a senator.[17]

William R. Meadows and John Gair, of Claiborne and East Feliciana parishes, respectively, were young members. Meadows was a man who owned a farm. John Gair, also a family man, was an effective political organizer in his home parish, and he became a leading legislator. The circumstances surrounding his death were among the most tragic of the Reconstruction era.[18]

The parish of Plaquemines was ably represented by a twenty-five-year-old clerk, Charles T. Thibaut, a native of this parish. He became a sheriff, tax collector, and recorder. John B. Lewis of De Soto was a youthful leader who organized a large political club near the town of Mansfield in his home parish. Natchitoches Parish was represented by a young political organizer named Charles Leroy. Leroy was elected to the conven-

17. *House Miscellaneous Documents*, 44th Cong., 2nd Sess., No. 34, Pt. 1, pp. 201–207, Pt. 3, p. 9. Victor Lange paid tax on a lot in East Baton Rouge valued at approximately $800 throughout the Reconstruction period. Tax Assessment Rolls, East Baton Rouge Parish, 1870, 1872, 1874–77, Clerk of Court Office, Baton Rouge; T. B. Tunnell, Jr., "The Negro, the Republican Party, and the Election of 1876 in Louisiana," *Louisiana History*, VII (Spring, 1966), 107–16.

18. *House Miscellaneous Documents*, 41st Cong., 2nd Sess., No. 154, Pt. 2, pp. 160–61; While his family helplessly watched, Meadows was murdered in his back yard in early 1869. Bossier *Banner*, May 16, 1868; John Gair to James Taliaferro, October 12, 1868, in James G. Taliaferro and Family Papers; *Senate Miscellaneous Documents*, 44th Cong., 2nd Sess., No. 14, p. 926; Gair, who was married and had two children, was killed, along with his sister-in-law, for allegedly plotting to kill a white doctor. While Gair was being taken to jail by sheriff's officers, he was taken from the deputy by a mob and murdered. The charges against him were never proved. Attempted assassination of Gair by his opponent during the November, 1874, election campaign indicates his political significance. New Orleans *Daily Picayune*, May 21, 1868, February 17, October 20, 21, 1874; New Orleans *Times*, October 15, 16, 1875.

tion because of his efforts to make equality before the law a reality. He would later serve as postmaster in Natchitoches. John Pierce of Bossier Parish and the farmer Frederick Marie of Terrebonne Parish were also active organizers.[19]

Rapides Parish sent two black men to the convention—George Y. Kelso and Samuel E. Cuney. Both were free men of color and continued in politics after the convention. Kelso was reelected to two terms as senator, 1868–1876. A former newspaperman and businessman, he lived in Alexandria until one of the terrorist groups forced him to leave his home during the 1876 election and seek refuge in Arkansas. Cuney served only one term after the convention in the lower House. The Alexandria *Democrat* listed Cuney as having paid his taxes amounting to $1.45 up to January 1, 1868, which indicates he had little property.[20]

Dennis Burrel, a delegate from St. John the Baptist Parish, was a former slave. Physically, he was tall and "well-shaped and dignified in his deportment." Before the war he was the slave of James W. Godbery, a sugar planter in the parish. He had not had much formal training but was shrewd and had unusual natural ability and he was a good speaker. Burrel had served as a poll watcher during "voluntary" election of November 6, 1865. When he and another former slave brought the returns to New Orleans, the two men were seized by the police and jailed. They were later freed at the urging of Union Association members. After the convention, Burrel was one of the strongest supporters of the constitution. He later represented the parish in the lower House before retiring to private life as a blacksmith.[21]

19. *House Miscellaneous Documents*, 41st Cong., 2nd Sess., No. 154, p. 531; Plaquemines *Protector*, January 8, 15, March 5, September 10, 1887; Custom House Nominations, Louisiana, New Orleans, June, 1869–May, 1870, Box 110, RG 56, NA; *Senate Documents*, 40th Cong., 1st Sess., No. 14, p. 224; Charles Leroy to James G. Taliaferro, July, 26, 1869, in Taliaferro Papers; Bossier *Banner*, June 13, 1868; New Orleans *Tribune*, January 25, 1866. Marie served as sheriff in Terrebonne, 1868–70.

20. Alexandria *Democrat*, January 8, June 17, October 2, November 20, December 11, 1868; *Senate Reports*, 42nd Cong., 2nd Sess., No. 457, p. 778; *House Reports*. 42nd Cong., 2nd Sess., No. 101, Pt. 2, p. 45.

21. St. John the Baptist Parish *Meschacebe*, April 11, 1868; Bossier *Banner*, September 12, 1868; Thomas J. Durant to Warmoth, January 18, 1866, in Warmoth Papers; St. James *Sentinel*, June 5, 1875.

Collectively, these men represented much of the political experience and wealth of the black population. Many had been business leaders before their election, and others became more prominent because of their service in the convention. They were men who, in several instances had gained employment in the highest paying professions then open to blacks. Their educations were certainly above average for their race and were at least equal to those of the white delegates.

On November 23, 1867, the convention met in New Orleans, and the requirements established by Congress for readmission of Louisiana to the Union were officially implemented. The contest in the sessions, as viewed by the New Orleans *Tribune*, was on a single principle—"the extension of equal rights and privileges to all men, irrespective of color or race." The deliberation of the convention did not involve the mere declaration of such a principle, but the "several applications of that principle to common life." Such a principle, the *Tribune* further reasoned, had been absent in the past political life of Louisiana.[22]

Black delegates to the Louisiana Constitutional Convention of 1868 took an active part in its deliberations. They were assigned to various committees, such as the Committee of Thirteen on Rules and Regulations, which had five black members. The Committee on Militia had seven black members, including the chairman, P. B. S. Pinchback. Four members on the Committee on Public Education were blacks, and five blacks served on the Committee to Draft a Bill of Rights. This committee was chaired by James H. Ingraham. Other committees were General Provisions; Enrollment; Internal Improvement; Executive, Legislative, and Judiciary Department; and Contingent Expenses. The last committee had a black chairman.[23]

In their efforts to establish a constitution, the new leaders of Louisiana tried, first of all, to frame laws which would ensure the

22. New Orleans *Tribune*, November 28, 1867.
23. *Official Journal of the Proceedings of the Convention for Framing a Constitution for the State of Louisiana* (New Orleans, 1867–68), 7, 13, 234–37, hereinafter cited as *Journal of the Proceedings of the Convention for Framing a Constitution*.

readmission of Louisiana to the Union. Following congressional stipulations, the convention did not place any racial restrictions on exercise of the franchise. Louisiana did, however, make exceptions of those who had been disfranchised by the Reconstruction acts and the Fourteenth Amendment, ratification of which became a prerequisite for readmission. Public office, according to the Fourteenth Amendment, was closed to persons who had "engaged in insurrection or rebellion" against the United States along with those who had "given aid or comfort to the enemies thereof." These exclusions applied both to state and national officers. The controversy over the franchise began with Robert I. Cromwell's resolution asking for the state to be "governed, controlled and directed by those who served it in time of its peril and who seek to preserve it with friendly hands from its foes." Cromwell was unrelenting in his efforts to have the Fourteenth Amendment and Reconstruction Act provisions placed in the constitution. Several days after introduction, the resolution was referred to the Committee on Bills of Rights and General Provisions. When this committee took no action on the resolution, another black delegate, P. G. Deslonde of Iberville Parish, wrote a similar amendment proposing universal suffrage for twenty-one-year-old male citizens of any race or color. Restrictions were placed, however, on persons committing felonies against the state. The congressional restrictions were also reiterated.[24] Indeed, it should be stated that several of the black delegates urged an end to penalties suffered by former Confederates. The framer of the constitution, although limited by congressional guidelines, had shown no inclination to place permanent suffrage restrictions on anyone. Black delegates frequently expressed the hope that any restrictions placed on former Confederates would be temporary. Pinchback and three other black delegates signed a petition against Article 98, which disfranchised former Confederates. It stated: "We are now, and ever have been advocates of universal

24. *Ibid.*, 15, 21–24, 157, 165, 172–76, 189, 191–92, 222; New Orleans *Daily Picayune*, December 4, 20, 21, 1867, for mild attitude of blacks.

suffrage, it being one of the fundamental principles of the Radical Republican Party."[25]

In the mind of the black delegates, the establishment of a system of public education ranked in importance with the granting of adult male suffrage. James H. Ingraham's resolution urged the establishment of at least one free public school in every parish. He also called for integrated schools under the guidelines established by the General Assembly. Another black delegate, David Wilson, proposed an amendment to give the legislature authority to provide for the education of all children in the state between the ages of six and eighteen years without regard to color or previous condition of servitude. These resolutions were referred to the Committee on Education.[26]

Those desiring integrated schools did succeed in obtaining them, at least in theory, since the convention provided that "there shall be no separate schools or institutions of learning established exclusively for any race in the state of Louisiana." This proposal was opposed by conservative elements in the state. The "Congo Convention," the New Orleans *Times* asserted, was trying to introduce "amalgamation" into the public schools. Such an attempt, the editor concluded, would never succeed and might "serve to destroy the public school system." He then called for a united effort of the conservatives to "defeat the Constitution." One white delegate, Judge W. H. Cooley of Pointe Coupee Parish, called the mixed school proposal "another attempt to establish by laws, the social equality of all classes and color."[27] These conser-

25. *Journal of the Proceedings of the Convention for Framing a Constitution*, 293. The other signers included A. Donato, Jr., O. C. Blandin, and J. B. Esnard. Pinchback also felt that two-thirds of the Negro population of Louisiana "did not desire disfranchisement to such great extent." *Ibid.*, 259. One Negro delegate, however, wanted to make the provision harsher by adding persons engaging in duels or acting as seconds after the constitution was adopted. This motion was tabled. *Ibid.*, 260; New Orleans *Daily Picayune*, January 25, 26, 28, February 28, 29, 1868. Several white radicals urged a harsher provision.

26. *Journal of the Proceedings of the Convention for Framing a Constitution*, 16–17, 45, 60–61, 154, 200–201. Anti-private-school appropriation provisions were also encouraged by black delegates.

27. *Ibid.*, 292. See Franklin, *Reconstruction*, 112–13; Roger A. Fischer, "Racial

vative views did not prevail, and the overwhelming opinion of the delegates was favorable to the provision of mixed schools. One Negro delegate, Victor Lange, stated that it "secures to my child and to all children throughout the state the education which their forefathers have been deprived of for two hundred and fifty years." Another Negro delegate voted "in the affirmative" because establishing public schools for all "will elevate and enrich the community, which ignorance dishonored and burthened."[28]

One of the most crucial matters debated by the constitutional convention was the establishment of a Bill of Rights. The push for articles to give everyone "equal protection" came early in the session from Robert I. Cromwell, James H. Ingraham, C. C. Antoine, and P. B. S. Pinchback. When the Committee on Drafting the Constitution presented its report, a separate report, presented by four black members, had twenty-two articles included in its Bill of Rights. The majority report, signed by five white members, presented a Bill of Rights with twelve articles. Both reports provided for the abolition of slavery and involuntary servitude, freedom of the press, the right of peaceable assembly, the right to petition the government, freedom of worship, the right to bail, trial by jury, and the protection of private property. But the minority report contained additional provisions. It established just compensation for all property taken for public use, protective laws for all church denominations, the subordination of the military to civil power, free elections and suffrage for all men (except those legally disfranchised), and a prohibition against the transportation of persons to other states for trial.[29] Such additional proposals, the black delegates felt, ensured full, equal rights for Louisiana's black citizens.

Some delegates demanded additional civil rights. Pinchback was author of the notable Civil Rights Article, which proved to

Segregation in Ante-Bellum New Orleans," *American Historical Review*, LXXXIV (February, 1969), 936–37.

28. *Journal of the Proceedings of the Convention for Framing a Constitution*, 201, 289.

29. *Ibid.*, 15, 21, 24, 26–27, 35–37, 40–41, 84–85, 96.

be one of the most far-reaching measures in the constitution. Introduced on December 31, 1867, this article granted blacks the same rights and privileges as whites on common carriers and in places of business or public entertainment. When the proposal came up for consideration on January 2 and 3, 1868, it was debated and then adopted by a vote of fifty-eight to sixteen. Minor improvements in wording were suggested by the Committee on Revision and accepted on February 22. As Article Thirteen of the ratified constitution, the measure stated: "All persons shall enjoy equal rights and privileges upon any conveyance of a public character; and all places as required by either State, parish or muncipal authority, shall be deemed places of a public character and shall be opened to the accommodation and patronage of all persons, without distinction or discrimination on account of race or color." This article was similar in wording and meaning to the subsequent Federal Civil Rights Acts of 1875. Both were designed to guarantee blacks protection and rights to the enjoyment of public accommodation; both also were inadequately enforced. The federal act was later rendered inoperative by the United States Supreme Court in 1883.[30]

Discussion of marriage laws and reforms was also crucial. The first request for stricter regulations came from James H. Ingraham. Early in the convention, he offered a resolution entitled "Matrimony." It urged persons: "formerly debarred by slavery from legally contracting matrimony in the state, who have lived together as husband and wife for three consecutive years prior to the adoption of this Constitution, shall be deemed, after the adoption of the Constitution, in all courts of justice, as husband and wife." Their children would then be "their legal heirs as though said disability had never existed." This resolution was referred to the Committee on Judiciary. After no action was

30. *Ibid*, 56, 57, 96–97, 121, 125, 234, 243; New Orleans *Daily Picayune*, December 4, 28, 1867, January 2, 4, February 25, 1868; *Constitution of the State of Louisiana with Amendments* (New Orleans: Republican Office, 1875), 4–5; Franklin, *Reconstruction*, 223; Kenneth M. Stampp, *The Era of Reconstruction, 1865–1877* (New York: Alfred A. Knopf, 1965), 140.

taken, another black delegate, Robert I. Cromwell, unsuccessfully proposed a similar measure, with stricter provisions. It ignored the number of years of "co-habiting," and legalized the relationship of husband and wife if the parties had lived together before or at the time the constitution was adopted. Their children, it further asserted, "shall be deemed legitimate, whether born before or after the adoption of the Constitution." Again, in late January, 1868, this issue appeared when a delegate urged the adoption of the article with the stipulation that women could sue for breach of promise. The measure was debated in the convention until it was finally laid on the table by a vote of forty-nine to nineteen. Robert H. Isabelle, a black delegate from New Orleans, tried unsuccessfully to have the amendment adopted because he felt that since the courts were open to all persons, it was unwise to deny the partners in common-law marriages an opportunity "to marry and legalize their children." The matter was not resolved during the convention, but Pinchback secured Senate passage of a bill legalizing common-law marriage. This bill later passed the House during the first legislative session.[31]

Other reforms centered around land, homesteads, labor laws, extension of the Freedmen's Bureau term, regular reports of auditor, noncompensation for former slaveholders, abolition of contracts "bounding" out children under the Freedmen's Bureau agents and their return, more rigid resident requirements, strict Assembly attendance rules, citizen-appointed policemen for New Orleans, the militia, the excise tax on liquor, relief for the veterans of 1812 and 1815, licensing of lotteries, and payment of the delegates. Pinchback pushed through the article setting the lieutenant governor's salary at $3,000 per annum. The black members, in accord with the *Tribune's* demands, wanted land redistribution in order to relieve the widespread destitution among Louisiana's black community. This involved

31. *Journal of the Proceedings of the Convention for Framing a Constitution*, 16, 48, 192, 198, 206–207; New Orleans *Daily Picayune*, December 1, 1867, February 5, 1868; Grosz, "P. B. S. Pinchback," 13; Chap. IV herein.

land purchased at nominal prices. The program did not materalize. Robert I. Cromwell was successful, however, in securing adoption of a provision that allowed "no person to buy more than 100 acres and not less than five." This measure was designed to aid the poor. Exemption for personal property from forced sale because of default on mortage payment, up to the value of five hundred dollars was urged by delegates; homestead tax exemptions for one thousand dollars and "eighty acres of land and dwelling houses theron" were likewise advocated. These measures were not passed, although Article 132 stated: "All lands sold in pursuance of decrees of Courts shall be divided into tracts of from ten to fifty acres." Abolition of imprisonment for debt further relieved the most unfortunate classes. Another black delegate, Arnold Bertonneau, urged a social welfare article. It read: "Institution for the support of the insane, the education and support of the blind and the deaf and dumb, shall always be fostered by the state, and be subject to such regulations as may be prescribed by the General Assembly." The proposal was adopted by the convention. Robert H. Isabelle promoted a resolution which taxed each delegate 30 percent of his pay "for charitable purposes." This article was adopted by a vote of forty to thirty-two.[32]

Since many of the delegates were former soldiers, the militia, in many instances, took priority over other matters, such as tax reform. The quickly organized Militia Committee held an early meeting, and presented its report to the session several weeks after the convention opened. This report gave the General Assembly power to organize a militia consisting of all able-bodied males between the ages of eighteen and forty-five and not disfranchised by the constitution. It further authorized the governor to appoint commissioned officers, with the confirmation of the Senate. All militia officers had to take an oath similar to the

32. *Journal of the Proceedings of the Convention for Framing a Constitution*, 16, 25, 29, 34–35, 44, 48, 79, 83, 115, 122, 151–52, 158, 169, 191–92, 204, 220–21, 237, 249, 260, 267, 271, 291, 299, 306.

one taken by officers of the United States Army. The article was eventually adopted.[33]

In general, the demands of the delegates were not of a revolutionary character. They envisaged no radical change in the structure of Louisiana's economic life or government. Yet some features of the new constitution were indeed different, however, and did pose numerous problems for the former Confederates. These involved administering such innovations as universal suffrage, charitable programs, and free public schools. Few of these changes pleased the conservatives and former Confederates, who disliked both the congressional measures and their advocates on the state level.[34] The black delegates' demands, if they were not put into operation then, were carried over into the General Assembly. These demands changed only slightly and provided some of the basic issues discussed during Reconstruction.

The constitutional convention completed its work on March 9, 1868. There were a number of basic differences between this constitution and the constitution of 1864. The new document provided that all persons should enjoy equal rights and privileges; it set up a state citizenship requirement; it provided that no public schools or institutions should be established exclusively for any race; and it enacted a new suffrage law providing disfranchisement of Confederate leaders, against which a few blacks dissented. The new suffrage law provided stringent disfranchisement of Confederate leaders. It permitted every adult male citizen of the United States, resident of Louisiana for one year, to vote except (a) persons convicted of crime or under interdict; (b) those who had held any office for one year or more under the so-called Confederate states; (c) registered enemies of the United States; (d) leaders of guerilla bands during the rebel-

33. *Ibid.*, 40, 205.
34. Franklin, *Reconstruction*, 118; Stampp, *The Era of Reconstruction*, 170–72; Roger W. Shugg, *Origins of Class Struggle in Louisiana* (Baton Rouge: Louisiana State University Press, 1939), 222.

lion; (e) those who, in the advocacy of treason, wrote or published newspaper articles or preached sermons during the rebellion; and (f) those who voted for or signed the ordinance of
secession in any state.[35] The constitutitn also prescribed an
oath, even for legislators, pledging state officeholders to accept
the political and civil equality of all men; it abolished the Black
Code labor laws passed by the Democratic legislature of 1865;
and it provided that representation in the General Assembly
should be based on total population.

Many of the convention delegates had had little experience in
exercising political power or personal independence. But these
limitations did not prevent them from establishing a workable
structure of government, a fact that not even the bitterest Confederates could justifiably deny. The constitution was adopted in
the convention by a vote of seventy-one to six. Various black
delegates voiced the ratification of their colleages in the document. "I vote *yes* with the profound conviction that the constitution secures to all people of this state equal justice," said James
H. Ingraham. William Murrell declared that "it embodied the
highest principles of justice, humanity and equality before the
law."[36]

The Negro delegates did not try to elevate the issue of race
above the matter of ability. The charge of the New Orleans
Crescent that they had "wrested" power from "the intelligent"
was unfounded. In fact, the conscientiousness of the blacks was
reflected in their desire to see that qualified men held important
posts in the convention and in their efforts to aid the freedmen.
The black delegates' clash with G. M. Wickliffe a white extreme
Radical, best illustrates their concern. Wickliffe urged that all
subordinate officers be taken equally from the two races. Pinchback argued that such a plan, placing color above merit, would
not necessarily ensure just decisions on matters of importance.

35. *Constitution of the State of Louisiana*, Title VI, Articles 98, 99.
36. Franklin, *Reconstruction*, 118; *Journal of the Proceedings of the Convention for
Framing a Constitution*, 277, 282.

He maintained that offices should be awarded not on the basis of race but on the basis of education.[37]

The ratification of the constitution and the selection of state officials opened new avenues for black political participation. Both ratification and election of state officials would occur on the same days. April 16 and 17 were the dates appointed for taking the popular vote on the constitution. General R. C. Buchanan, who had replaced General Hancock, was in charge of the ratification and selection of officers. Earlier, on March 25, 1868, General Buchanan had issued an order that the recent act of Congress (March 12) should be applied—that a majority of votes cast should decide the election without reference to the number of registered voters. His decree included a warning against dismissing black laborers who voted Republican, and he ordered the military to prevent unfairness.[38]

Ratification and election of state officials were the next steps to ensure the operation of their programs. Much opposition and many scare tactics were used by the Democratic newspapers. Blacks and radicals hastily organized nominating conventions and selected local and state officials. In Alexandria, Rapides Parish, the "black and tan chiefs" set March 21 as their date of selecting nominees. The *Democrat* said of the laborers: "It mattered not the snap of a . . . finger to them, that our planters were very much behind with their work owing to the bad season; not at all; they quit the plow, dropped the shovel and the hoe, mounted their broken down mustangs and made Headquarters in time to take active parts in the initial meeting of the season. We may look for such gatherings and such neglect of crops from this time to November."[39]

37. New Orleans *Crescent*, November 22, 1867; Dunbar-Nelson, "People of Color in Louisiana, Part II," 74. Wickliffe's proposal was tabled by a vote of forty-seven to thirty-eight. *Journal of the Proceedings of the Convention for Framing a Constitution*, 4.

38. Ficklen, *Reconstruction in Louisiana*, 201; Pinchback had offered a "Memorial resolution" early in the convention to be sent to the national Congress urging a majority vote for approval. This resolution was adopted. *Journal of the Proceedings of the Convention for Framing a Constitution*, 27–28.

39. Alexandria *Democrat*, March 25, 1868; New Orleans *Times*, March 14, 15, 17,

Others who had not registered still had time. The New Orleans *Times* of April 9, described the following at City Hall: "About fifty freedmen—the lame, maimed, and sick—at the Marine Hospital were this morning forced into three furniture carts and conveyed to the registration office at City Hall, for the purpose of being qualified for the coming election. These men in all stages of illness, parched with fever, emaciated with long confinement, prostrated with debility, many of them on crutches, standing in the hall all morning awaiting their turn."

White efforts to prevent ratification were widespread. In Bellevue, Bossier Parish, one newspaper used scare tactics to stir sentiment to vote down the constitution. The paper asserted: "The issue before the people of the State in the coming election is a single one—*Negro equality*. Will all men, whigs, democrats, rebels, Americans and Union men, unite on that one issue and VOTE DOWN THE CONSTITUTION!" Ratification was often equated with black equality. To others this meant integration. One paper used the example of a local bar to scare whites into opposition: "How would you feel sitting at the table of the Ice House, between a brace of big bucks? The way to effectively put a stop to such infamies is to vote against the Constitution." It urged a total involvement—"every white man, every white lad, every white woman, every white lass . . . to be up and doing." Other tactics included listing the registration figures: "3101! 1300!" The editor then asked his readers to see if they could reduce the large total of the foe to a mere fraction.[40]

There was, however, little chance of defeating the constitution or the Radical Republican candidates. On January 4, 1868, the Republicans met to nominate candidates for the April election. The uncompromising Radical faction, led by Dr.

April 4, 1868. The April 9 issue has local registration figures for the various wards. New Orleans *Daily Picayune*, April 7, 8, 10, 17, 1868.

40. Bossier *Banner*, March 21, 28, 1868; Carroll *Record*, March 28, 1868; New Orleans *Times*, April 16, 17, 18, 28, 1868; Louisiana *Democrat*, April 8, 15, 22, 1868; Lafourche *Sentinel*, June 27, 1868.

Louis C. Roudanez, founder and owner of the New Orleans *Tribune*, wanted a black nominated for governor. On the first ballot Francis E. Dumas, a black nominated by this faction, received more votes than any of the other candidates. Dumas received forty-one votes; Henry Clay Warmoth received thirty-seven; W. M. Wickliffe received four; James G. Taliaferro (president of the convention) received three; and W. J. Blackburn received three. After the lowest three nominees were dropped, and the second ballot was held, Warmoth defeated Dumas by only two votes, forty-five to forty-three. Dumas then received the nomination for lieutenant governor; but he refused it. Oscar James Dunn was nominated instead.[41]

The uncompromising Radicals were unsatisfied with this arrangement. They nominated their own candidate, James G. Taliaferro, for governor. Taliaferro received votes and support from various and strange political sources—some Democrats, several conservative newspapers, the German element, and the uncompromising Republicans.[42]

The election passed off quietly, Warmoth defeating Taliaferro by a vote of 65,270 to 38,118. Taliaferro carried fifteen parishes out of forty-eight. Of these fifteen, nine had more registered white voters. Warmoth carried thirty "black parishes" and only three parishes where a majority of registered voters were whites. The constitution was also ratified by a vote of 66,152 to 48,739 against.[43]

41. Warmoth, *War, Politics and Reconstruction: Stormy Days in Louisiana*, 51–59; Alexandria *Democrat*, January 22, 1868.

42. Wynona G. Mills, "James G. Taliaferro (1798–1876): Louisiana Unionist and Scalawag," (M. A. thesis, Louisiana State University, 1968), 76–81; New Orleans *Daily Picayune*, March 7, April 11, 1868.

43. Bossier *Banner*, April 25, 1868; New Orleans *Times*, April 18, 21, 1868; Mills, "James G. Taliaferro," 82–85. F. Wayne Binning, "Carpetbagger's Triumph: The Louisiana Election of 1868," *Louisiana History*, XIV (Winter, 1973), 31–38, contends that the Warmoth faction had successfully scored a coup to the Roudanez faction in controlling the party. Thomas Conway to Warmoth, February 15, 1868, in Warmoth Papers; Donald W. Davis, "Ratification of the Constitution of 1868—Records of Votes," *Louisiana History*, VI (Summer, 1965), 301–305; Martin Abbott (ed.), "Reconstruction in Louisiana: Three Letters," *Louisiana History*, I (Spring, 1960), 156–57.

Louisiana's black leaders and their white allies had accomplished the first step of their program. They had written a nondiscriminatory constitution that would protect the rights of all. Now they had to specifically implement its provisions with legislative measures. Another struggle would face them in the General Assembly.

CHAPTER IV

Education and Civil Rights, 1868–1870

The election held on April 16 and 17, after the ratification of the constitution elevated blacks to public office for the first time in Louisiana. Whites, not yet recovered from having blacks assist in the framing of the constitution, now turned their attention to the legislature. What would be the black legislators' demands? How would they vote and what laws would they request? Whites seemed not to be concerned with the fact that blacks were a minority in both houses, or that they would continue to be, or that they were a fairly well-educated group. Most of the black legislators were freeborn and were educated at the professional level or in trades. Even among the few who had been slaves, none can be identified as completely illiterate.

The percentage of blacks in the two houses varied. In 1868, although there were more blacks in the House than in the Senate, they never constituted more than slightly over one-third of the total—35 out of a membership of 120. The Senate had only 7 blacks out of 38 members.[1]

A large number of Negro delegates to the constitutional convention were elected to the first legislature. However, there were twenty-four blacks—over half—who had not served in the

1. Warmoth, *War, Politics and Reconstruction*; xii, states that there were six senators. Franklin, *Reconstruction*, 134–35, says there were forty-two blacks in the first legislature. The New Orleans *Republican*, March 20, September 15, 1870, lists long-term senators and short-term senators.

convention. The representatives elected from Orleans Parish were generally all businessmen of varied wealth. Representative Octave Belot, thirty-five years old and a native of New Orleans, was a leading businessman in the city. A cigar maker, he also owned a coffeehouse and several "property houses." He could not speak English well because of his African-French heritage. His brother, who was later a representative, and his father were also prominent citizens of New Orleans; they testified later that they were often objects of abuse and discrimination.[2]

Other Orleans representatives listed as businessmen included the following: Jerry Hall, a thirty-year-old saloonkeeper and native of Philadelphia; Joseph Mansion, a thirty-year-old cigar-store operator; Frank Alexander, a blacksmith; and Curron Adolphe, a grocer. Representative Felix C. Antoine of the Third District was the younger brother of Senator Caesar C. Antoine and a man of considerable wealth. Born in New Orleans in 1839, Antoine had served as a second lieutenant in the Seventh Louisiana Colored Voluntary Infantry; he was a mechanic.[3] New Orleans furnished eight representatives to the legislature of 1868, including Robert Isabelle, the dyer, who had attended the constitutional convention.

The other parishes selected men of varied backgrounds and abilities. Typical of this class was David Young of Concordia, a parish that was 92.8 percent black in 1870. Young was the political leader in his home parish for over twelve years. He was born a slave in Kentucky on February 4, 1836. While a boy he

2. See Appendices B and F, herein; *Gardner and Wharton's New Orleans Directory, 1858*, 37; *House Miscellaneous Documents*, 41st Cong., 2nd Sess., Pt. 1, No. 154, p. 253. Belot was later awarded $27,000 damages by a jury in New Orleans for property damaged in the political excitement of the fall, 1868, Carroll *Record*, March 6, 1869; New Orleans *Times*, February 26, 1869.

3. *Senate Miscellaneous Documents*, 44th Cong., 2nd Sess., No. 14, p. 760; *House Miscellaneous Documents*, 45th Cong., 3rd Sess., No. 34, Pt. 1, pp. 189, 190–92; New Orleans *Weekly Louisianian*, January 28, 1882; *Gardner and Wharton's Directory, 1858*, pp. 59, 201, *1866*, pp. 37, 189, 268; Succession Papers of Lucien Mansion, United States Court House, New Orleans; Civil War Pension Files, Records of the Veterans Administration, RG 15, NA. Representative Antoine was married in November, 1859; See also, *Edwards' Annual Directory . . . City of New Orleans For 1870*, p. 44.

ran away and escaped to Ohio. There he was captured and brought to Natchez, Mississippi, in 1850. Subsequently, he was taken to Vidalia in late 1851. A natural leader, Young rose rapidly in Concordia Parish after emancipation. He was elected to the House in 1868, 1870, and 1872. He and his brother John, who was the sheriff of the parish, dominated the politics of Concordia during the 1870s. He owned a clothing store and published a newspaper in which he featured the slogan Equal Rights to All Men. The *Eagle* was published until the mid 1880s and was designated the Official Journal of Concordia. After six years in the House, Young was elected to an equal number of years in the Senate. In addition, he was a member of the town council and later treasurer of the school board.[4]

De Soto Parish also sent a former slave as one of its representatives, Stephen Humphreys. He had become a carpenter and owned a "shop downtown." Humphreys was not freed until the surrender. While still a slave he learned to read and write in Prince Georges County, Maryland; he later moved to Mansfield, De Soto Parish, where he was living when elected to the legislature. He was well respected, and he ran for office only because his neighbors urged him to. During the voting in April, Humphrey had to hide out to save his life from enraged whites. Unlike Young and Humphreys, Harry Lott of Rapides Parish, was a northern-born free black. Lott was a leading businessman in

4. Concordia *Eagle*, October 2, 1875, March 3, 1877; William Ivy Hair, *Bourbonism and Agrarian Protest: Louisiana Politics, 1877–1900* (Baton Rouge: Louisiana State University Press, 1969), 96–97; *Senate Reports*, 45th Cong., 3rd Sess., No. 855, pp. 131–38. Young's service on the school board (1871–73) earned him condemnation from blacks and whites in Concordia Parish when the school fund totaling $30,000 disappeared. Court suits were instituted against him, but after Governor Kellogg intervened a nolle prosequi was issued by the district attorney. *Senate Reports*, 46th Cong., 3rd Sess., No. 855, pp. xviii, 368–73; *House Miscellaneous Documents*, 44th Cong., 2nd Sess., No. 34, Pt. 1, pp. 57, 158, 162, 226–29, 255–56; New Orleans *Daily Picayune*, February 5, 1875; New Orleans *Republican*, October 29, 1874; The 1870 Census listed Young as a thirty-three-year-old "Grocer Rt." He owned real estate valued at $5,000 and $3,000 worth of personal property. His wife was thirty-seven years old and also a native of Kentucky. They had a three-year-old daughter, a domestic servant, a clerk, and a laborer living with them. U. S. Census Population Schedule, 1870, Concordia Parish, Vidalia, Ward 4, p. 54; *Louisiana Annals*, 158.

Alexandria. As a barber, he served both blacks and whites. He was born in Wheelerburg, Ohio, near Portsmouth, and moved to Alexandria in May, 1862. His father came from Philadelphia and his mother from Maryland. Educated in Ohio, Lott attended schools in Cincinnati and Cleveland. He was thirty-five years old when the legislature convened in 1868.[5]

Gloster Hill of Ascension served from 1868 until 1870 and was returned for two more years, 1874–1876. He was born free in New Orleans, February 15, 1840. Apprenticed as a carpenter, Hill joined the Union army on August 20, 1863, and was honorably discharged in December, 1865, at Tallahassee, Florida, with the rank of first sergeant of Company K, Ninety-ninth Regiment, United States Colored Volunteer Infantry. He later qualified for a pension because of injuries received and illness contracted in the War. Hill lived in Ascension Parish until he was removed to Charity Hospital in New Orlenas where he died in 1919 at the age of seventy-eight.[6]

Less biographical information survives other representatives who served during 1868–1870. The remaining ten representatives were almost invisible men. But the following information, although vague, can be documented: Emile Honoré of Pointe Coupee served two terms and was a member of an influential political family. The brothers Robert and Victor Lange were members from East Baton Rouge. Robert died in 1870 after gangrene infested his leg which he had injured in a riding accident. Both had entered the legislature after contested election disputes. The thirty-five-year-old Moses Sterrett, of Caddo Parish, who had been a steward, served only one term. H. C. Tournier, of Pointe Coupee, was copublisher of the Pointee Coupee *Republican*. Tournier's colleague from the same parish,

5. *House Miscellaneous Documents*, 41st Cong., 2nd Sess., Pt. 1, No. 154, pp. 319–23. Humphreys testified that blacks in his parish did not look for "forty acres and a mule" but only wanted honest work. See also *ibid.*, 44th Cong., 2nd Sess., No. 34, Pt. 1, pp. 348–50; Lott was also a depositor in the Freedmen's Saving and Trust Company. See Register of Signature of Depositors in Branches of the Freedmen's Saving and Trust Co., 1865, RG 101, NA; Alexandria *Democrat*, June 17, 1868.

6. Civil War Pension Files, Records of the Veterans Administration, RG 15, NA.

William Smith, died suddenly on October 5, 1868. Robert Taylor, of West Feliciana Parish, was a newcomer who served one term, as did East Feliciana's black representative, William C. Williams. St. James Parish also sent two black representatives in 1868, Adolphe Tureaud, who remained until 1874, and Charles Gray, 1868–1870. George Washington would serve Assumption Parish throughout the Warmoth regime. Another black representative, Noel Douglas, of St. Landry, did not appear until late in the session because of a contested election, and he served only one term.[7]

Of the seven senators who served in the 1868 session, five—over half—had served in the constitutional convention. These included: Senators Caesar C. Antoine, of Caddo, who entered the senate after a contested election on September 24, 1868; George Y. Kelso, a businessman from Rapides; Curtis Pollard, the part-time minister from Carroll; Robert Poindexter, a farmer from Assumption; and P. B. S. Pinchback of the Second District, Orleans Parish; Pinchback's seat was also contested. Alexander E. François of St. Mary, East and West Baton Rouge, and Julian J. Monette of Orleans, former captain in the Sixth Louisiana Volunteers for the Union, were beginning on their first elective offices. Monette, who was one of the incorporators of the Mississippi River Packet Company in 1870, dropped out of politics after his brief term in the Senate.[8]

7. New Orleans *Times*, April 26, 1868; Baton Rouge *Tri Weekly Advocate*, March 4, 1870; *Official Journal of the Proceedings of the House of Representative of the State of Louisiana* (New Orleans: A. L. Lee, 1868), 254, hereinafter cited as *House Journal* with date indicated; *Weekly Louisianian*, June 22, 1871; *Weekly Iberville South,* December 26, 1868; Custom House nominations, Louisiana, New Orleans, January 1, 1868–June, 1869, Box 109, RG 56, NA; New Orleans *Crescent*, October 7, 1868; Interview with the late A. P. Tureaud, Summer, 1970; *House Miscellaneous Documents,* 44th Cong., 2nd Sess., No. 34, Pt. 2, p. 628. Tureaud sent his children to private schools. *House Journal, 1870*, pp. 270, 300.

8. New Orleans *Crescent*, September 13, 17, 25, 1868. Antoine's opponent, John R. White, was declared ineligible for office by the Senate (the writer used the Senate proceedings and general debates as published in the *Picayune* and *Crescent* for the 1868 session). For Pinchback's contest see, Thibodaux *Sentinel*, September 5, 1868. Pinchback unseated E. L. Jewell of Orleans. Monette paid taxes on $700 worth of real estate in Orleans Parish, *Register of Taxes*, 1871, L to P, New Orleans Public Library, New Orleans.

François had a short and tragic career. Before going into politics he had followed various occupations. Born a free black in St. Martin Parish, he had been a butcher, merchant, and planter. After his death in early May, 1869, Senator Pinchback eulogized him with the following words: "He bore a character there [St. Martin] of honesty and integrity that entitled him to the respect of the people. As to his character upon the floor of the Senate, I believe none can complain of that, either as political friends or opponents. He was ever a quiet, unostentatious, gentlemanly, courteous member of this body."[9]

François' death, which came after he served only one year of his four-year term, went almost unnoted in the conservative newspapers in the parishes he represented. The *Weekly Iberville South* carried only several small items. One article was entitled "A Senator Cowhided." Reportedly Senator François had addressed a letter to the citizens of St. Martin during the campaign of 1868, giving his family background. The report also stated that for generations a white family (allied with three others) in the parish had ruled as a hereditary monarchy. François named the members and further asserted that there had been few evil deeds committed there without the involvement of a member of one of these families. Several weeks later two men of the family approached Senator François in the town of St. Martinville and beat him severely with a cowhide and hickory stick. He was taken to New Orleans where he died approximately three weeks later.[10]

The legislature convened on June 29, 1868, with apparent harmony between black and white members. The atmosphere

9. *Debates of the Senate of the State of Louisiana* (New Orleans: A. L. Lee, 1870), 6, hereinafter cited as *Senate Debates*, with date indicated; New Orleans *Daily Picayune*, May 14, 1868.

10. *Courier of the Teche* quoted in the *Weekly Iberville South*, May 13, 1868; *Ibid.*, May 29, 1868; *House Miscellaneous Documents*, 41st Cong., 2nd Sess., No. 154, Pt. 1, p. 634, Pt. 2, pp. 490–91. His teenage son witnessed the incident. The senator's other son was justice of the peace in Saint Martinville before he was forced to leave. Senator François had earlier served as an agent of the New Orleans *Tribune* in St. Martinville and "the whole Attakapas," New Orleans *Tribune*, October 15, 1865. Apparently no action was taken against the guilty persons.

was particularly cordial after the test oath conflict was settled. In the forty-four House seats contested, only six blacks were involved. Five of the blacks were eventually seated. They were Moses Sterrett of Caddo, Jerry Hall of Orleans, Noel Douglas of St. Landry, and Victor and Robert Lange of East Baton Rouge. Another black, Samuel Wakefield of Iberia, was not seated. Senators Antoine and Pinchback were involved in contested elections but were seated; two other blacks claiming seats failed.[11]

The first responsibility of the assembly was to ratify the Fourteenth Amendment and to select United States senators to fill the seats that had been vacant since John Slidell and Judah P. Benjamin had resigned in 1861. Without much dispute, the legislature voted to send William P. Kellogg, a lawyer of Vermont, and John S. Harris, a native of New York, to Washington; both were white and carpetbaggers. They took their places along with the five elected members of the House, one of whom, J. Willis Menard, a northern-born, educated black creole, however, who was not admitted.[12]

11. Oscar J. Dunn of the Senate and Robert H. Isabelle, temporary chairman of the House, declared that since the state was still under military law as well as under Reconstruction law, they deemed it necessary for members to take both the stringent test oath and the new oath of the constitution. The test oath request was soon dropped in favor of a milder oath. Ficklen, *Reconstruction in Louisiana*, 203–204. See critical comments in New Orleans *Times*, July 4, 1868; New Orleans *Daily Picayune* July 1, 24, August 2, 4, September 1, 17, 1868. See *House Journal, 1868*, p. 3, 252, 254; New Orleans *Crescent*, September 17, 1868.

12. The Census of Concordia Parish, 1870, lists John S. Harris, a native of New York, as owning no personal or real estate in the parish. United States Census Reports, Schedules, Concordia Parish, 1870. Vidalia, Ward 4, p. 56; Bossier *Banner* July 18, 1868. *House Journal, 1868*, p. 19; Cromwell advised black legislators to vote for senators who would be "true to the Negro race." New Orleans *Times*, June 28, 1868. Menard, who had served as a clerk in the Department of Interior and later published two newspapers, had also authored a book of poems. In 1868 he was nominated and elected on the Republican ticket to fill the unexpired term of James Mann, Second District of Louisiana, who had died in late August, 1868. A conflicting three-way contest for the seat evolved when Caleb S. Hunt, Democrat, challenged Menard's election and Simon Jones, Republican, contested the right of the deceased James Mann to have held the seat. The lower House of Congress decided against all three and the seat remained vacant until March 4, 1869. All three men, however, were given $2,500, an amount equal to their salary if they had been seated. Although Menard was not seated, he had the distinction of being the first Negro to speak on the floor of the House of Representatives. Edith Menard, "John

With these matters out of the way, the legislature turned to performining its principal function, enacting laws. Most descriptions of its work are exaggerated and reflect prejudices or preconceptions of the writers. The classic picture of the Louisiana legislature, and other Reconstruction legislatures, depicts a body controlled by evil whites and ignorant Negroes who combined to steal the state blind. There was corruption in the Louisiana legislature, and blacks have some responsibility for it. Some of them engaged in corruption simply because they were corrupt men and saw a chance for quick money. Others succumbed to the temptations offered by powerful corporate forces, the same forces that corrupted other legislatures. Thus blacks supported the chartering of the Louisiana Lottery Company, a gigantic gambling concern that had been used in antebellum Louisiana, and rechartered, by the all-white legislature of 1866; the Louisiana Levee Company, which was to control and repair levees on the Mississippi River financed by heavy taxes; and the Canal Monopoly granted the New Orleans and Ship Island Canal Company charter that authorized it to construct a canal from the Mississippi River in Jefferson Parish just above New Orleans, through the Rigolets to Ship Island in the Mississippi Sound. For tolls the corporation could charge any amount it wished. It should be noted, however, that not all legislation favoring corporations was corrupt. Some members of both races supported subsidiaries to corporations as a means to close the economic gap separating the South from the North.

Typical accounts of the Louisiana legislature also emphasize the autocratic powers voted to Governor Henry Clay Warmoth, implying or stating that lawmakers assented to these powers because the ambitious governor purchased or forced their consent. Warmoth was a man with dreams of empire and on numer-

Willis Menard, First Negro Elected to the U.S. Congress, First Negro to Speak in the U.S. Congress: A Documentary," *Negro History Bulletin*, XXVIII (December, 1964), 53–54; Bossier *Banner*, May 8, 1869; J. Willis Menard to Henry C. Warmoth, November 19, 1868, in Warmoth Papers; New Orleans *Times*, January 23, 24, February 3, 28, March 2, 7, 1869.

ous occasions did pressure the legislature to do his bidding. He doubtless used pressure to get the power laws passed. But both he and the legislature felt they had justification for supporting them. Warmoth, for example, feared that his power base would be in danger without additional controls. He secured the passage of four acts. The Registration Act empowered the governor to appoint the registrar of voters, who in turn appointed the polling officials. The Election Act authorized him to appoint commissioners of election to preside at the ballot boxes. The Constabulary Act gave him power to appoint constables in all parishes except Jefferson and St. Bernard. The Militia Act made him commander in chief of all the state militia; he could organize, arm, equip, and uniform as many able-bodied male citizens between the ages of eighteen and forty-one as he deemed necessary. Senator Pinchback, speaking on the election bill, revealed the reason for his assent. The current law, Pinchback maintained, did not provide for "honest expression of the opinion of the people of the state at the ballot box." Whites felt free to intimidate black voters, he declared, citing violence that occurred during the November, 1868, election as proof. Vesting power in Warmoth was the lesser of two evils, Pinchback concluded. He was not a "lover or worshipper" of the governor, but violence against blacks had to be stopped.[13]

Blacks were willing to entrust the governor with even greater powers. Senator Curtis Pollard introduced a bill authorizing the governor to issue a warrant for the arrest of any person committing a crime punishable by death or imprisonment if parish authorities failed to seize him. he was to be tried by a parish or district court. Critics of the bill said it gave the governor the

13. *Acts Passed by the General Assembly of the State of Louisiana* (New Orleans: A. L. Lee, 1870), Nos. 99 (Registration), 100 (Election), 74 (Constabulary), 75 (Militia), hereinafter cited as *Acts* with appropriate year; New Orleans *Times*, February 25, 1869; New Orleans *Republican*, January 12, 15, 24, 1871; *Senate Debates, 1870*, pp. 169–75. The election bill passed the Senate 20–12 without a single black dissent, and the registration bill met with no black opposition. *Official Journal of the Proceedings of the Senate of the State of Louisiana* (New Orleans: A. L. Lee, 1870), 72, 74, 110, 136, 139–40, 150 hereinafter cited as *Senate Journal* with appropriate date.

power to disregard parish lines, but the law won approval in both houses.[14]

Black legislators were convinced that a strong militia was necessary to preserve Republican and Negro power. Conversely, they feared that extralegal white military organizations might attempt to overthrow the Warmoth administration. Consequently, Representative J. B. Esnard proposed an act to "prohibit the formation and continuance of military organizations, except such as were established by law," that is, were part of the militia. Attempts to form unofficial military units were to be regarded as felonies, and the persons instigating them were liable to imprisonment for not less than one year or more than three years. The bill passed the House with no black dissent by a vote of 49 to 11, and won easy approval in the Senate.[15]

In addition to supporting legislation extending favor to corporate or other economic interests, blacks sometimes championed bills to gain narrow personal profits. At least three black representatives and two senators secured legislation giving them ferry privileges in their districts. One such act granted Curtis Pollard and Henderson Williams ferry rights across the Mississippi River near the town of Delta in Madison Parish. They had to pay the parish a tax of $300 and the rate they charged had to be approved by the parish. When first introduced and adopted in the House, the privilege was assigned to Albert Housinger and Henderson Williams; in the Senate, Pollard's name was substituted for Housinger's.[16]

Another act authorized black representative Milton Morris and a J. E. Warren to operate a ferry for a distance of two miles above and below Donaldsonville on the Mississippi River. Although ferry charges were to be set by the police jury, other

14. *Senate Journal, 1870,* p. 25; *Acts of 1870, Extra Session,* No., 40
15. *House Journal, 1868,* pp. 101, 109, New Orleans *Crescent,* August 12, 1868; *Acts of 1868,* No. 38, pp. 44–46.
16. *Senate Journal, 1869,* pp. 22, 203–204, 214; *Senate Journal, 1870, Extra Session,* 319; *House Journal, 1869, Extra Session,* 383; *Acts of 1869,* pp. 73–74.

ferries in the area were prohibited. For this monopoly the operators had to pay the parish a tax of only $125.[17]

Another black legislator, William Murrell, shared the ferry privilege across the Bayou Lafourche at Donaldsonville with a Marx Shomberg. The charter granted them a twenty-year right at a monthly rate of forty dollars, payable to the police jury. Unlike the other ferry privileges granted, this charter stated the amount to be charged: one footman, five cents; a single horse or mule, five cents; a cart or one-horse wagon, twenty cents. This ferry was operated until 1882 when a bridge on Bayou Lafourche was constructed.[18]

The ferry privilege at Napoleonville was secured by Senator Robert Poindexter. The charter granted him fifteen years of operation; rates charged were to be the same as that of other ferries throughout the parish, but schoolchildren could cross free of charge. The only restriction on the operation of these ferries was that they were responsible for damages. Although the promoters of these enterprises were seeking profits, they may have had an additional motive. Some legislators thought that only black-operated ferries would assure blacks of passage at these locations. Certainly black leaders realized that their people were often subjected to restrictions in traveling. Thus a desire to guarantee travel rights may have influenced Senator Pinchback when he managed the passage of an act establishing the Mississippi River Packet Company, which catered to blacks. On the other hand Pinchback was one of the incorporators and stood to gain money on the transaction. Later he helped to

17. *House Journal, 1870,* 29, 33, 49, 99, 130, 205, 225; *Senate Journal, 1870,* 103, 109, 156, 157. Representatives Robert H. Isabelle introduced this bill in the House; *Acts of 1870,* No. 35, pp. 62–63. This bill became law without the governor's signature.

18. *House Journal, 1870,* p. 102; *House Journal, 1870, Extra Session,* 359; *Senate Journal, 1870,* pp. 205, 108, *1875,* p. 28. This bill, as first introduced, did not include two names rather one name, a Charles Robinson; Charles Nordhoff, *The Cotton States in the Spring and Summer of 1875* (New York: D. Appleton and Company, 1876), 62. Sidney A. Marchand, *The Story of Ascension Parish Louisiana* (Donaldsonville: Sidney A. Marchand, 1931), 93–94. A resolution, offered by black Senator Pierre Landry in 1875, urging a special committee to investigate ferry privileges was not adopted.

secure an appropriation of twenty-five thousand dollars from the state government to aid the corporation. The only benefit the state received, according to one source, was to appoint three directors of the company.[19]

It is the corporate and corrupt legislation that had drawn the attention of historians of Reconstruction. They were right in characterizing many of these laws as injurious to the state, but in their haste to stigmatize the legislatures they missed part of the story. In addition to the bad laws, many acts were passed that were forward looking and that benefited the state, particularly in the areas of education and internal improvements. This part of Reconstruction has been recognized only recently by historians. It is not yet sufficiently appreciated that in enacting either bad or good laws, blacks did not have as much influence as has been thought. An examination of the places held by blacks on important committees in the Louisiana legislature will illustrate the point. Nearly all the committees created in the 1868 session had a majority of white members. This was especially true of such powerful committees as the one on finance. Generally, blacks were assigned to the less important committees. Thus, the Committee on Banks and Banking consisted of two blacks, Milton Morris and Robert Taylor, and five whites. Representative J. B. Esnard sat on the Committee on Railways with six whites. Of the three members composing the Penitentiary Committee, Gloster Hill was the only black. The powerful House Ways and Means Committee consisted of two blacks, Emile Honoré and Adolphe Tureaud, and three whites. Milton Morris, Henderson Williams, and Theophile Mahier joined four whites on the Public Building Committee. Three blacks, Robert

19. *Senate Journal, 1869*, pp. 67, 68, 86, 123, 242–43; *Acts of 1869*, No. 129, p. 68; Grosz, "P.B.S. Pinchback," 16–17; *Acts of 1870*, No. 93, pp. 128–30; *Senate Journal, 1870*, pp. 137, 158, 177, 213; *House Journal, 1870*, pp. 230, 257, 284; Senator C. C. Antoine purchased twenty shares of the capitol stock of the company for $200 on March 12, 1870. The officers included Pinchback as president and George Y. Kelso as secretary. C. C. Antoine Scrapbook. See Burch's plea in New Orleans *Republican*, February 25, 1871. The *Republican* printed the debates for the 1871 Session.

H. Isabelle, John Gair, and Samuel Cuney and four whites formed the Federal Relations Committee. Three blacks, three whites, and two vacancies were listed on each of the following seven-man committees: Claims, Contingent Expenses, Public Lands and Levees, Public Health and Quarantine, Charitable and Public Institutions, and Penitentiary Committee.[20] The Committee on Agriculture listed four members and three vacancies when it was set up. Only two members were blacks, but later Stephen Humphreys and Henderson Williams were added. William Murrell was the sole black on the five-man Printing Committee. Unlike the Committee on Militia in the constitutional convention, which had a majority of blacks, the Militia Committee of the 1868 session included only two, Frank Alexander and John Pierce, as opposed to five white members.

Blacks fared better in assignments to education-oriented committees. The House Committee on Education consisted of three blacks, Joseph Mansion, P. G. Deslonde, and F. C. Antoine and three whites. The former slave Dennis Burrell and four blacks, Curron Adolphe, Deslonde, Mansion, and Moses Sterrett and two whites comprised the State Library Committee, leaving three seats vacant.

Blacks were chairmen of only four of the twenty-one appointive committees. Octave Belot headed the Committee on Registration, which consisted of Ulger Dupart and two whites and listed three vacancies. F. C. Antoine was chairman of the Committee on Pensions; its membership consisted of Henderson Williams, three whites, and it had two vacancies. The four-man committees on the constitution and immigration were presided

20. No reason was found among records as to why vacancies were listed on many committees when first appointed, but most vacancies were filled before the session ended. *House Journal, 1868*, pp. 34, 43–44. The memberships of several committees were increased in late August, 1868. This led to Harry Lott's appointment to the Judiciary Committee on August 22. Other blacks filled vacancies on the following committees almost two weeks before the session ended: Parochial Affairs, Charitable and Public Institutions, State Library, Registration and Pensions. See September 30, 1868 session, *ibid.*, 154, 250.

over by John Gair and Harry Lott respectively; their rosters included two blacks each, one white, and three vacancies. Only one House committee had no black members. This was the powerful Judiciary Committee that listed five white members.[21]

Blacks were more numerous on the House special committees but were seldom a majority. The three-man committees named to examine the auditor's accounts and to check on the issue and disposition of levee bonds had one black each, Octave Belot and Harry Lott respectively. The committee assigned to investigate the conduct of the recent election listed William Murrell of Lafourche and two whites. A committee appointed to revise the police bill had two blacks, Mansion and Alexander, and five whites.[22]

In the Senate in 1868, blacks were generally assigned to minor committees. Robert Poindexter was the only black on the three-man Committee on Public Works. No blacks were represented on Visiting the Penitentiary, on Banks and Banking, or on Examining of Vouchers committees. The Committee on Public Education had only one black, George Y. Kelso, and four whites. The three members of the Committee on Federal Relations were whites.[23]

In the 1869 House session, blacks attained a somewhat more favorable representation on committees. Two seven-man committees, Agriculture and Registration, were chaired by blacks and had a black majority of four to three. Samuel Cuney of Rapides was head of Agriculture; his black colleagues were Dupart, Douglas, and Morris. Octave Belot was chairman of the Registration Committee; Douglas, Dupart, and Sterrett were the other blacks. Four other committees had black chairmen. They included the seven-man committees on Corporation (Isabelle), Penitentiary (Lange), Federal Relations (Deslonde), and Constitution (Taylor). The total number of blacks on these

21. *House Journal, 1868*, pp. 21–22, 43–44.
22. *Ibid.*, pp. 21, 22, 25, 34, 43, 250; New Orleans *Daily Picayune*, July 28, August 1, 1868.
23. New Orleans *Daily Picayune*, July 26, 27, 29, 1868.

committees varied, including the chairmen, from three of seven, to two of seven. The other committees generally had fewer blacks. Each of the seven-member committees on Ways and Means, Banks and Banking, Judiciary, Election and Qualification, and Immigration had only one black member. Three blacks were on the seven-man Committee on Public Health and Quarantine, including the black chairman, Charles Gray of St. James. Two blacks were on the seven-member committees on Appropriation, Drainage and Canals, Railroads, Public Building and Internal Improvements. The six-man Committee on Financial Affairs of the Metropolitan Police Board did not have a black among its membership.[24]

In the 1869 Senate session, blacks did not comprise more than one-third of any standing committee, except the Committee on Auditing and Supervising the Expenses of the Senate, where there were two blacks and two whites. Only one black was listed on the following three-man committees: Militia (Pinchback), Claims (Pinchback), Commerce and Manufacturers (Antoine), Unfinished Business (Antoine), Federal Relations (Kelso), Charitable Institutions (Pollard), and Public Buildings (Poindexter). Two five-man committees also listed but one black: Public Education (Pinchback), and the Corporation and Parochial Affairs (Monette). Two blacks, Kelso and Pinchback, and three whites sat on the Committee of Railroads. Three Senate committees had no black members. They were the committees on Internal Improvements, Printing, and Visiting the Penitentiary.[25]

By 1870, blacks apparently were able to exert more influence. In the House session of that year blacks were assigned to every committee, and blacks held a greater number of chairmanships. However, they still were not a majority on any committee. One six-man committee was, however, equally divided. Thirteen

24. Blacks were later selected to fill vacancies on the following committees: Education (Gair), Commerce and Manufactures (Tureaud), Parochial Affairs (Hill), and Library (Lange and Honoré). *House Journal, 1869*, pp. 15, 33, 48.
25. *Senate Journal, 1869*, pp. 15, 82.

committees had Negro chairmen. Two blacks, including chairman Joseph Mansion, served on the seven-man Enrollment Committee. Three other seven-members committees had one black member each: Election and Qualification (Mahier), Federal Relations (Taylor), and Emigration (Lott). Blacks headed several seven-member committees: Parochial Affairs (Cuney), Pension (Belot), Agriculture (Burrell), and Public Printing (Hall); these groups contained one additional Negro member. The eleven-member Committee on the State Library was chaired by George Washington and included three other blacks and seven white members.

The six-man Committee on Corporations was equally divided and had a black chairman, Harry Lott. Black representatives Robert H. Isabelle and John Gair were chairmen, respectively, of the seven-member committees on Railroads and Internal Improvements. Both committees had two black and five white members. V. M. Lange chaired the six-man Committee on the Penitentiary, while Frank Alexander headed the eight-member Committee on Public Health and Quarantine. There was one additional black serving on each agency.

The number of blacks on the more important committees was generally smaller. The seven-member Judiciary Committee included only Harry Lott. The seven-member Committee on Banks and Banking listed Robert Taylor and John Gair. Three blacks did, however, serve on the powerful seven-member Committee on Contingent Expenses. Two blacks were assigned also to the seven-member Committees on Appropriation, Ways and Means, Commerce and Manufacturing, Canal and Drainage, Public Land and Levees, Claims, Militia and Constitution. Three blacks served on the nine-man Committee on Charitable and Public Institutions, but only one black was listed on the same numbered Committee on Education. Of the nine members serving on the Committee on Public Building, two were black. Other special committees had at least one black member.

For instance, the three-man Committee for Equal Distribution of Room in the State House, and the five-member special Committee on Metropolitan Police Affairs had one black.[26]

In the Senate in 1870 blacks did not fare much better in committee assignments than in previous sessions. No blacks were chairman of senate committees, nor was a black assigned to the powerful Judiciary Committee or to the Committee on Public Health and Quarantine. Blacks never composed more than one-third of the committees, and on most committees they held only a fourth of the membership. The one-third-black-membership committees were Militia, Claims, Commerce and Manufactures, Unfinished Business, Federal Relations, and Libraries. Blacks made up one-fourth of the committees on Finance, Enrollment, Auditing and Supervising the Expense of the Senate, Public Education, Printing, Banks and Banking, Visiting Penitentiary, Corporation and Parochial Affairs, Charitable Institutions, Public Lands and Levees, and Railroads.[27]

In the main, the legislative programs offered by the blacks in the General Assembly were similar to their demands in the constitutional convention. They were especially interested in educational reform and civil rights. One of the first efforts of the legislature was directed at reviving the educational system. Early in the 1868 session the six-man Committee on Education, a majority of whose members were blacks, set to work on legislation to establish an improved public educational system. The committee first drafted a bill providing for a board of directors for the schools of New Orleans. But something more comprehensive was necessary. Next, it prepared a bill providing

26. Negro membership was also included in the Committee on Address, and to fill vacancies on the Commerce and Manufactures Committee. *House Journal, 1870*, pp. 18, 20, 24, 45.

27. *Senate Journal, 1870*, p. 24. The committee assignments remained the same during the 1870 extra session. *House Journal, 1870, Extra Session*, 321–22; *Senate Journal, 1870, Extra Session*, 244.

assistants for the superintendent of education and a broader measure regulating the whole educational system.[28]

While the committee was working on the latter bill, documented reports were presented to the House, at the request of black Representative Robert H. Isabelle, on the current condition of the public school system that had operated in the state since 1847. One report declared, "The entire school system needs remodeling. Your superintendent is perfectly powerless to do anything in the way of improving the school system." A more specific indictment came from Oneze A. Guidry, treasurer of the St. Landry Parish school board: "Generally, the teachers are scholastically bad and morally worse, the Directors uneducated and . . . incompetent to judge the requirements of applicants." The "present condition of public schools," another report stated, "calls loudly upon the legislature for some revision and modification." One of the reports concluded that the old school system "has proved to be a failure and should be discontinued. . . . An entirely new system is needed."[29]

The existing system had been subjected to various strains during the war. Both General Butler and General Banks had attempted to impose on it their ideas of education. Butler wanted to centralize control. Until Union control, the school was organized into four independent school districts presided over by four superintendents. Each district maintained a high school for each sex, and the school day consisted of five and one-half hours. Butler abolished the four existing districts and substituted a bureau of education and a superintendent of public schools. Many teaching positions were given to Union sympathizers.

General Banks retained in office John B. Carter, who had been appointed by Butler, but gave him the added responsibility of promoting education for the freedmen. During Banks's regime, probably thousands of blacks received the rudiments of an education. Carter was succeeded by John McNair (February

28. *House Journal, 1868*, pp. 25, 38, 91.
29. *Ibid.*, 147, 152; Shugg, *Origins of Class Struggle in Louisiana*, 67–75.

1864–December 4, 1866) and Robert M. Lusher (December 5, 1866–April 1868), who revealed himself as a supporter of white supremacy. In 1868 Lusher was defeated by Thomas M. Conway. Conway, who had formerly headed the Bureau of Free Labor under General Banks, was not a native Louisianian. After his election to the office, he set about preparing legislation to establish a school system.[30] Many parts of the current legislative bill came from his ideas.

By September 9 the legislative bill was engrossed by the House Committee, several amendments were made, including the chairman's plan for administration, and passage was recommended. On February 27, 1869, the bill was passed by both chambers; in the Senate the bill was adopted by an overwhelming twenty-one to one vote under a suspension of the rule. In the House much of the debate centered on a proposal to separate control of New Orleans city schools and the country schools. Representative Dennis Burrell thought that both the New Orleans and country schools should be under the same control. Isabelle agreed and spoke of the evil of separating the control, especially since blacks would be hurt in the process.[31] This law, Act No. 121, became law on March 10, 1869.

Act 121 brought into operation a new educational program. The first section of the act placed the schools of the state under management of a State Board of Education consisting of the state superintendent of education, and one member appointed from each congressional district and two members from the state at large. The appointments were made by the governor with the

30. Leon O. Beasley, "A History of Education in Louisiana During the Reconstruction Period, 1862–1877" (Ph. D. dissertation, Louisiana State University, 1957), 45–95, 130–31; Betty Porter, "The History of Negro Education in Louisiana," *Louisiana Historical Quarterly*, XXV (July, 1942), 736–39; New Orleans *Republican*, March 29, October 26, 1870, February 8, 1871; Hilda A. Kohler, "A History of Public Education in Louisiana During Reconstruction" (M. A. thesis, Louisiana State University, 1938), 8–10; New Orleans *Times*, March 29, 1870.

31. *House Journal, 1868*, p. 217; *Senate Journal, 1869*, pp. 198–99. The New Orleans *Tribune*, February 14, 1869, considered education "our great need" in the state. *Debates of the House of Representatives of the State of Louisiana* (New Orleans: Republican Office, 1869), 239–47, hereinafter cited as *House Debates* with the appropriate date.

advice and consent of the senate. The board members were to serve four-year terms; the original appointees were to serve terms of two and four years to initiate rotation of half the board each biennium. Each division superintendent had to organize and conduct conferences, encourage and assist teachers' association, and report the number of students in schools. In addition, teacher standards were raised; certification of qualifications had to be signed by the division superintendents; certificates were valid for only one year, and class rolls were required.[32]

In the extra session of 1870 an amending act abolished the State Board of Education. The division superintendents, instead of receiving their appointments from the board, were now to be nominated by the state superintendent and appointed by the governor with the consent of the Senate. Therefore, the division superintendent held ex-offico status on the board. Other changes made the superintendent, not the state auditor, apportioning officer for the school funds.

Black legislators favored this modification. Senator Pinchback recommended giving the state superintendent even more power over appointments. The superintendent would best know the members appointed and how to work with them, Pinchback suggested.[33] In the House two blacks spoke on the bill. Representative Burrell opposed taking out the provision making the reading of the Bible compulsory. He and George Washington were most insistent in demanding a specific provision forbidding segregation of children in the schools. Washington feared that blacks would "have no schools, or next to none, if this section is not inserted." Burrell was equally as forceful in his pleas. In his remarks he added a new dimension to the question:

> I fear if this is not put in, distinction will be made against poor white children as well as colored; that poor white children will be debarred

32. *Senate Journal, 1869*, p. 193–98; Beasley, "History of Education," 134–140.
33. *House Journal, 1870*, pp. 164–66, 177, 227; *Senate Journal, 1870*, p. 234; New Orleans *Republican*, March 1, 11, 13, 31, 1870; *Senate Debates, 1870*, pp. 760–61.

from the educational institutions provided for in this act. That there shall be no distinction on account of race, color, or previous condition, is not enough. It does not cast the mantle of the law around the schools of the state. I want this law to be perfect in this respect. I want to see poor white and colored children admitted to all the blessings that must flow from a perfect system of education.[34]

Another black Representative, Robert H. Isabelle, urged integration. He told his colleagues in the legislature that integration was a way of making the races respect one another. He asserted in early 1870: "I want to see the children of the state educated together. I want to see them play together; to be amalgamated (laughter). I want to see them play together, to study together and when they grow up to be men they will love each other, and be ready, if any force comes against the flag of the United States, to take up arms and defend it together."[35] Senator Pinchback feared that separate schools would cause white children to "look upon colored children as inferiors" and the black schools would suffer because of lack of government support and poor teachers.

Black legislators demonstrated an interest in almost every area of education. In 1868 Senator Robert Poindexter presented a bill granting free passage to all school children on public ferries, roads, and bridges. This bill passed the Senate on August 30, and passed the House in early September. The act granted free right of passage and conveyance over the public ferries, bridges, and roads except the ferries on the Mississippi River which were rented out by state and parish or for which license fee is paid. The free privilege was granted to all children on foot attending public schools. No attendants at such ferries or bridges could demand tolls between the hours of seven and nine A.M. and four to six P.M. On Sundays and holidays, however, "no scholar" was permitted to cross such ferries, bridges, and roads except on terms similar to other passages. This law went into

34. *House Debates, 1870*, pp. 183–84.
35. New Orleans *Daily Picayune*, February 9, 1870, quoted in Blassingame, "A Social and Economic Study of the Negro in New Orleans, 1860–1880," 216.

effect immediately but did not apply to contracts on leases prior to the date of its enactment.[36]

Straight University (presently Dillard) often received the favors of the black legislators. C. C. Antoine promoted an act to aid the medical department of the university in the Senate, and Representative Robert Isabelle guided it through the lower House of the assembly. However, the act was vetoed by the governor on the grounds that it was a private institution and aid to it conflicted with Article 140 of the constitution which forbade state appropriations to private institutions.[37]

Relocation of the state library was another matter drawing the interest of black legislators. Two weeks after its appointment, the Committee on the State Library issued a report in which the reestablishment of its former location in the law university was advocated; repairs at the site had caused its removal to an area inconvenient to members of the legislature. When the state librarian gave the annual report two years later, the library had been moved to the previous location which was at a "more central position in the city" and adjacent to the legislature building.[38]

Black legislators began a drive for a civil rights law in 1868. Apparently many of them took the word *democracy* in its literal sense. Representative Robert H. Isabelle introduced a bill called "an act to protect all persons in their civil and public rights." The purpose of the bill was to enforce the thirteenth article of the constitution by making segregation a criminal offense and by demanding that all persons, "without regard to race, color or previous condition shall enjoy equal rights and privileges in, their traveling" and on public conveyances, in public resorts, or

36. New Orleans *Daily Picayune*, August 14, 21, 30, 1868; *Acts of 1868*, 212–13.
37. *Senate Journal, 1870*, pp. 303, 306, 324; *House Journal, 1870*, 266, 271, 313; *House Journal, 1870, Extra Session*, 377; *Senate Journal, 1871*, p. 7
38. *House Journal, 1868*, pp. 43, 84; "Annual Report of the State Librarian to the General Assembly of Louisiana," *Louisiana Legislative Documents* (New Orleans: Office of the Republican, February, 1871), 2.

businesses where a license was required by the state. Fines ranging from one hundred dollars to five hundred dollars and imprisonment from three months to one year were imposed on convicted violators.

The Isabelle bill passed the first reading on the day it was introduced. Five days later, on July 15, it was referred to the House Judiciary Committee; on August 24, the committee reported favorably. Four days later, the House passed the measure by a vote of fifty to fourteen. The bill was sent to the Senate the next day. On September 1, it was made the special order of the day, read twice, and referred to the Senate Judiciary Committee. Two weeks later it passed the Senate by a fifteen to seven vote.[39]

Governor Warmoth almost immediately vetoed the measure. In his veto he attacked the bill on four counts. He asserted that (1) the rights proposed by the bills were already safeguarded in the new state constitution; (2) the penalties imposed were impracticable and pernicious; (3) the provision relating to railroads and steamships impinged upon congressional authority to regulate interstate commerce; (4) the governor felt that with the November election approaching, the bill would inflame racial tension. The veto message was received in the House on Friday, September 26, but Isabelle had consideration of it postponed until Monday, September 28. On the latter day the House refused to override the veto in a thirty-two–thirty-two vote.[40]

The New Orleans *Tribune* disagreed with the governor's reasoning. The black newspaper asserted that the bill was a forward piece of racial legislation. The governor had "proved

---

39. *House Journal, 1868*, pp. 26, 39, 172–74. See also Roger A. Fischer, "The Segregation Struggle in Louisiana, 1850–1890" (Ph.D. dissertation, Tulane University, 1967), 66–67; New Orleans *Daily Picayune*, August 25, September 15, 1868; Ficklen, *Reconstruction in Louisiana*, 208.

40. *House Journal, 1868*, pp. 246–49. See also T. B. Tunnell, Jr., "Henry Clay Warmoth and the Politics of Coalition" (M. A. thesis, North Texas State University, 1966), 8–9; St. James *Sentinel*, September 29, October 3, 1868; Carroll *Record*, October 3, 1868.

unfaithful to the principles upon which he was elected" and had borrowed the argument from the Democrats, the *Tribune* charged. Representative Isabelle, author of the bill, was extremely critical of Governor Warmoth's veto. According to several reporters, he stated that foreigners received the same treatment in public places that whites did, but blacks, who defended the American flag, did not. He expressed the view that "during the war he and his race were told that they should have all the rights and privileges of the white man, and he wanted to see the promise kept."[41]

This veto did not stop the black legislators' drive for a civil rights law. Some of them had expected a veto and were ready with a counter strategy. The date set to discuss the veto measure, Septemeber 28, Representative Dennis Burrell introduced a bill entitled An Act to Enforce the Provisions of the Thirteenth Article of the Constitution of Louisiana. The Burrell bill reiterated the public accommodations provisions of the constitution and provided recourse of civil suits to injured parties. Such suits would also have preference upon the docket of the court in which they were instituted, provided the right to jury trial was not impaired. The bill was read twice and referred to the Judiciary Committee but was buried as the session adjourned.[42]

When the legislature reconvened in 1869, the push for civil rights came from blacks in both the upper and lower houses. Pinchback gave notice that on a future day he would present a bill entitled An Act to Enforce the Thirteenth Article of the Constitution. A week later, he introduced a bill entitled An act to

---

41. New Orleans *Tribune*, January 7, 8, 13, 1869. The *Tribune* was briefly revived in January, 1869, after financial difficulties forced it to close down in April, 1868. New Orleans *Daily Picayune*, July 7, 1868, September 27, 1869; Fischer, "The Segregation Struggle in Louisiana," 70. Representative Dennis Burrell supported the veto.

42. *House Journal, 1868*, pp. 248–49. Earlier, on August 17, 1868, Burrell had introduced a House bill "repealing all articles on civil code and all laws of the State of Louisiana making a distinction on account of race or color." The next day it was referred to the Committee on Judiciary and never reappeared. *Ibid.*, 131, 136.

Enforce the Thirteenth Article of the Constitution, and to Regulate the Licenses Mentioned in Said Thirteenth Article. The Senate Judiciary Committee was unable to reach a decision on the bill and reported back on January 28 with a tie vote. The next day Pinchback called up the bill, ordered it printed, and made it the special order for Thursday, February 4. On that date an adjournment motion was adopted pending discussion of the bill. The next day two Democratic senators attempted to get the bill recommitted, while another one urged postponement; both proposals were tabled on Pinchback's motions. The Senate then resolved itself into a Committee of the Whole; the bill was eventually postponed as special order of the day, February 7, at one o'clock. On this date, Pinchback and other black senators fought off efforts to amend the bill, but the effort failed as the Senate adjourned. Finally, on February 9, the bill came up and was adopted twenty-to-nine vote.[43]

In the House, Isabelle and Burrell acted as managers of Pinchback's bill. Isabelle, who had previously championed civil rights, suggested three amendments to strengthen the measure. The first imposed additional penalties for damages "exemplary as well as actual." The second provided that suits to enforce the act would take preference in both the "inferior and superior courts." His last amendment stipulated that acts inconsistent with the provisions of the bill be repealed and that it should become law as of April 1, 1869. Rejecting motions to postpone the bill, the House passed it by a vote of sixty-one to fifteen; black members gave it solid support.[44]

43. *Senate Journal, 1869*, pp. 10, 67, 73, 91, 93, 95–96, 98; New Orleans *Tribune*, January 8, 1869; New Orleans *Times*, February 11, 27, March 2, 1869. The *Times*, on March 2, 1869, accused Lieutenant Governor Dunn of not consenting to sign legislation favorable to Warmoth supporters until the governor signed the civil rights law. Dunn denied the charges.

44. *House Journal, 1869*, pp. 20, 41, 55, 159. Burrell's bill had passed its second reading and was in the Judiciary Committee. Fischer, "Segregation Struggle in Louisiana," 79–80. There is no current "exemplary" provision in Louisiana laws. The black Reconstructionist leader wanted violators to suffer beyond the light punishment meted out for some offenses; with the word *exemplary* included the violators could be

When the civil rights bill came back to the Senate, Pinchback was unable to secure concurrence in the House amendments. The Senate voted down the sections giving civil rights cases preference and setting April 1, 1869 as the enforcement date. However, it retained the provision recovering damage "exemplary and actual." The black senators voted for all these sections but were joined by few whites. A message was sent to the House from the Senate, accepting only one of the amendments, the "exemplary" provision. Not wanting to risk losing the entire bill, the blacks in the House agreed to the Senate plan and the bill passed. During the debate, the *Tribune* declared unqualified support of the bill, maintaining that under the "present order of things, our manhood is sacrified. The broad stamp of inferiority is put upon us." In a rebuke to white moderates, the paper pointed out, "The civil distinctions which are insisted upon by our white brethren are an indignity put upon themselves as well as upon us." Governor Warmoth signed the measure into law on February 23, 1869. To many blacks the law went a long way toward fulfilling the promises of the constitution.[45]

The act looked good on paper, but enforcement of it was difficult. Hence, in the 1870 session blacks moved for a strong law. Representative Isabelle introduced an act "prohibiting unjust discrimination on account of color or race." This bill forbade segregation to licensed places of business and on common carriers. Criminal prosecution was called for in enforcement, and violators would be fined from fifty dollars for each infraction, and their businesses were to be closed until compliance was enforced. Local justices of the peace, as well as parish recorders, were to try cases. The bill was referred, on Isabelle's request to a special committee of three, of which he was chairman. Reported favorably to the House by a vote of two to one, the bill

forced to forfeit their licenses, as well as subject to fine. *House Journal,1869*, pp. 159–60; New Orleans *Tribune*, February 7, 9, 12, 13, 18, 19, 21, 1869; *House Debates, 1869*, pp. 205, 206, 254, 260.

45. *Senate Journal, 1869*, pp. 139, 142; *Acts of 1869*, No. 38, p. 37.

was quickly adopted. In the Senate, Pinchback guided its passage and with few alterations. Governor Warmoth received the bill in late February but held it on his desk for nine months before vetoing it. He stated among other reasons, that further legislation in the area of civil rights was unnecessary.[46] The legislature sustained the veto.

Black legislators did not share the governor's opinion that enough had been done for civil rights. Pinchback and Isabelle were insistent on legislation giving preference in the courts to enforcement cases arising under Article Thirteen of the consitituion. Isabelle had placed a provision to this effect in the Pinchback bill of 1869, but the Senate had refused to concur in it. Now in February, 1870, Pinchback proposed a similar measure, and it became law with Warmoth's approval.[47]

In the sessions of 1868–1870 black legislators were competent, persistant, and had achieved significant success in winning recognition of the rights of their people. They had not accomplished all that they had sought, but they had made a beginning and would continue their efforts.

46. *House Journal, 1870*, pp. 80, 106, 211–12, 215; New Orleans *Tribune*, January 16, 19, 1869; *Senate Journal, 1870*, p. 278; *Senate Debates, 1870*, pp. 807–808; *Senate Journal, 1871*, pp. 4–5.

47. *Senate Journal, 1870*, pp. 186, 191, 202–203; Representative Octave Belot was the principal spokesman in the House, as it passed during the extra session 49 to 8. *House Journal, 1870, Extra Session*, 346; *Acts of 1870, Extra Session*, No. 39, p. 93.

CHAPTER V

Economic and Social Reforms, 1868–1870

Although most blacks of the Reconstruction era were concerned with obtaining civil rights, those living in cities or towns were more determined to push the issue. Most blacks, however, lived in rural areas, where their daily lives were bound to the land. Their primary demand was for an equitable reward for their labors; beyond this, they wanted to become owners of land. Their aspirations were known to black legislators, many of whom came from country parishes and were eager to join economic reform to civil rights.

The 1868 House session was barely underway when George Washington, of Assumption, gave notice that he would introduce an "Act extending protection to the laborers upon plantations." Washington's bill was revised somewhat by the Judiciary Committee and emerged as a measure prohibiting planters, managers, or overseers from discharging laborers because of political beliefs. The penalties for such discharge were to be a fine of not less than $500 and not more than $1,000, one half of which was to be paid to the informer of the violation and the remainder to the school treasurer, or imprisonment for not more than two years. The bill passed the House by a fifty to twenty-one vote; no black legislators voted against it.[1]

1. *House Journal, June 29, 1868*, pp. 45, 51, 120; New Orleans *Crescent*, August 14, 1868 (the writer is using the 1868 Senate proceedings and general debate as published in the New Orleans *Crescent* and New Orleans *Daily Picayune*).

The bill struggled through the Senate with the Democrats fighting it at every stage. Democratic Senator E. L. Jewell, of New Orleans, called it "new in jurisprudence and unparalleled in the history of this Legislature" and threatened to "take the stump and call upon the people to resist them [the laborers] at the point of the bayonet." In rebuttal, Senator Curtis Pollard proclaimed that the laborers needed the protection provided by law. He asserted that if a laborer contracted to work for a year and attempted to leave the plantation on election day to vote "against the will of the planter, he would be discharged and receive nothing for his labor." Such action toward workers was not justice, Pollard declared. Seeking to make the bill look ridiculous, one Democratic senator urged an amendment to allow "any officer in this state having power to remove another office-holder because of his political opinion." He maintained that whites needed protection as well as blacks. Jasper W. Blackman, Democratic Senator from Claiborne, offered a similar amendment. He proposed making the penalty apply to "any man promising a mule to colored men or land, or intimidating them by asserting that if they voted the Democratic ticket they would be forced into Slavery." These and other amendments failed, and the bill passed seventeen to seven in August.[2]

Governor Warmoth approved the bill on September 4, 1868. This law, as finally passed, became Act No. 54 entitled Extending Protection to Laborers in the Exercise of Their Privileges of Free Suffrage. It prohibited "any planter, managers, overseer, or other employer of laborers" in Louisiana from discharging or attempting to control the votes of employees under their control "previous to the expiration of the term of service of any laborer in their employ."

The penalty for a violation of the Act was to be a fine of not less than one hundred dollars or more than five hundred dollars to be recovered in court of competent jurisdiction. The district attor-

2. New Orleans *Daily Picayune*, August 14, 20, 25, 26, 1868.

ney for the judicial district or the district attorney *pro tempore* of
the particular parish in which the violation was committed was
to receive 25 percent of the fine, and the remainder was to be
paid into the common school fund of the parish.[3]

Several other measures to aid laborers were also offered in the
1868 session. Charles Gray of St. James secured passage of a bill
repealing the law authorizing planters to sell goods to their hands
without a license. Another black legislator, A. C. Hill, of Ascension proposed a bill limiting a legal working day to eight hours. It
was referred to the Judiciary Committee and apparently buried
there.[4]

In the 1869 session blacks returned to their effort to remove
discriminations against plantation laborers. They were disturbed
to learn that certain pre-1868 labor laws, presumably annulled by
the constitution, were still being applied. One such law enabled
employers to secure the arrest of a laborer found "visiting
another plantation," and this practice aroused the ire of Senator
Robert Poindexter of Assumption. In January, 1869, he introduced an "act to repeal such laws or statutes as make it a
misdemeanor or tresspass to be found on or visiting at a plantation." The bill received a favorable report from the Judiciary
Committee, but Poindexter met repeated delays when he called
it up for final passage. Eventually he had to admit failure.[5]

A similar fate befell an effort in the 1870 session. A bill was
introduced in the House that permitted laborers to bring lawsuits
for payments from employers who refused to pay laborers who
might live in different parishes. A white Republican, Charles
Harper, of St. Charles, urged passage of the bill, for he felt the
present situation of making laborers move to the parish of
employment was a hardship for laborers, especially for those

3. *Acts of June 29, 1868*, No. 54, p. 68
4. New Orleans *Daily Picayune*, July 26, August 29, September 12, 15, 1868; *Acts of 1866*, No. 123, p. 236; *Acts of 1868*, No. 89, p. 119; *House Journal*, 1868, p. 65.
5. *Senate Journal*, January 4, 1869, pp. 43, 46, 88, 138, 162–63, 165. The act Poindexter wanted to repeal was No. 11, To Prevent Trespassing, approved December 20, 1865. *Acts of Extra Session, 1865*, p. 16.

living close to parish boundaries. The bill easily passed the House but failed in the Senate, which frequently seemed less responsive to black demands than the House.[6]

The Senate did, however, assent to a bill permitting laborers the right to provisional seizure of an employer's property if he did not render them the agreed-upon compensation. Complaints of black workers often appeared in the newspapers. When Democrats spoke against the bill, Curtis Pollard vigorously defended it. He asserted that the agreement between planter and laborer "did not amount to anything for the laborer, as he got nothing." This was especially true, he maintained, in cases where the landowners promised to provide the necessities and give the laborer half the crop. Adroitly, Pollard called on his Democratic "friends" to support the measure, reminding them that he had "lived amongst" them all his life harmoniously.[7] This measure failed in the House.

White leaders, disturbed at the growing demands of black laborers, preached the benefit of encouraging white immigrants to come to the state. Although these whites would presumably compete with blacks for jobs, black legislators were not hostile to the proposal. The chairmen of the committee on Immigration in 1868 and 1870—Harry Lott and P. G. Deslonde respectively—favored legislation to encourage immigration. During the first week of September, 1868, the committee (under Lott) reported that continuing the Bureau of Immigration had become a necessity for developing agricultural resources of Louisiana. Since the state had the commercial and agricultural

6. *House Journal, 1870*, pp. 47, 48; *Senate Debates*, 1870, p. 42. Bills providing for homestead exemptions and land reforms were offered, but they failed to win the approval of both houses or were buried in committees. See *House Journal, 1868*, p. 74; New Orleans *Daily Picayune*, September 20, 1868. Incorporation of the Labor and Homesteads Association and of the Land Office was approved in 1870. Pinchback pushed the 1868 homestead exemption bill into the 1869 session. He urged repeal of the Civil Code laws governing the exemption, but his law never materialized. *Senate Journal, 1869*, pp. 123, 135, 142.

7. New Orleans *Daily Picayune*, August 26, 1868; New Orleans *Times*, June 3, 1868; Bossier *Banner*, December 17, 1870.

advantages to draw immigrants, the committee suggested that an "adequate appropriation be made" to continue the function of the bureau. Speaking in opposition, Senator Pollard suggested it was wrong to invite immigrants to come since many would be unable to earn a living.[8]

With blacks strongly in support, the 1870 legislature enacted a law to organize the Bureau of Immigrants and gave it an appropriation of $20,000.[9] Blacks also supported a measure to incorporate an agency to be known as the Louisiana Commercial Agricultural and Emigration Association. Introduced by a white Republican, Anthony W. Faulkner, of Caldwell Parish, the bill was designed to encourage direct ocean communication from the Port of New Orleans to ports in Great Britain and Europe. Supporters of the bill argued that it would bring to Louisiana a vast influx of the best portion of inhabitants from the Old World, create an industrial population, and enhance the economy of the state.

Most of the opposition to the bill came from Democrats who contended in old-fashioned Jeffersonian rhetoric that the project was an improper exercise of state power and would cost too much money. Black representatives and senators voted unanimously for passage in the House, and the bill passed the Senate during the extra session.[10]

While championing the economic rights of their constituents, black legislators were equally intent on removing various social discriminations to which their people had been subjected. The

8. *House Journal, 1868*, p. 202; New Orleans *Daily Picayune*, August 14, 1868; New Orleans *Tribune*, February 25, 1869, for favorable comments on immigrants; William E. Highsmith, "Louisiana During Reconstruction" (Ph.D. dissertation, Louisiana State University, 1953), 198–99; E. Russ Williams, Jr., "Louisiana's Public and Private Immigration Endeavors, 1866–1893," *Louisiana History*, XV (Spring, 1974), 157–59.

9. Ella Lonn, *Reconstruction in Louisiana after 1868* (Gloucester, Mass.: Peter Smith Reprint, 1967), 39–40. During the extra session of 1870, one black representative urged repealing the act and transferring the assets to the German Society of New Orleans. The bill failed. *House Journal, Extra Session, 1870*, pp. 365–366.

10. *House Journal, 1870*, pp. 33, 169–70, 186–87, 290. On the motion of Representative Gray of St. James to strike out the section setting the quota at 20,000, one-half of which were to be Africans, the blacks split their vote. *Senate Journal, Extra Session, 1870*, p. 287.

most resented of these stigmas was that under slavery, marriage was not recognized; hence a Negro family had no legal basis or existence. Consequently, in the 1868 session Representative Burrell introduced a bill that he called an Act Relative to Marriage. Becoming law in November, it revolutionized the marital status of blacks. Its first provision validated all private or religious marriages contracted before it passed, provided no other impediments than color existed. The second section legalized children of these unions. Other sections legalized interracial marriage, which formerly was prohibited, and provided a way to legalize common-law marriages. The enforcement date for the act was set immediately after passage.[11]

Black legislators wanted to make the legitimacy of children born of slave unions doubly certain. Representative Robert H. Isabelle introduced bills to guarantee this result in the 1868 and 1870 sessions. The 1870 act was entitled To Authorize Natural Parents to Legitimate Their Natural Children. It provided that natural fathers and mothers who were prevented from legitimizing their children because of slavery could now do so simply by declaring their intentions before a notary public and two witnesses. This act was not to conflict with the act relative to marriage (approved November 5, 1868) and was to take effect immediately.[12]

Not satisfied to remove social discrimination against their race, blacks were also active in pushing measures of broad social

11. *House Journal, 1868*, pp. 131, 153, 182, 218; New Orleans *Crescent*, September 16, 19, 1868. Pinchback pushed the bill through the Senate and added the section legalizing common-law marriage. Grosz, "P.B.S. Pinchback," 13; *Acts of 1868*, No. 210, pp. 178–79; Senator Poindexter had advocated a measure providing imprisonment and fines for cohabition between unmarried couples; the measure failed. New Orleans *Crescent*, July 29, 1868.

12. The act of 1869 was designed to amend Art. 221 of the Civil Code of the state, which dealt with the acknowledgment of an illegitimate child. See *Civil Code of the State of Louisiana with Statutory Amendments from 1825 to 1866, Inclusive, and Reference to the Decisions of the Supreme Court of Louisiana, to the 17th Volume of the Annual Reports, inclusive, with an Exhaustive Index* (New Orleans: B. Bloomfield Co.; New York: John F. Trow, 1867), 37; *House Journal 1869*, 223, *1870*, pp. 22, 33, 166, 275; *Senate Journal, 1870*, p. 209; *Acts of 1870*, No. 68, p. 96; see *Louisiana Civil Code; Revision of 1870, Edited with Annotation* (Indianapolis: Bobbs-Merrill, 1932), 76.

reform, some of them beneficial to whites as well as blacks. Black support for charitable institutions was constant and almost unanimous. In the 1868–1870 sessions most of the bills for hospitals, insane asylums, deaf and dumb schools, and charitable societies were introduced by black members.[13]

The blacks, adhering to a traditional American pattern, often introduced appropriation bills to benefit their particular districts. Thus, Senator Pinchback, of Orleans, suggested and secured an appropriation of three thousand dollars instead of three hundred for Freedmen's Charitable Hospital of New Orleans. Senator Antoine and Representative Moses Sterrett, of Caddo, promoted a bill to establish Charity Hospital of Shreveport. Their act allowed the state to issue one hundred bonds of one thousand dollars each to support the Hospital. Representative Sterrett also sought passage of an act for the relief of the Shreveport Medical and Surgical Infirmary.[14]

Some blacks demanded that the charity hospitals be integrated. The issue arose during debate on a bill appropriating five thousand dollars to pay the cost of removing blacks from the Freedmen's Marine Hospital to the Charity Hospital. Although the Charity Hospital board of administrators had forbidden segregation of the facilities in September, 1868, the hospital officials were slow to admit blacks. Some of the Democratic senators did not want blacks housed even temporarily in Charity Hospital. Representative Isabelle favored the bill although he labeled it "class legislation." The bill, as finally passed, required Charity Hospital to immediately make provisions for admittance of black patients.[15]

13. *House Journal, 1868*, pp. 118, 176, 206, 263; New Orleans *Crescent*, August 21, 1868; *Senate Journal*, 1869, p. 206; *House Debates, 1869*, pp. 116–19, 488–90, 195. See appropriation bill in *Acts of 1868–1870*.

14. *Senate Journal, 1869*, 123, 191, 206–207, 223, 225–26, 243; *House Journal, 1868*, 192, *1870*, pp. 250–51; *Acts of 1869*. No. 149, pp. 24–26; *House Journal, 1870, Extra Session*, 374.

15. Fischer, "The Segregation Struggle in Louisiana, 1850–1890," 93–94; *House Debates, 1869*, pp. 116–19; *Acts of 1869*, No. 19, p. 16; New Orleans *Times*, February 10, 1869.

The care of orphan children interested several blacks, and especially Representative Isabelle, who became a leader in this field. His most ambitious project was an orphan asylum and vocational home for black youths. This scheme involved 110 orphans who had been removed from the Marine Hospital in New Orleans to the Bertha Plantation in St. Mary Parish. A philanthrophist in France had agreed to give ten thousand dollars if others (probably the state) would give twenty thousand dollars. The proposed building, an old sugar house, was in need of repairs, including a new roof. Representative Isabelle eagerly supported a resolution for the twenty thousand dollars appropriation since it would give young black people a chance to learn to make shoes, become tailors, and learn other trades. The bill passed the House and was endorsed by the Senate.[16]

Black legislators, like their white colleagues, introduced many relief bills. The bills included relief for individuals, for parishes, for victims of the riot of 1866, and for black veterans of the War of 1812. An especially interesting relief act concerned the African Methodist Espiscopal Church of New Orleans. An ordinance of the city council in April, 1858, had confiscated the property of the church, and white hostility had subjected the members to "gross indignities and heavy fines." An appropriation of three thousand dollars was awarded the church.[17]

At this time the need for reform in the state penitentiary did not seem to interest black legislators. The 1869 legislature ratified the lease arrangement with John Huger and Colonel Charles Jones. Under the act, the "direction and control of the health and religious" regulations of the convicts was vested in a board of control consisting of five gubernatorial appointees. In 1870

16. *House Debates, 1869*, pp. 130–32, 134, 309; *Senate Journal, 1869*, p. 142, 172, 233, 235; New Orleans *Republican*, February 19, 1871.

17. *House Journal, 1868*, pp. 58, 170, 217–18, 227, 301, *1869*, pp. 20, 80, 89, 96, 107, 118, 293, *1870*, pp. 89, 98, 102, 118; *Senate Journal, 1870*, pp. 24, 80, 170; New Orleans *Crescent*, September 16, 23, 1868; *Acts of 1869*, No. 169, pp. 228–69. This law was promulgated on October 20, 1868; efforts to extend relief to the AME Church in 1869 failed. *Senate Journal, 1869*, pp. 168–69, 178.

the lease was sold by Huger and Jones to Samuel L. James and Company. The bill authorizing the new lease was favored by black legislators in both houses. The lessee had to pay a graduated annual rental—five thousand dollars the first year, six thousand the second year, until twenty-five thousand dollars was paid to Louisiana in 1891. Unnoticed by some, the bill made no reference to the board of control.[18] To many, the lease served a twofold purpose: first, it eliminated the cost and responsibility of the state government in taking care of prisoners; secondly it provided an income through the lease for the state. Later many black legislators would alter drastically their attitude toward the leasing of prisoners, most of whom were blacks.

The new state services and the welfare programs supported by blacks cost more than the state received in revenue. Some projects had to be financed by bonds, and the public debt rose steadily standing in 1870 at $23,427,952.29. Demands for tax reform were loud, and they found a response among white legislators. Unfortunately, nobody in either group seemed to know how to effect reform or to have the political courage to attempt fundamental change. Several black legislators, for instance, introduced so-called reform plans, but these dealt with only small local taxes. As state expenditures increased, some taxpayers, principally whites, tried to resist payment, forcing the government to recognize a new and serious problem.[19]

Black legislators did advocate taxes on corporations. They had been among the strongest supporters of pro-railroad legislation, and they seemed to reason that the recipients of their favors could bear a greater share of the tax burden. A succinct rep-

18. Mark T. Carleton, *Politics and Punishment: The History of the Louisiana State Penal System* (Baton Rouge: Louisiana State University Press, 1971), 16–18; Blacks attempted to delay the vote on the 1869 proposal to ratify the lease, but the effort failed. *House Debates, 1869*, pp. 300–301; *House Journal, 1870*, pp. 119–20, 158, 165, 169.

19. *House Journal, 1868*, pp. 38, 53, 85, 94, 132, 289, 299, *1869*, pp. 94, 116, 132; *Senate Journal, 1869*, pp. 145, 149. The floating of a New Orleans bond to liquidate its debt won almost complete black support, and Governor Warmoth later vetoed an act to liquidate the taxes of New Orleans. Lonn, *Reconstruction*, 82–84; New Orleans *Daily Picayune*, August 6, 1868.

resentation of their action came from Representative Isabelle: "It is property in this state; it should pay a tax in this state. Seven of the northern States derived immense revenue from their railroad tax. Under an equitable law there is nothing wrong in taxing these wealthy companies. . . . The state cannot afford to lose any of those sources from which she is entitled to draw a revenue. . . . The State of Illinois has no debt. She taxes her railroads, and I am in favor . . . of taxing ours.[20]

Much legislation proposed by blacks was designed with a public rather than a racial purpose in mind. For example, internal improvement and environmental bills had a high priority with blacks, but these measures would benefit members of both races. Blacks took the lead in advocating improved sewage disposal in New Orleans, a city whose system was so obsolete as to cause widespread disease and death. Representative Frank Alexander, chairman of the Committee on Public Health and Quarantine, advocated a bill that would improve the sanitary conditions of the city of New Orleans and grant certain privileges to the New Orleans Sanitary and Fertilizing Company. The bill made it unlawful to dig or construct any sink or privy vault within the city limits; and all existing vaults had to be filled by the owners of the property. It was, perhaps, Louisiana's first postwar antipollution law.[21]

Other internal improvement schemes also appealed to blacks. Harry Lott of Rapides urged the building of a new courthouse in Alexandria. Blacks supported the bill authorizing the state to purchase stocks in the Mississippi Navigation Company. Lott also urged the creation of a board to provide the construction of

20. *Senate Journal, 1868*, p. 116, *1870*, pp. 108, 119, 130, 162, 166, 200, 226, 241, 243, 249, *Extra Session,* 287; *House Journal, 1870*, pp. 54, 120, 133, 237, 308, *Extra Session,* 251, 333, 357, 374, 377; Lonn, *Reconstruction*, 34–35; New Orleans *Times*, February 12, 26, 28, 1869. Isabelle and others opposed taxing benevolent societies. Isabelle felt that burden of supporting the state government would fall heavily on poor working men if the state failed to tax wealthy companies. *House Debates, 1870*, pp. 93, 96–97, 346; New Orleans *Republican*, March 10, 1870.

21. *House Journal, 1870*, 302, *Extra Session,* 331–32, 369; *Senate Journal, 1870, Extra Session*, 324; New Orleans *Republican*, March 11, 1870.

state roads. Representative Burrell introduced a House bill authorizing the state to contract a company to dig a canal from the Mississippi River to Lake Pontchartrain in St. John the Baptist Parish. The bill reached the Senate but died in committee near the end of the session. A measure to establish the Mississippi Valley Levee Company passed the House with black support; but the Senate adopted Pinchback's resolution to have it returned to the House and placed on the secretary's desk. A substitute proposal was later adopted. Many of these companies received money but did not complete their work; such companies, along with those chartered to clean bayous and rivers, often committed many swindles.[22]

In other areas of legislation, blacks showed a surprisingly modern cast of mind. This is best exemplified in their efforts to pass a law to prohibit the sale of drugs by unlicensed dealers and to enact a gun-control (concealment) law. Both measures failed to pass, though the gun concealment measure caused considerable debate.[23]

The problem of vagrants came before the legislature for a solution.[24] A bill, Relative to Vagrants in the Metropolitan Police District, passed the House late in the session amidst apprehensive comments from black legislators. The Metropolitan Police District then included the parishes of St. Bernard and Jefferson, as well as the cities of Carrollton and Jefferson. Representative Murrell urged its indefinite postponement because it arose from "rebellious hands." He further felt that in the rural parishes

22. *House Journal, 1869*, pp. 11, 159, 174, *1870*, 32, 33, 100, 121, 157, 158, 160, 201, 229–30, 259, 283, 298–99, 301, 306–307, 363–364, *Extra Session*, 363, 364; *Senate Journal, 1870*, 186, 201, 220–21, *1870, Extra Session*, 327. *House Debates, 1870*, p. 225; Many proposals for incorporation of manufacturing associations and levee companies were offered, but few passed. *Senate Debates, 1870*, pp. 748–50; Charles Nordhoff, *The Cotton States in the Spring and Summer of 1875* (New York: D. Appleton Co., 1876), 60–61; New Orleans *Times*, January 16, 17, 22, 23, March 3, 4, 1869.

23. *House Journal, 1870*, pp. 158, 168; *Senate Debates, 1870*, pp. 113–14.

24. New Orleans *Times*, February 16, 1869, See letter from George L. Cain, superintendent of Metropolitan Police urging harsh punishment.

blacks would need passes to travel the roads, and many unfriendly local officials would try to return them to peonage. Representative David Young proposed a substitute bill that was lost. Another black, Harry Lott, expressed less alarm. He favored the bill because he felt that it was not directed at black men necessarily but was a much needed measure against both black and white vagrants.

Black senators also expressed apprehension over the bill. Senator Pinchback wanted the bill read and adopted section by section. His major criticism was over the definition of *vagrant*. This criticism prevented passage, and several days before the session closed, a three-man committee—including Pinchback and Pollard—was appointed to establish an equitable definition. The committee reported the next day by way of a substitute proposal that won approval in both houses.[25]

The vagrancy law of 1869 was quickly signed by Governor Warmoth. It defined a vagrant as a person apprehended with a picklock or another felonious instrument and who had no visible means of support. Such a person could be arrested by a justice of the peace, constable, sheriff, or policeman and taken before the Metropolitan Police Board. Conviction carried a sentence of commitment to the workhouse for six months at hard labor. The convicted person was entitled to jury trial; he could be released if he was from another parish or town (other than the ones specified) or a foreigner. For harboring vagrants, a person was charged not less than fifty dollars and not more than one hundred dollars. This money was receivable in the name of the Metropolitan Police Board.[26]

The next session saw a vigorous effort to repeal the above law. Apparently the law was being applied to make arrests outside the Metropolitan Police District. Early in the session, Senator

25. *Senate Journal, 1869*, pp. 82, 228, 234, 236; *House Debates, 1869*, pp. 366, 368–69, 519.
26. *Acts of 1869*, No. 87, pp. 87–89.

Pinchback introduced a bill to repeal the vagrancy law. He desired a law that would be applied exclusively to the city of New Orleans, since the 1869 law included the parishes of St. Bernard, Jefferson, and the cities of Carrollton and Jefferson. He opposed a vagrancy law for the parishes or the state at large and vowed to oppose the move for such a law. His bill was reported favorably by the Judiciary Committee, but it was amended to include the parish of Orleans and was adopted section by section. In the House, the bill passed the third week in February, 1870.[27]

The vagrancy law of 1870 held several revisions. As its title indicated, it was limited to Orleans Parish and the city of New Orleans. In defining *vagrant*, it deleted from the first section the provision that a person had to have a picklock or other instruments. The bill lay on the governor's desk until January, 1871, when it was signed.[28]

Many other issues of a local nature came before the legislature. Blacks favored most proposals for the centralization of local authority, and to give the governor more power over local appointments; they voted for the bill to amend the city charter of Jefferson which instituted an administration consisting of a mayor and seven administrators who were to be appointed by the governor and hold office until the election in November. The act also provided for detaching a portion of Jefferson Parish and annexing it to New Orleans.[29] The mayor of Shreveport was given additional powers through an act championed by Representative Moses Sterrett and Senator Antoine. Other bills to incorporate towns were offered and supported by blacks.[30]

27. *Senate Journal, 1870*, pp. 40, 47, 173; *Senate Debates, 1870*, p. 564.

28. *Acts of 1871*, No. 99, pp. 11–13.

29. *House Journal, 1870*, pp. 157, 219, 227, 295–96, 356, *Extra Session*, 268–69, 284–86, 345, 375. The *Tribune* was extremely critical of the bill and asserted that the proposal placed too much power in the governor's hand and placed the interest of the blacks in "serious danger" because the measure was offered by Democrats. New Orleans *Tribune*, January 12, 19, 21, 22, 27, 28, February 13, 20, 28, 1869.

30. Representative Sterrett advocated a measure in 1870 giving the mayor and trustees power to establish workhouses and correction homes for vagrants. Senator Curtis Pollard promoted the measure to incorporate the town of Delta in Madison

Removal of restrictions on the franchise naturally had the support of black legislators. As in the constitutional convention, black leaders favored universal suffrage. But since the restriction on the franchise was a constitutional amendment, it could only be removed by an amendment to the constitution. Article 99 forbade the following persons from voting: (1) criminals; (2) those holding offices under the Confederacy; (3) leaders of guerilla bands during the war; (4) those advocating treason; (5) and those who voted for or signed the ordinance of secession of any state. The issue came up in the assembly in 1868 and in 1869, and Warmoth had urged removal in his annual message. In 1868 Pinchback supported removal of the restriction because it was in conflict with the Fourteenth Amendment. An amendment for removal came up for a vote in 1870. It passed almost unanimously in both houses at a single sitting, and in the November election was accepted by a large majority.[31]

The performance of black legislators in the first session had been marked by success and failure and was characterized by a mixture of idealism and selfishness. Blacks had secured their greatest triumph in the passage of civil rights legislation. They had won only very partial victories in attempting to enact measures that would benefit blacks economically, attempts that a later generation would call *gut* issues. In pursuing their goals, black legislators had displayed on some occasions progressive action and a capacity to rise above race. On other occasions, they had been self-seeking and amenable to special interests and corruption. In their varied and contradictory qualities, they were

---

Parish. Senator Poindexter failed to incorporate the town of Napoleonville in Assumption; he did, however, guide a bill through the Senate incorporating Donaldsonville in Ascension Parish, but the bill was vetoed by the governor and sustained by the legislature. *House Journal, 1869*, p. 132, *1870*, p. 227, *Extra Session*, 356; *Senate Journal, 1869*, pp. 121, 137, 138, 159, 161, 165, 171, 176, 191, 204, 222, 229; *Acts of 1869*, No. 109, pp. 139–40, No. 50, pp. 27, 28.

31. New Orleans *Crescent*, September 16, 1868; Lonn, *Reconstruction in Louisiana*, 57–58; William A. Russ, Jr., "Disfranchisement in Louisiana (1862–70)," *Louisiana Historical Quarterly*, XVII (July, 1935), 578–80; also by the same author, "Registration and Disfranchisement Under Radical Reconstruction," *Mississippi Valley Historical*

much like white legislators in the Reconstruction or later periods. The election of 1870 would alter somewhat the influence of blacks in the legislature, but it would not cause them to change their demands significantly.

Review, XXI (September, 1934), 177. Other amendments enacted made the governor eligible for another term, secured the safety of the public fund, and limited the public debt. See *Senate Journal, 1870*, pp. 115–16, 221; *House Journal, 1870, Extra Session*, 379, 381; New Orleans *Daily Picayune*, August 14, 1868.

CHAPTER VI

Legislation and a Lame Duck Governor

The legislative session of 1870 brought several changes to the political situation in Louisiana. The most significant change was a rift in the Republican party, caused by opposition to Governor Warmoth. According to one source, the opposition was largely personal and can be traced to the proposed removal of the clause in the constitution making the governor ineligible to succeed himself. This caused great alarm "to other Republican aspirants for that honor." Another writer lists a combination of reasons for the opposition to the governor. His veto of the civil rights bills of 1868 and 1870 and his refusal to enforce the public education law aroused apprehensions among both black and white Republicans. White Republicans also resented his support of President Grant's brother-in-law, James F. Casey, as the Customhouse collector, and his support of the Constabulary, Registration, Militia, Election, Warrant, Judiciary and City Charter acts.[1]

1. Lonn, *Reconstruction in Louisiana*, 73–74; Althea D. Pitre, "The Collapse of the Warmoth Regime," *Louisiana History*, VI (Spring, 1965), 162–63. See Dr. R. I. Cromwell's critical letter on Warmoth in New Orleans *Republican*, October 17, 1871. In a letter to the New York *Tribune* Lieutenant Governor Oscar J. Dunn claimed that "nineteen-twentieths of the Republican party" in Louisiana was opposed to Warmoth. Francis B. Harris, "Henry Clay Warmoth, Reconstruction Governor of Louisiana," in *Louisiana Historical Quarterly*, XXX (April, 1947), 622–23. Black political leaders in New Orleans, who earlier organized the Union Progressive Club, called a meeting on June 20, 1870, for the purpose of protecting the "political interest of the colored people" of Louisiana. Committees were appointed to communicate with blacks in other parishes and draw up a constitution. Apparently, the club became defunct several years later. See handwritten proceedings, P. B. S. Pinchback Papers, Moorland-Spingarn Research Center.

At the state Republican convention in 1870 the Warmoth forces met defeat at the hands of the rival faction, the Customhouse Republicans. The latter group represented a combination of the forces of Lieutenant Governor Oscar J. Dunn, the Customhouse jobholders headed by United States Marshal S. B. Packard and the newly organized Christian Republican Association—the latter organized by Negro religious leaders in support of the Radical Republican party. These groups were able to organize the convention, elect Dunn as permanent chairman and to control the choice of party nominees in the House and local elections. In retaliation, the governor's forces refused to support some of the nominees. They organized an auxiliary committee and began a canvass of their own to promote several candidates not regularly nominated by the party.[2]

The November, 1870, election was a sweeping Republican and Warmoth victory. The governor described it as the "quietest and fairest election ever held in the State of Louisiana up to that time." The Republicans elected every one of their candidates for Congress, Benjamin F. Flanders as mayor of New Orleans, and gained a working majority in both houses of the state legislature. Moreover, the voters approved all four of the proposed constitutional amendments, including the one making the governor eligible for reelection.[3]

The election brought a turnover in black (and white) membership in the House. Although there were more black members in 1870—thirty-six as opposed to thirty-five in 1868—twenty-six of the members were new.[4] Thus, only ten returned from the 1868–1870 sessions. Apparently, many blacks were not re-

2. Lonn, *Reconstruction*, 74; Charles Dufour, "The Age of Warmoth," *Louisiana History*, VI (Fall, 1965), 348–49. Opposition to the appointment of Democrats as officers in the Customhouse was heated. See B. P. Blanchard to H. S. Vanderbilt, January 6, 1870, Custom House Nominations, Louisiana, New Orleans, January 1, 1869–June, 1869, Box 109, RG 56, NA; Teddy B. Tunnell, Jr., "Henry Clay Warmoth and the Politics of Coalition" (M.A. thesis, North Texas State University, 1966), 30–32.

3. Warmoth, *War, Politics and Reconstruction*, 101–102.

4. See Appendix C herein; also comments by Pinchback in New Orleans *Republican*, January 22, 1871.

selected by the Republican party caucus in their districts. One of the new House members, R. G. Gardner (Jefferson Parish), had served in the constitutional convention of 1867–1868, but the other twenty-five were new politicans on the state level.

The two leaders among the new House members were J. Henri Burch of East Baton Rouge, and Raiford Blunt of Natchitoches. Burch, who had taken the 1870 census for the city of Baton Rouge, would be a political leader for over ten years in the parish. He rejected a relatively secure life in the North to come South to aid his fellow blacks. The son of a wealthy Negro minister, he was born in New Haven, Connecticut, in 1836. He attended college at Owega Academy in New York, where he was the only black student. Burch sincerely believed that education and political leadership were the two most pressing needs of the freedmen. After attending an abolitionist meeting of the Garnet League, he wrote an article in *Freedmen's Appeal*, the journal of the League, urging northern educated blacks to go South. Upon reading the article, the Reverend Charles Burch, who was then preaching in Louisiana, advised his son to put his faith to work and come South for the cause of education. In April, 1868, J. Henri Burch arrived in Baton Rouge and two weeks later took charge of the local Negro school until he was elected to the lower House.[5]

A journalist and musician by training, Burch demonstrated great diversity of ability. One of his earliest ventures in the newspaper business was as a correspondent of the *Republican Standard* published at Carrollton. Along with Pinchback and several others, he was copublisher of the *Louisianian* in 1870. One year later, he purchased the Baton Rouge *Courier* and edited and published it until the latter part of 1878,[6] under the title *The Grand Era*.

5. Baton Rouge *Weekly Advocate*, May 7, 1870; *Senate Reports,* 46th Cong., 1–2 Sess., No. 163, Pt. 2, pp. 217–18; New Orleans *Semi-Weekly Louisianian*, January 8, February 16, 19, September 28, 1871.
6. *Senate Reports*, 46th Cong., 1–2 Sess., No. 163, Pt. 2, p. 219; A. E. Perkins, "James Henri Burch and Oscar James Dunn in Louisiana," *Journal of Negro History*,

Raiford Blunt of Natchitoches was, like Burch, not a native of Louisiana. He came to Natchitoches Parish in March, 1853, from Thompsonville, Georgia. Blunt, a Master Mason, had enjoyed some educational advantage and was a well-to-do Baptist preacher and schoolteacher. His property holdings included several houses and lots within the city and similar property outside the town. His church services were well attended. Church membership was listed at 507, despite the fact that there were approximately twenty-nine other Baptist churches in Natchitoches. His family consisted of a wife and daughter.[7]

Henry Demas of St. John the Baptist Parish was another leader elected in 1870. He defeated a former slave Dennis Burrell for the position. Demas was also born a slave in St. John the Baptist Parish in 1848 and not freed until the Civil War. His master was a medical doctor. In addition to freedom, the war brought him a chance to increase his education. He served from August, 1864, until March, 1867, in Company H, 80th Regiment. Attending the regimental schools for black troops, he welcomed all opportunities for education. Young Corporal Demas returned to civilian life confident of his abilities. In 1868 he was elected constable of his parish, organized the voters, and remained in executive office for the next two decades, serving in the House for two terms and serving one of the longest senatorial terms of any of the blacks. He was later a member of the school board of St. John the Baptist Parish and parish treasurer. Slightly above average height, and a good speaker, Demas always commanded close attention whenever he gained the floor.[8]

XXII (July, 1937), 321; *Senate Reports*, 42nd Cong., 3rd Sess., No. 457. p. 778; *House Reports*, 43rd Cong., 2nd Sess., No. 101, Pt. 2, pp. 44–45; Burch was listed as paying taxes on a horse and buggy in Baton Rouge valued at $225. Tax Assessment Rolls, East Baton Rouge Parish, 1872, 1874, Clerk of Courts Office, Baton Rouge. Burch married the widow of Oscar Dunn and was a Master Mason before his death from cancer in 1883. Baton Rouge *Daily Capitolian-Advocate*, July 31, 1883; New Orleans *Times-Democrat*, July 30, 1883.

7. *Senate Reports*, 45th Cong., 3rd Sess., No. 855, pp. 131–38; *House Reports*, 43rd Cong., 3rd Sess., No. 261, pp. 214, 218; Natchitoches *Vindicator*, January 16, May 8, June 12, 19, 1875.

8. Emerson Bentley to Warmoth, December 8, 1871, in Warmoth Papers; Philip

MEMBERS OF THE CONSTITUTIONAL CONVENTION, 1868

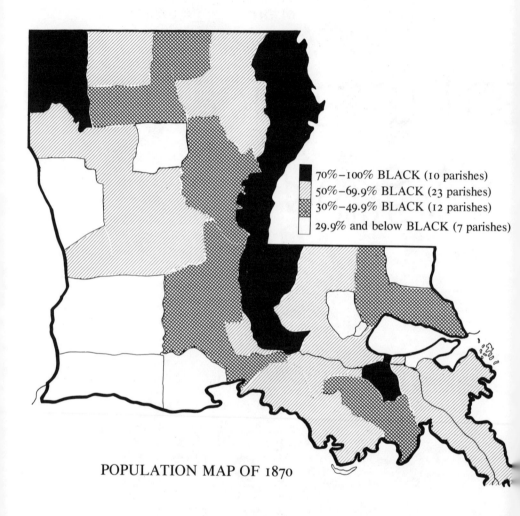

70%–100% BLACK (10 parishes)
50%–69.9% BLACK (23 parishes)
30%–49.9% BLACK (12 parishes)
29.9% and below BLACK (7 parishes)

POPULATION MAP OF 1870

PARISH MAP OF 1870

CAESAR C. ANTOINE

Courtesy Lillian Landry Dunn

PIERRE LANDRY

P. B. S. PINCHBACK

Courtesy Lillian Landry Dunn

T. T. ALLAIN

OSCAR J. DUNN

Courtesy president's office, Southern University

WILLIAM BROWN

Courtesy C. C. Dejoie, Jr.

ARISTIDE DEJOIE

Another former slave elected to the Lower House in 1870 was Harry Mahoney of Plaquemines Parish. He had been purchased in New Orleans by the Wyche family of New Iberia. During the war, he served as a body servant of Major Wyche in the campaigns west of the Mississippi. A self-educated man of great fortitude, Mahoney once saved his master from drowning. Mahoney later served in several political posts in Plaquemines Parish. While a school board member he was accused of embezzling funds but was found innocent.

William Harper of Caddo Parish was also a self-educated former slave elected to the legislature in 1870. Harper was born in Tennessee in 1834 and came to Louisiana with his master in 1845. He was married and a man of good native ability and an effective speaker. A close friend of Senator Caesar C. Antoine of Caddo, Harper served in the lower House only one term before succeeding to Antoine's vacancy in the Senate in 1872. Outside the legislature, he engaged in several occupations. He farmed, operated a grocery store, and did "about everything a man ever did to try to make a living." When "bulldozers" took the ballot from the blacks in 1877, Harper did not return to political office but remained in Shreveport. He continued, however, to carry his pistol and refused to be personally intimidated.[9]

Uzee, "Republican Politics in Louisiana , 1877–1900" (Ph.D. dissertation, Louisiana State University, 1950), 141–42; Demas to William P. Kellogg, September 11, 1876, in Kellogg Papers, Department of Archives and Manuscripts, Louisiana State University, Baton Rouge; New Orleans *Times*, June 3, 1868; *Semi-Weekly Louisianian*, February 20, 1875; *Meschacebe* (St. John the Baptist Parish), April 10, June 5, 1875. Demas was accidently shot in the abdomen by a friend. *Meschacebe*, June 5, 1869; For Demas's defeat of Burrell in 1872, see the *Meschacebe*, November 16, 1872; Burrell contested Demas' election but later withdrew his complaint. *House Journal, 1871*, 48. Demas married in October, 1871, and had four children. Civil War Pension Files, Records of the Veteran Administration, in RG 15, NA; New Orleans *Times Picayune*, April 20, 1900.

9. Mary P. Wyche to John R. Ficklen, February 28, 1903, Harry Mahoney to Ficklen, January 30, 1904, Mahoney to Mary P. Wyche, February 10, 1903, all in John R. Ficklen Papers, Box 1, Folder 1, Department of Archives and Manuscripts, Louisiana State University, Baton Rouge; Register of Signature of Depositors in Branches of the Freedmen's Saving and Trust Co., 1865, in RG 101, NA; New Orleans *Republican*, January 18, 1871; Nordhoff, *The Cotton States in the Spring and Summer of 1875*, 51–52; *Senate Documents*, 44th Cong., 2nd Sess., No. 855, pp. 24–26. Harper had one daughter. His will and succession are filed in Caddo Parish courthouse, Shreveport.

St. Mary Parish's representative, John J. Moore, was a literate thirty-four-year-old former slave. Born in Edgefield, South Carolina, in 1836, Moore had moved to St. Mary Parish at the age of eleven with his master. Wishing to be free but thinking the Emancipation Proclamation did not apply to his parish, he ran away from his plantation. In talking with Union soldiers, he discovered that he was free and thenceforth supported the Union war efforts although he was not a soldier. Politically, he considered himself a "radical republican." He was also a member of the Republican executive committee for the parish and a former supervisor at one of the polls during the April, 1868, election. Because of his political activities, Moore was often threatened by whites and lived in fear of death. He was married, owned several horses, and, for a living, worked cane on George Cleveland's plantation. He had also chopped wood for "anybody who would hire me." Before becoming a representative, Moore had served as a porter for a Senate enrolling committee during the 1868 session.[10]

Eugene V. Macarty of Orleans Parish had enjoyed more advantages than had Harper, Mahoney, Demas, or Moore. Macarty was a freeborn native Louisianian, educated in Paris; he was a tragedian actor and musician. When elected in 1870 he was approximately fifty-three years old and was a member of one of the most prominent creole families in the city. After his one term in the House, he retired and turned to teaching youth in Baton Rouge. Representative Macarty married and had three children.[11]

T. B. Stamps of Jefferson Parish, former coroner, was a leading black businessman and wealthy commission merchant. In fact, he was one of the leading businessmen in south Louisiana. When Stamps established his commission house, he sent a circular to all the black ministers to be read in their congregations

10. *House Miscellaneous Documents*, 41st Cong., 2nd Sess., No. 154, pp. 634–35, 638; New Orleans *Times*, November 11, 1870.
11. *Weekly Louisianian*, July 2, 1881.

urging black planters to support black business. His advertisement in the *Louisianian* promised quick sales, goods at the
"lowest rates," and liberal rates to his customers. After a term in
the lower House and one term in the upper House, he spent full
time at his business. He took personal tours of the parishes and
into Mississippi and Arkansas seeking business for his commission house and cotton factorage. He built a thriving enterprise
and was strongly recommended by the *Louisianian*.[12]

Captain William B. Barrett, of the Seventy–fourth Regiment,
Company A, First United States Colored Infantry, would serve
for only one term 1870–1872, as representative from the third
district (Orleans). Approximately thirty-seven years old when
elected in 1870, Barrett was born in Cincinnati, Ohio, where he
attended school (and was a schoolmate of Pinchback and William Weeks, later assistant secretary of state). The son of a white
woman and black man, Barrett spent his early years as a barber
on the Mississippi River, on many of the same boats with Pinchback, and was considered by friend and foe as a "Man's Man."[13]

Less biographical information was found on the other nineteen new House members to the 1870–1872 legislative session.
Nine were from Orleans Parish. Curron Adophe and Felix Antoine returned for their second term. Armand Belot was new but
was the brother of Octave Belot who served in 1868. The other
representatives were Edgar Davis, a wealthy thirty-seven-
year-old creole, who had offered to raise a regiment of soldiers
for General Butler in 1862 (Fifth Representative District), R. J.
M. Kenner, a native Louisianian (Fourth Representative District), and E. C. Morphy (Seventh Representative District),

12. New Orleans *Daily Picayune*, April 30, 1868; *Weekly Louisianian*, August 9,
September 13, 1879; January 31, March 6, 1880, April 2, May 1, July 30, 1881; Blassin-
game, "A Social and Economic Study of the Negro in New Orleans, 1860–1880," pp.
155–56. Later Stamps served as a school board director. Register of Signature of
Depositors in Branches of the Freedmen's Saving and Trust Co., 1865, in RG 101, NA.
13. Civil War Pension Files, Records of the Veterans Administration, in RG 15, NA;
Custom House Nominations, Louisiana, New Orleans, January 1, 1868–June, 1869, in
Box 109, RG 56, NA.

former assistant alderman, who would later serve as recorder of births, marriage, and deaths for Orleans Parish. Charles W. Ringgold (Fourth Representative District) was the son of a wealthy broker for a Cuban sugar planter; later, Ringgold served as postmaster in New Orleans. Benjamin Buchanan's seat (right bank) was declared vacant and he was unseated on February 11, 1871. Thomas Murray (Second Representative District) was born in Baton Rouge and later moved to New Orleans. Another Orleans representative, and former constable in the First District, was J. W. Quinn (Third Representative District) who was later appointed to the police board in New Orleans.[14]

The other eight representatives came from various parishes. Anthony Overton, of Ouachita, was a former coroner; he also owned a large boardinghouse and a "provisionstore" in Monroe. William Crawford of Rapides, Prosper Darinsburg of Pointe Coupee, John Nelson, former justice of the peace from Lafourche, George Washington of Concordia, Joshua Wilson of East Baton Rouge, and Joseph Lott of Rapides, who was later a law student at Straight University, served only one term each. Cain Sartain, a former justice of the peace in Carroll Parish, served three consecutive terms. The twenty-seven-year-old Sartain lived in the neighborhood of Goodrich's Landing and produced one of the largest crops of cotton in the parish. He was a slave in, and native of, Pike County, Mississippi, where he was

14. *House Miscellaneous Documents*, 41st Cong., 2nd Sess., Pt. 1, No. 154, pp. 253–54; Belot paid taxes on $1,500 worth of real estate and personal property in Orleans Parish. Tax Ledgers, 1870, A–L, City Archives, New Orleans Public Library; Desdunes, *Our People and Our History*, 118–19; Pension Files, Records of the Veterans Administration, in RG 15, NA; Register of Signature of Depositors in Branches of the Freedmen's Savings and Trust Co., 1865, in RG 101, NA; New Orleans *Republican*, January 10, 11, 1874; Custom House Nominations, Louisiana, New Orleans, January, 1868–June, 1869, and June, 1869–May, 1870, in Box 109, RG 56, NA; New Orleans *Republican*, January 18, February 4, 17, 1871; *House Journal*, 1871, pp. 94, 102, 147, 172, 193–95. Upon his death in 1895, Murray had acquired over $3,000 worth of property that he left to his daughter and grandson. Succession Papers of Thomas Murray, U.S. courthouse, New Orleans; *Weekly Louisianian*, February 18, May 11, 1872; New Orleans *Times*, April 23, 1868; New Orleans *Daily Picayune*, April 24, 1868.

born in 1843. He served in the Civil War as a private in Company K, Seventieth United States Colored Infantry.[15]

The 1870 Senate also experienced several changes. Three senators did not return; one, Alexander François, had been killed in 1869; Julian J. Monette of Orleans and Robert Poindexter of Assumption were not reelected. Three new senators were elected, maintaining the total black membership in the Senate at seven out of thirty-six.[16] Two of the new senators were from New Orleans, James H. Ingraham and A. E. Barber. The other senator, Edward Butler, was from Plaquemines Parish and Orleans (right bank).

James H. Ingraham was, perhaps, the leader among the three new senators. He had been politically active before the Reconstruction acts, and he remained in the Senate until 1874. He aspired to become a United States congressman but failed and was for a while disenchanted with the party. Visiting with President Grant in the spring of 1872, he impressed the president greatly and was appointed surveyor of the Port of Customs at New Orleans, a position he held until early 1874.[17]

15. New Orleans *Times*, April 25, 1868; *Senate Documents*, 44th Cong., 2nd Sess., No. 2, pp. 412–13; Another black man, Joseph L'Official, was also elected from East Baton Rouge, but he was killed on election day by a mob. *Weekly Advocate*, August 6, November 12, 1870. Representative Burch urged a resolution granting relief for L'Official's wife, Mrs. Leontine L'Official. Both the Senate and House adjourned on January 7, 1871, out of respect for him. *House Journal, 1871*, 16, 18, 84, 103. New Orleans *Republican*, January 7, 1871. Wilson was listed as owning 225 acres of land, several horses, and buggies, all valued at $4,797. Tax Assessment Rolls, East Baton Rouge Parish, 1872, 1875, 1876, Clerk of Courts Office, Baton Rouge. The value of his property fluctuated during the period. New Orleans *Times*, June 3, 1868. Representative Sartain was one of the strongest black men in his parish. He often lamented the assassination of blacks in Mississippi and urged blacks to unite. The Democratic press accused him of drawing the "color line." Carroll *Watchman*, January 8, August 12, December 25, 1875, February 19, 1876; Richland *Beacon*, January 1, 1876; Pension Files, Records of the Veterans Administration, RG 15, NA; Military Service Record, RG 94, NA.

16. See Appendix F. herein.

17. New Orleans *Tribune*, January 10, 1865, July 31, 1867; Chap. 3, *n*4, herein; *Semi-Weekly Louisianian*, April 4, 1872. He often contributed to his church's support of Straight (Dillard) University. Charles H. Thompson to the Reverend E. M. Cravath, April 16, 1874, in Louisiana files, Amistad Research Center, Dillard University; New Orleans *Republican*, October 11, 1874.

A. E. Barber was also an Orleanian and former Union soldier. A native of Kentucky, he spent his early life in Louisville and on steamers on the Mississippi River, where he obtained much of his education. During the war, he secured the rank of an officer. When the fighting ended, he was in New Orleans, where he entered politics, served as president of the Union National Brotherhood of New Orleans in 1864, and during 1870–1874 served as state senator. His strong character and agreeable personality were admired by many, including Frederick Douglass, who, after meeting Barber declared that the South had capable native leaders. Douglass further felt that with such men in the South, "it will not be easy to reverse the wheels of liberty in that region."[18]

As a close friend of Governor Warmoth, Senator Barber was appointed harbor master of New Orleans, made brigadier general of the state militia, and was often designated to attend Republican party meetings in the North. His death at the age of forty-six, on October 25, 1875, undoubtedly left the state poorer in political leadership.[19]

Senator Edward Butler, a native of Massachusetts who served from 1870 until 1874, had lived in Plaquemines Parish only four years before he was elected to the Senate. As a supporter of the Warmoth faction, he held many offices after his senatorial term; he was a parish recorder and a member of both the police jury and school board.[20]

---

18. *Weekly Louisianian*, October 30, 1875; New Orleans *Daily Picayune*, November 24, 1871; New Orleans *Tribune*, August 13, 16, 1864; *New National Era*, May 10, 1872, quoted in *Semi-Weekly Louisianian*, May 11, 1872.

19. *House Miscellaneous Documents*, 42nd Cong., 2nd Sess., No. 211, p. 392. Barber was apparently a man of some means. In early May, 1872, he had a large house party with a band to provide the music. *Weekly Louisianian*, May 4, 1872, October 30, 1875; Custom House Nominations, Louisiana, New Orleans, January 1, 1868–June, 1869, in Box 109, RG 56, NA; Charles H. Thompson to the Reverend E. M. Cravath, April 16, 1874, in Louisiana files, Amistad Research Center.

20. As a school board member, Butler was charged with fraud, but a nolle prosequi ruling ended the matter. New Orleans *Weekly Democrat*, October 5, 1878; *House Miscellaneous Documents*, 44th Cong., 2nd Sess., No. 34, Pt. 5, pp. 286, 323, 337, 349;

The politics of the 1871 session presented a scene of rival factions fighting for control. In the House, a coalition of Democrats and Republicans reelected Mortimer Carr as Speaker; a similar coalition in the Senate attempt to rob the lieutenant governor of his patronage by taking the appointment of committees from his hands. These arrangements did not last. By the middle of the session, dissatisfaction with Speaker Mortimer Carr's ruling was loudly expressed, and Colonel George W. Carter was elected in his place. This change caused a shift in the personnel of committee appointees. Initially, when the house standing committees were appointed on January 9, and 13, there were nine black chairmen out of thirty committees. Approximately four weeks later, when the same standing committees were reconstituted, there was only one black chairman, and there were fewer black members on important committees. Black Representative F. C. Antoine chaired the seven-man Committee on Elections and Qualifications, which included two other blacks.[21] Whites had a majority vote on all committees except the Committee on Charitable and Public Institution which had four blacks and three whites; the Committee on Penitentiary was equally divided in membership—four blacks and four whites.

The most important committees had from one to two blacks. For instance, the committees on Appropriation, Canals and Drainage, Unfinished Business, and Registration had two blacks and five whites. The Judiciary Committee consisted of two blacks and four whites, while the Committee on Banks and Banking had only one black and six whites. The committees with

Nordhoff, *The Cotton States*, 51–52; Register of Signature of Depositors in Branches of the Freedmen's Saving and Trust Co., 1865, RG 101, NA.

21. Representative Burch was also nominated but received only seven votes to Carr's eighty-five. Carter received sixty votes and Burch received thirty-five. New Orleans *Republican*, February 1, 1871; Lonn, *Reconstruction*, 75–76. The committees included: Constitutional, State Library, Federal Relations, Registration, Canals and Drainage, Pensions, Corporations, Public Printing, and Enrollment. *House Journal, 1871*, pp. 3, 30–31, 34, 48, 61, 64, 78–79, 92, 111–12.

three blacks and four whites were the following: Railroads, Enrollment, Immigration, Corporation, Militia, and Agriculture.[22]

No Senate committee had a black chairman. Moreover, only one committee had a majority black membership. This was the Committee on Federal Relations, that included Senators Pinchback and Butler and one white. Two three-man committees had one black. These were the committees on Parish and Parish Boundaries (Barber) and on Manufacturing (Kelso). Blacks had one member on the following four-man committees: Claims (Ingraham), Public Education (Antoine), Printing (Antoine), Penitentiary (Ingraham), and Public Lands (Kelso). Senator Pinchback was the only black on the seven-member committees of Enrollment, Apportionment and Election District. The Committee on Health and Quarantine, as well as the Committee on Engrossing Bills consisted of two blacks and three whites. Only Senator Butler was represented on the Committee on Retrenchment and Reform. No blacks were represented on the following powerful Senate committees: Judiciary, Finance, Militia, Banks and Banking, Appropriations, Auditing and Supervising the Expenses of the Senate, Corporation, Charitable Institutions, Parks and Public Buildings, Railroads, Pensions and Gratuities, Drainage, Canals and Inland Navigation, "to Compare Bills in Third Readings," and Levees.[23]

Along with the interparty strife, the legislative session of 1871 was one of the most extravagant of Warmoth's administration. It cost the state almost a million dollars. Many needless appropriations were made, and the compensation and contingent expenses of the General Assembly amounted to $250,000. The

22. *House Journal, 1871*, pp. 92, 111–12.
23. Pinchback later sponsored a resolution to increase the membership of the Committee on Election to seven. This was offered in connection with his resolution to authorize such a committee to send for persons and papers in all contested elections when requested by the contestees or their attorney. Pinchback was added to the committee. Representative Harry Lott sponsored a similar resolution in the House, authorizing the Committee on Election to send for persons and paper. It was adopted.

most extravagant of these were usually offered by white members. The bill making an appropriation for general expenses was offered by Senator McMillen, but blacks, generally, supported the measure. The appropriation bill was increased by such items as $1,000 for the "Family of Widows" of St. Bernard Street and $3,000 for Institutes for Les Orphelins Indigents located at Dauphine, near Union Street; both items were sponsored by Senator Ingraham. Other increases were urged by Senator Antoine; these included $800 for the Morning Star Benevolent Association of Shreveport and $5,000 for the Sisters of Charity of Shreveport.[24] But when the bill returned from the House, many additional items were attached; in the Senate, other items were added. The contingent expense was increased from $60,000 to $125,000 at the request of Senator John Lynch. These amendments as well as the bill were adopted on the last day, with three of the five black senators who were present opposing the bill. Senators Antoine and Ingraham criticized it, and Antoine voted for it under protest, "being convinced that the Senate had better concur in the amendments, unjust as they were in part, rather than endanger the final passage of the bill." Senator Ingraham refused to vote for it under any circumstances, thus risking his sponsored items. He explained his vote:

> The undersigned votes 'no' because of the vast amount of uncalled for items in the appropriation bill, appropriating the peoples money to various objects and purposes which I believe to be unworthy of any state aid, and calculated to cause all respect for civil government in this state to cease on the part of the people.
>
> Respectfully Submitted
> James H. Ingraham[25]

24. Appropriations to pay expenses amounted to $625,000; however, this sum was exhausted. Outstanding warrants totaled over $200,000. Total appropriations made during the session came to $16,185,322.99. Pitre, "Collapse of Warmoth Regime," 166–67; *Senate Reports*, 42nd Cong., 2nd Sess., No. 41, Pt. 1, pp. 356–60; New Orleans *Republican*, March 1, 3, 1871; *Senate Journal, 1871*, pp. 29–30, 59–62, 80–81, 84–85, 183, 191, 192, 197, 199, 212; *Acts of 1871*, No. 72, p. 186; *House Journal, 1871*, pp. 15, 16, 31, 220–21.

25. *Senate Journal, 1871*, p. 222.

Several other unusual bills were passed in this session. Two were sponsored by black members. On the last day of the session Representative F. C. Antoine of Orleans urged the resolution allowing the Committee on Election and Qualification to sit after adjournment for thirty days with pay, and to visit the Parishes of Bossier, Iberville, Martin, and Sabine. Representative William E. Barrett of Orleans sponsored a resolution authorizing the Committee on Charitable and Public Institutions to examine the financial and general affairs of such institutions, within a sixty-day period with pay.[26] Both members were on these respective committees, and F. C. Antoine was chairman of the Committee on Election and Qualifications.

Many bills were offered that were constructive and directed toward aiding the entire citizenry. Blacks continued to support education, and a supplement to the law of 1870 was passed. This act simplified administration of school matters by abolishing the ward boards. Through this law the parish and town-board members lost their positions, and new ones were appointed in their places by the state board.[27]

A civil rights measure also was passed by both houses. The measure adopted in 1871 grew out of an amendment that Representative Robert Isabelle had tried to attach to Senator Pinchback's civil rights bill of 1869. The Senate had refused to concur in the proposal.

This bill originated in the House and passed in mid-February. Senator A. E. Barber managed the measure in the Senate and by refusing to permit delay tactics, secured its enactment in one day. As Act Number 23, the title best summarizes its

26. *House Journal, 1871*, pp. 222–23. Warmoth acquired an injuction against these committees and others. They were prevented from receiving the warrants for payments. Lonn, *Reconstruction*, 93–94. Professor Lonn further assumes that these measures were necessarily corrupt; but many public institutions actually needed investigation; in a number of specified parishes elections were held at gunpoint and through other intimidations.

27. *House Journal, 1871*, pp. 38, 109–11; *Senate Journal, 1871*, pp. 90, 157. This bill was introduced in the House by Emerson Bentley, white Republican from St. Mary; in the Senate, Ingraham called it up. *Acts of 1871*, No. 8.

objective: "To regulate the mode of trying cases arising under the provisions of Article Thirteen (13) of the Constitution of Louisiana, or under any acts of the Legislature to enforce the said Article Thirteen of the said Constitution, and to regulate the licenses therein mentioned."[28]

In addition to civil rights, the issues of relief, internal improvements, and incorporation of towns received the attention of blacks. Legislation in these areas had been urged in the governor's annual message. Internal improvements were a crying need in Louisiana. Senator Ingraham introduced an act to authorize the city of New Orleans to construct a shell road from the Marigny Canal to Lake Pontchartrain. The city would also authorize the collection of a toll for the use of the road. The Senate passed the bill on the day it was introduced, and the House concurred a week later, on the last day of the session. This act became law on the first day of the 1872 session without the governor's signature. It leased the road to the city of New Orleans for a period of fifteen years. Other internal improvement schemes were not as successful. Representative Ringgold sponsored an act to provide protection for New Orleans from overflow by constructing a levee. The bill passed several House readings but was buried in a committee. Representative Harry Lott urged a similar bill to protect Alexandria by constructing a "break water on the Red River." Mahoney of Plaquemines Parish urged repeal of the act granting certain contracts to the New Orleans Sanitary and Fertilizing Company, an agency that had been contracted by the legislature to clean the city sewage but had not fulfilled the work. The bill died in the Judiciary Committee. Representative Demas championed a bill, providing state aid for the cleaning out to Bayou Portage and Bayou Mayer, and digging a canal from the latter

28. *House Journal, 1871*, p. 139; *Senate Journal, 1869*, pp. 133, 161, 165–66; *Acts of 1871*, No. 23, pp. 57–58; "Noline" to Henry C. Warmoth, February 27, 1871, in Warmoth Papers. "Noline" thought that the governor should sign it to show blacks that he would "stretch a point to secure them their rights." New Orleans *Republican*, February 5, 16, 23, 1871.

Bayou to Bayou Yorkely to secure better drainage in St. Mary Parish. Senator Butler promoted a bill to incorporate the Metropolitan Drainage Company to provide drainage for New Orleans and Carrollton. The bill was read twice and died in the Committee on Drainage.[29]

In addition to constructing new internal improvements, there was a desire to investigate old canals and companies not operating but holding state bonds. Representative David Young vigorously pushed for the dissolving of the New Orleans and Ship Island Canal Company. On January 9 he introduced a resolution to appoint a committee to investigate the condition of the company and to determine whether it had complied with the conditions of the charter. Three days later the measure was called up, amended to include the affairs of Lake Borgne and the Mexican Ship Canal Company, and adopted. Four days later a three-man committee was appointed, including David Young, Adolphe Tureaud and S. Marvin. A month later, February 16, the Committee issued its report. The report stated that the company had complied fully, but since the consolidation of portions of Orleans and Jefferson parishes, the latter parish refused to execute the endorsement of its bonds. Therefore the committee recommended dissolving the charter by an act of the legislature.

The next day, a House bill was introduced to dissolve the corporation. David Young championed it; but when no action was taken a new five-man committee was appointed. Of the five members, Young was the only black. The committee favored the bill; however, the efforts to pass it were last in the end-of-session debates to pass the Appropriation Bill.[30]

An issue of special concern to black legislators was the quality of local government in their districts. Thus Caddo Parish's (black) senator and representative sought various

29. New Orleans *Republican*, February 25, 1871; *Acts of 1872*, No. 108, p. 22; *House Journal, 1871*, pp. 37, 40, 50, 53, 60, 100, 195, 204, 205, 217; *Senate Journal, 1871*, pp. 87, 109–10, 165, 174, 181.
30. *House Journal, 1871*, pp. 17, 32, 38, 145–46, 152, 189, 193, 220–21.

changes in the government of Shreveport. Senator Antoine introduced in late January a bill to incorporate the city of Shreveport and to provide it with police and municipal agencies. It was read twice and referred to the Judiciary Committee and reported favorable on February 1; on Antoine's motion, it was made the special order for February 11 and was passed. In the House, it was called up by Representative William Harper, read twice, and referred to a special committee composed of representatives from Caddo, Bossier, DeSoto, and Natchitoches. After a favorable report, the bill was passed with minor amendments. In its final form, it provided for a city council government for Shreveport vested in a mayor and four administrators (Finance, Improvement, Public Accounts, and Assessments). The governor appointed all members until successors were elected in November, 1872. The administrators of Finance and Assessments were to be elected in November, and every two years thereafter; the following November (1873), there was to be an election for mayor and for the administrators of Improvement and Public Accounts. All officers were to take the oath prescribed by Article 100 of the constitution.[31]

This act has been criticized by a historian of Shreveport. But contrary to the critic's claims, progress ensued under the new system. It was responsible for building the first city hall in Shreveport and for other improvements. The Democrats repealed the act in 1878, but their supplanting bill was similar in wording. It provided for the city government to be vested in a mayor and eight trustees.[32]

Other city governments were modified by legislation. Senator Butler promoted a bill to locate the courthouse in Plaque-

31. Senator Antoine also championed a bill, which became Act No. 101, confirming a compromise made between the city of Shreveport and the representatives of the Shreveport Town Company on certain property in the city. *Senate Journal, 1871*, pp. 61, 107, 114, 122, 130, 218; *House Journal, 1871*, pp. 150, 162, 192, 208; *Acts of 1871*, No. 98, pp. 218–28, No. 101, pp. 235–36.

32. Maude O'Pry, *Chronicle of Shreveport* (Shreveport: Journal Printing Company, 1928), 173–74; *Acts of 1878*, No. 25, pp. 283–95.

mines Parish at Pointe-a-la-Hache, its present location. Senator Barber sought passage of a measure to amend the act of 1852 extending the limits of Orleans, and to change the boundaries of Orleans and Jefferson; the bill never returned from the Judiciary Committee. Senator Reagan and Representative Burch joined to seek changes in the governmental affairs of East Baton Rouge.[33]

Relief measures also received priority in this session. Many relief items were included in the appropriation bill, but others did not receive committee approval or did not come up for a vote. Several were important enough to require individual acts, as in the case of Act No. 107 authored by Representative T. B. Stamps. Introduced ten days after the start of the session, it passed the house in late February, entitled "Act of the Relief of the Parish of Jefferson, Right Bank." It quickly won approval in the Senate. The act authorized the auditor of public accounts to issue warrants on the treasurer in the amount of $28,332.27 to pay the police jury of Jefferson Parish, right bank, for building the Jardos levee in the parish. The construction was completed in 1867.[34]

Railroad legislation continued to be quickly passed. An act to amend the charter of the Southeastern Railroad Company, giving it a second mortgage on bonds if the company would begin work within six months, received few dissenting votes from black lawmakers. A joint resolution to permit the New Orleans, Mobile and Chattanooga Railroad Company (charered in 1869) to change its name to the New Orleans, Mobile and Texas Railroad Company passed. The company retained its same rights to issue bonds. The Alexandria, Homer, Fulton Railroad Company was incorporated; the company was to con-

33. *Senate Journal, 1871*, pp. 13, 17, 30–31, 35–36, 41, 55, 76–77; *House Journal, 1871*, pp. 101, 157, 173, 187–88; *Acts of 1871*, No. 12, p. 48.
34. *House Journal, 1871*, pp. 33, 43, 50, 52, 53, 60, 93, 96, 144, 169, 173, 205; *Senate Journal, 1871*, pp. 12, 21, 31, 42, 100, 105, 116, 172, 184, 189; *Acts of 1872*, No. 107, pp. 21–22.

struct a railroad from Alexandria northward to Homer and to connect with a railroad in Arkansas. The company's bonds were guaranteed by the state to the amount of $12,500 each mile. A similar incorporation act for this road had been adopted in 1870 but was vetoed by Warmoth because it had granted the company unlimited powers.[35]

In many cases, legislation creating new parishes was supported by the black legislators. When the Senate voted for passage of the act creating Webster Parish, no black senators voted in the negative. The black representatives were not similarly united, but the bill eventually passed its third reading. Earlier in the House session, Raiford Blunt had championed an unsuccessful measure to stop legislation creating new parishes unless "authorized by an election of the voters of the parishes to be divided." He obviously did not change many opinions since the Senate passed a bill to create Red River Parish.[36]

One Orleanian, Representative E. C. Morphy, attempted to deal again with the problem of the status of children of unwed parents. Previous legislation had proved insufficient in this area. During the first week of February, he introduced an act to legitimatize children born of common-law partners. The bill was read twice and referred to the Judiciary Committee which reported it favorably. It was adopted and sent to the Senate, which took no action since the bill was received near the close of the session.[37]

Many days of the session were spent discussing the Louisiana Lottery Company. Representative George Washington of

35. *House Journal, 1871*, pp. 134–35, 148, 182–83, 204, 206–207; *Senate Journal, 1871*, pp: 7, 140, 157, 170; Senator Antoine held a certificate for one hundred shares at $100 each in the Southeastern Railway Company pending passage of the act. The certificate was dated February 10, 1871. C. C. Antoine Scrapbook; *Acts of 1871*, No. 28, pp. 66–72, Joint Resolution No. 94, p. 211; New Orleans *Republican*, February 7, 25, 1871. Another railroad company to get a second mortgage was the Northeastern Railroad Company, but the bill was apparently vetoed. *Senate Journal, 1871*, p. 170.

36. *Senate Journal, 1871*, pp. 149, 168; *House Journal, 1871*, pp. 58, 59, 68, 129, 198; New Orleans *Republican*, January 27, 31, February 3, 9, 24, 1871.

37. *House Journal, 1871*, pp. 104, 142, 175, 178; *Senate Journal, 1871*, p. 171.

Assumption sponsored a resolution to authorize a three-man committee to examine the books of the company. But the powerful gambling concern easily mobilized enough black and white legislators to table the resolution. Representative Charles Ringgold urged an act to incorporate the Charity Hospital Lottery Association of New Orleans, claiming it would bring additional revenue to the hospital; the proposal never reached a committee hearing. David Young offered a measure to incorporate the New Orleans Consolidated Lottery Company arguing that another lottery would benefit the state financially. But his effort was opposed by the lottery forces and eventually met failure.[38]

Blacks took the offensive in championing the cause of Negro candidates in contested elections, demanding investigation whenever fraud was suspected. Senator Pinchback opposed the seating of J. R. Gallup to replace Senator Alexander François, who had been killed by a mob, but failed to prevent Gallup being seated. Representative Tureaud, in an attempt to acquire testimony, unsuccessfully presented a resolution to pay the mileage and per diem of contestants for seats from Iberville and Saint Martin parishes. Representative Harry Lott secured a resolution requiring the Committee on Elections to notify a contestant in writing of the time when his case would be heard. The resolution was adopted but the House adjourned in heated debate before completing the seating. In another case two black contestants forfeited their claim, withdrew, and commended their opponents. Another contested election case found no winner; and the committee's resolution was adopted declaring the seat vacant and requesting the governor to order an election to fill the vacancy.[39]

38. *House Journal, 1831*, pp. 35, 38, 143, 144, 175; Berthold C. Alwes, "The History of the Louisiana State Lottery Company," *Louisiana Historical Quarterly*, XXVII (October, 1944), 978.

39. Pinchback later introduced a bill relative to elections, but it did not get a committee hearing. *Senate Journal, 1871*, pp. 3, 30–31, 33, 48, 223; *House Journal, 1871*, pp. 14, 48, 75–77, 94, 102, 147, 172, 193–95. For a case involving two black men seeking the representative's seat from Orleans District (right bank), see New Orleans *Republican*, February 4, 7, 28, 1871.

In this session black legislators had begun to feel the strength of their unity; their most serious handicap was the turnover of members. One term did not provide adequate time to enable members to learn their business or to become helpful to their supporters, although a few learned to fill their own pockets. The lack of political stability in the black membership (as well as white membership) was a symbol of the factionalism in the Republican party.

The struggle in the party for power continued during the summer of 1871 and became bitter. Professor W. E. B. DuBois aptly described Reconstruction politics in Louisiana when he said it was a "continuation of the Civil War."[40] By June the Customhouse faction of the Republican party was gaining strength. It now included Lieutenant Governor Dunn and his cohorts, Marshal S. B. Packard, chairman of the Republican state committee, and his followers; Collector Casey and his Customhouse gang; Postmaster Lowell and his employees of the post office of New Orleans; and Speaker Carter and his legislative friends. During the absence of Warmoth in Mississippi, because of a foot injury in late June, the leaders of the Customhouse group called a state convention to meet at the state capitol, Mechanic's Institute, on August 9. The purpose was to organize the party against Warmoth. The proceedings had not started before Warmoth returned and attempted to attend the convention; whereupon Packard, on August 8, changed the convention site to the Customhouse, a building which he controlled. Packard gathered his forces and summoned the deputy United States marshal from Texas to prevent the governor's entrance.

Warmoth was not to be outdone. When he arrived with his delegates and was denied admission, the governor advised his followers to withdraw to a place where they would hold their own convention without interruption. Of the 118 delegates 95

40. W. E. B. DuBois, *Black Reconstruction in America: 1860–1880* (New York: Harcourt, Brace and Co., 1935), 482.

convened with him at Turner's Hall (across the street). Listed among the delegates following Warmoth were Thomas Isabelle, Judge Henry C. Dibble, Francis J. Herron (secretary of state), and Pinchback.

The Turner's Hall faction endorsed Warmoth's administration and the state and national administration.[41] In other resolutions they denounced the Customhouse faction and the officials who had attempted to pack the convention with their followers. Then the president-elect of the convention, Pinchback, appointed a committee of twenty members to present the "facts" to President Grant. This resolution called for replacement of Marshal Packard, Collector Casey, Postmaster Lowell, and other federal officials who supported the Customhouse faction.

The "facts" accepted by President Grant were those of the Customhouse faction and of his brother-in-law, Collector Casey. The president accepted the view of Packard that it was necessary to destroy Warmoth's influence in the Republican party. Moreover, the president was aware that many Negroes and whites were disenchanted with the governor. The president's decision to side with one faction meant an irreparable rupture in the party. The division was now clear: the Warmoth-Pinchback combination versus the Customhouse faction led by Dunn and Packard.[42]

Both sides now prepared for the 1872 election. The Customhouse forces began by establishing the *National Republican* newspaper edited by Speaker George W. Carter. Fifteen days later this same faction was practically disbanded when Lieutenant Governor Dunn died unexpectedly on November 22, 1871. Several leading black legislators claimed foul play in Dunn's death. Senator Ingraham stated that Dunn's body was exhumed and arsenic was found in his stomach. No one was charged with

41. P. A. Morse and William M. Levy to Thomas J. Simms, November, 1871, in Warmoth Papers.
42. Pitre, "Collapse of the Warmoth Regime," 167–69; Warmoth, *War, Politics and Reconstruction*, 112–19; *House Miscellaneous Documents*, 42nd Cong., 2nd Sess., No. 211, pp. 299, 323–24.

the deed, but his death was a significant loss to the anti-Warmoth forces in Louisiana. Dunn's death presented an opportunity for the governor's faction to fill the office of lieutenant governor with a strong supporter. After consulting several lawyers, the governor issued a proclamation on November 24 calling the Senate into an extra session on December 6 for the purpose of filling the vacancy. His candidate was Pinchback. When the session convened, opponents of the governor protested its legality and threatened impeachment, but Warmoth had the strength to force a vote. On the first ballot the vote stood seventeen for Pinchback and seventeen for the anti-Warmoth candidate, T. V. Coupland, an official in the Customhouse. When Senator J. B. Lewis, a disenchanted Customhouse supporter changed his vote to Pinchback, the Warmoth faction was victorious and Pinchback was elected eighteen to sixteen. The Senate then adjourned sine die on December 7.[43]

The Customhouse faction was not willing to let the Warmoth people entrench themselves in power. Moreover, many blacks opposed the governor. United States Senator William P. Kellogg, who operated with the Customhouse faction, contended that Pinchback did not represent the black masses; Ingraham and Burch, he maintained, were the leaders who controlled more blacks.[44]

Events soon disclosed that blacks were far from united. When the legislature met in January, 1872, the struggle for political supremacy found blacks on both sides. Some cooperated with

43. Dufour, "The Age of Warmoth," 352–53; Pitre, "Collapse of the Warmoth Regime," 169–71; Senator Lewis later brought suit to recover the money for his vote. Alcee Fortier, *A History of Louisiana, 1861 –1904* (New York: Goupil and Co. of Paris, 1904), IV, 117–18. Numerous endorsements of Pinchback can be found in *Weekly Louisianian*, December 10, 14, 17, 21, 31, 1871, January 4, 1872. According to the newspapers, Ingraham refused to support Pinchback. For comments on Dunn's death, see L. B. Jenks to Warmoth, December 9, 1871, in Warmoth Papers; Perkins, "Oscar James Dunn," 116–17.
44. William P. Kellogg to S. P. Packard, December 7, 1871, in Warmoth Papers. Senator Antoine later called the session illegal since only the Senate met in session; but he felt that Pinchback would represent the interest of the black people in Louisiana. *Weekly Louisianian*, January 25, 1872.

the coalition of Democrats and Customhouse members who hoped to remove Warmoth from office. The first objective of the coalition was to organize the Senate against Warmoth, then to declare Pinchback's election illegal, and finally to impeach Warmoth. In the House, the Warmoth faction took the offensive and tried to remove Speaker Carter. After succeeding in this move, the Speaker attempted to establish a rival house in the Gem Saloon, but its meetings were later broken up by General W. H. Emory and the military forces.[45]

The Senate encountered similar strife. The anti-Warmoth senators tried to prevent a quorum by cruising on the steamboat *Wilderness* on the Mississippi River. However, on January 15 a sufficient number of members was present to make a quorum, and after the governor's message was received, the Senate proceeded to repeal the election, registration, constabulary, and printing acts. This ensured the governor of support from disenchanted Republicans and some Democrats. The Senate then confirmed the measures of the extra session (Pinchback's election). Moreover, the Gem house group (Carter's cohorts) was left powerless.[46]

Although blacks participated with both factions, few wanted to see autocratic measures giving almost unlimited powers to Warmoth abolished. Senator Pinchback was perhaps the most vocal in his opposition to such action. He felt that the legislature might as well repeal the Civil Rights Act as the others. If this were done, he said, the blacks of Louisiana could "bid farewell to

45. Blacks often voiced criticism of the Republican party leadership—carpetbaggers, and scalawags. In the Labor convention of blacks, which met in New Orleans in the spring of 1872, several black delegates expressed sympathy for the Liberal Republican movement. *House Miscellaneous Documents*, 42nd Cong., 2nd Sess., No. 211, pp. 310–11; *Weekly Louisianian*, January 14, 18, 21, 28, February 8, April 11, 14, 18, 24, May 11, 1872; Lewis, "The Political Mind of the Negro, 1865–1900," 199–200; New Orleans *Republican*, January 3, 4, 5, 20, 21, 25, 1872.

46. F. Wayne Binning, "Henry Clay Warmoth and Louisiana Reconstruction" (Ph.D. dissertation, University of North Carolina, 1969), 270–90. A Select Committee of the United States House of Representatives arrived during the dispute. *House Miscellaneous Documents*, 42nd Cong., 2nd Sess., No. 211, p. 16. The *Weekly Louisianian* was extremely critical of Speaker Carter; see December 31, 1871, January 7, 11, 25, 1872.

your right to public education; bid farewell to the right to hold office from police juror up to the highest office in the gift of people. . . ." He concluded by urging blacks to prepare "for condition of servitude second only to that which you knew before the war. . . ." Other senators called for block voting to oppose changing or modifying the measures.[47] This view did not prevail.

Occupation with party strife left little time for legislative matters. In fact, the session was half over before the House met properly. Among reports were those on railroads—their compliance with their charters and their discrimination practices. The New Orleans, Mobile and Texas Railroad Company had not complied with section one of its charter by beginning work within six months. Black Representative Eugene V. Macarty's wife had been ejected from her first-class seat; although not ejected himself, Macarty joined his wife in the smoking car on their trip to Bay St. Louis, Mississippi. The Louisiana and Texas Railroad (from New Orleans to Brashear City) was in good condition and working on schedule. Another railroad, the New Orleans, Jackson and Great Northern, was reported in "fairly fine condition."[48]

Late February saw the addition of a new election law. It continued the returning board, which was now made elective by the Senate. New printing and police laws were passed but were apparently vetoed. The Democratic press criticized the lack of relief measures or financial reforms as the strife-ridden legislature adjourned.[49] The approaching conventions and elections would bring new faces, but the old antagonism would continue to hinder reforms.

47. *Weekly Louisianian*, January 25, 1872.

48. *Ibid.*, February 2, 29, March 3, 1872; John F. Stover, *The Railroads of the South, 1865–1900* (Chapel Hill: University of North Carolina Press, 1955), 95, says Louisiana was relatively free of railroad scandals.

49. *Weekly Louisianian*, February 8, 29, 1872; New Orleans *Daily Picayune*, March 1, 1872; Lonn, *Reconstruction,* 135–37.

CHAPTER VII

Factionalism
Under
Governor Kellogg

The division in the state Republican party reflected a similar division in the national Republican organization. The state factions accordingly affiliated with one or the other of the national factions. In 1872 the national Republicans nominated Grant for President and Henry Wilson for vice-president. The Liberal Republicans selected as their standard-bearer Horace Greeley and for vice-president, B. Gratz Brown. Governor Warmoth decided to support the Liberal group because Grant had not upheld him in the state struggle. Originally, Lieutenant Governor Pinchback intended to support the Liberal Republicans but only if Charles Sumner received the nomination. But with Greeley's nomination, Pinchback broke with Warmoth and united with the Customhouse faction in supporting Grant.

During the spring and summer of 1872 three distinct parties emerged in Louisiana: the Customhouse, or Radical Republicans; the Reformers; and the Democrats.[1] Each group held one

1. The Reform party grew out of a committee of fifty-one citizens of New Orleans who met in December, 1871, to promote reform in the city administration. Lonn, *Reconstruction*, 140. Senator Burch was a member but later resigned when the party attempted to deceive black voters in the 1872 election. Another reform effort was promoted by the hereditary free black element in New Orleans who supported the wealthy philanthropist Aristide Mary for governor; the movement failed, however. Desdunes, *Our People and Our History*, 140–41; Lewis, "The Political Mind of the Negro," 198–99; New Orleans *Republican*, March 20, April 12, 13, May 10, June 7, 9, 1872, January 15, 16, 1873, October 6, 1874.

or more conventions and set up the usual committees. The Customhouse party was the first to hold a convention, meeting in New Orleans from April 30 until May 1, for the purpose of selecting delegates to the Republican convention. Resolutions denouncing Warmoth were introduced, but at this point Pinchback appeared and urged harmony. Milder resolutions were then adopted, and the meeting adjourned before delegates were chosen. Four weeks later the Warmoth Republicans who leaned toward the national Liberals met in the statehouse. The convention voted to wait on the outcome of the Liberal Republican national convention before endorsing candidates. Since many of the delegates were officeholders under Warmoth, official approval of the governor was voted overwhelmingly; Pinchback also won the praise of the convention. After endorsing the Republican platform of 1868, the convention adjourned to meet again on June 19 in Baton Rouge. Meanwhile, on June 3, the Democratic and Reform parties convened in New Orleans and managed to effect a fusion. John McEnery became the gubernatorial candidate of the combined factions that later united with the Liberals.

On June 19 the two wings of the Republican party met at Baton Rouge, hoping to effect a coalition. The hope was stillborn, however, and the factions adjourned to meet again in New Orleans on August 9. Conference committees from each group were appointed to confer with the other side. The Pinchback wing of the party found it impossible to approve the state Liberal platform and pledged itself to support Grant and Wilson. It first forwarded a ticket headed by Pinchback, with A. B. Harris in the second spot. However, negotiations continued with the Packard wing, and concessions were obtained. By August 27 a coalition of the two wings was a reality. The Republicans also came to agreement on a ticket: William P. Kellogg for governor (Customhouse); C. C. Antoine for lieutenant governor (Customhouse); Pierre G. Deslonde for secretary of state (Pinchback); Charles Clinton for auditor (Customhouse); W. G. Brown for superintendent of education (Pinchback); and P. B. S. Pinchback for congressman-at-large.[2]

The election was held in early November in accordance with the registration and election laws of 1870 It was described as quiet; but the outcome was disputed and resulted in a period of dual government for the state. Fraud and systematic denial for the rights of black voters were undoubtedly practiced bringing vigorous protests from blacks.[3] The results were not final until ratified by a returning board that canvassed and counted the votes. The board consisted of five members, but two of them were found to be ineligible, and therefore the governor replaced them with two of his supporters. One of the members, Senator John Lynch, refused to agree to the new appointments and named two men of his own. These maneuvers gave rise to two different returning officials—the Lynch, or Republican, board and the Warmoth, or Fusion, board. Both claimed legitimacy, and each brought suit to sustain itself in the Eighth District Court in New Orleans before Judge H. C. Dibble. A recent Republican candidate for reelection, Judge Dibble eventually ruled in favor of the Lynch board and enjoined the Warmoth group.

The governor then attempted a flank maneuver by signing into law a new act. This law had been passed by the legislative session of 1872 and remained on his desk unsigned. Although it eliminated some of his powers over election machinery, it pro-

2. Binning, "Henry Clay Warmoth and Louisiana Reconstruction," 297–307; Lonn, *Reconstruction*, 145–65; New Orleans *Weekly Louisianian*, May 21, 28, 30, April 4, May 4, 18, 25, June 1, 8, 15, 22, 29, June 6, 13, 20, 27, August 3, 10, 17, 24, 31, 1872; Baton Rouge *Weekly Advocate*, October 19, 1872, for rallies organized by J. Henri Burch.

3. Warmoth, *War, Politics, and Reconstruction*, 199–202; Allie B. Windham, "Methods and Mechanisms Used to Restore White Supremacy in Louisiana, 1872–1876" (M.A. thesis, Louisiana State University, 1948), v, 1–27; *House Miscellaneous Documents*, 42nd Cong., 3rd Sess., No. 91, pp. 26–27, 119–30; Lonn, *Reconstruction*, 169–80. Black politicans in New Orleans held several meetings at Lieutenant Governor Pinchback's home to protest "the political wire pullers" who proposed to deny blacks the right to vote. Fifteen hundred affidavits were filed in the circuit court, and a report was written by blacks. *Weekly Louisianian*, November 23, 30, 1872, January 11, 1873; New Orleans *Republican*, January 7, 1873.

vided for a new returning board and abolished all existing boards. This new board, known as the DeFeriet board, canvassed the returns and declared John McEnery's Democratic ticket to be elected. Alert to every contingency, Warmoth, before the count was completed, named a supporter of his, W. A. Elmore, as presiding judge of the Eighth District Court and excluded Dibble from serving in this jurisdiction.[4]

In the midst of the confusion, Governor Warmoth issued a call for the General Assembly elected on November 4 to convene in extra session on December 9. It was rumored that he sought to be elected United States senator; but if this was his purpose he failed. Gubernatorial candidate William P. Kellogg filed a chancery bill against McEnery and the official journal of the state, claiming black voters had been excluded from the polls on account of race. The Lynch board was then ordered to canvass the return. After Warmoth's board ignored the court order, Judge E. H. Durrell of the United States Circuit Court ordered seizure of the statehouse by the United States marshal on December 5 and forbade the assembling of any legislative body except those returned according to the Lynch board.[5] The McEnery faction met as a legislature in Lyceum Hall.

Thus members of the legislature whose election was certified by the Republican returning officers (Lynch board) were permitted to meet and take the oath of office. Pinchback contributed to the rising anti-Warmoth sentiment by revealing that the governor had approached him and offered him $50,000 and the appointment to any number of offices if he agreed to organize the legislature according to directions. The lieutenant governor claimed he had declined the offer.[6]

Immediately after the House had organized itself, it resolved

4. Grosz, "P.B.S. Pinchback," 36–39; *Weekly Louisianian*, November 23, 1872; Lonn, *Reconstruction*, 185–90.
5. Warmoth, *War, Politics, and Reconstruction*, 205–13; Grosz, "P. B. S. Pinchback," 35; Lonn, *Reconstruction*, 192–95.
6. P. B. S. Pinchback to Henry C. Warmoth, December 9, 1872, in Warmoth Papers.

on the extreme step of trying to remove Warmoth from office. The possibility of impeaching him had long been discussed by many Republicans, and at last they acted. By an overwhelming vote of fifty-eight to six, the members adopted seven articles of impeachment against the governor for "high crimes and misdemeanors in office," including his attempt to bribe Pinchback. The charges included: his forcible ejection of George Bovee, secretary of state and an elected official, from his office; Warmoth's appointment, in April, 1870, as a tax collector for Tangipahoa Parish after the appointee's nomination had been rejected by the Senate; Warmoth's commissions to Henry Nash Odgen as attorney general, W. S. Elmore as judge of the Eighth District Court, and W. P. Harper as sheriff, as well as to other commissions, all before the returns of the election had been promulgated; the attempted bribe of the supervisor of Saint Charles Parish to make false returns; and Warmoth's issuance of proclamations after his impeachment.[7]

Shortly after the action of the House was announced, the Senate resolved itself into a court of impeachment to hear the charges by a vote of seventeen to five. Warmoth was suspended from office, and Pinchback was named as acting governor. Black legislators were instrumental in the attempt to impeach Warmoth. James H. Ingraham was active in persuading the Senate to hear the charges and was chairman of the five-man committee appointed to prepare and submit rules of procedures on the impeachment case of the House. In the House, Representative William Murrell offered the motion for an appointed committee to bring impeachment charges against the governor.[8] Chief Justice J. T. Ludeling organized the court of impeachment. The trial

7. *House Journal*, January 6, 1873, pp. 6, 20–22, New Orleans *Republican*, December 14, 1872.
8. *House Executive Documents*, 43rd Cong., 3rd Sess., No. 91, pp. 14–15; *Proceedings of the Senate Sitting as a Court of Impeachment in the State of Louisiana versus Henry C. Warmoth in Senate Journal, Extra Session, 1872*, pp. 1–4, 20–21; *Weekly Louisianian*, December 28, 1872; *Senate Journal, Extra Session, 1872*, pp. 5, 17, 18, 25; *House Journal, Extra Session, 1872*, p. 26; New Orleans *Republican*, February 1, 1873.

continued slowly from December 9 until January 27, 1873, when on the advice of the chief justice, the Senate decided to discontinue it. Meanwhile this extra session produced ten legislative acts that bore the signature of P. B. S. Pinchback as governor.

In the makeup of the legislature as finally recognized by the federal authorities, the number of blacks in the House had increased by one, with an increase of seven black senators.[9] The 1872–1874 House included thirty-seven blacks, of whom twenty-seven were new members.

Among the new members, Theophile T. Allain of West Baton Rouge Parish proved to be an outstanding representative. Born on Austrialian plantation in West Baton Rouge Parish, October 1, 1845, the son of a white planter and a slave mother, Allain knew few of the burdens of slavery. Traveling extensively in the North and in Europe with his father, he enjoyed the luxury of private tutors in New Orleans and attended college in New Brunswick, New Jersey.

In 1869 he returned to Louisiana and entered the grocery business in his home parish and in Iberville. Four years later he invested in sugar and rice cultivation. His ventures were extremely profitable and brought him into contact "with some of the leading commercial men of the South." He had an income of over fifteen thousand dollars yearly and employed thirty-five laborers. Within a few years, he was shipping large quantities of rice, sugar, and molasses out of New Orleans. Almost every business exchange in New Orleans was open to him. These interests also caused him to take a lead in the fight for good levees in the state. At one time, Allain held a bond and contract with the state of Louisiana to construct 150,000 yards of levee along the Mississippi River.

Allain was as much a humanitarian as a lawmaker. He had organized schools for whites as well as blacks following the war, and in the legislature, he had a hand in encouraging the establishment of black institutions of higher learning. He was also one

9. See Appendices D and F.

of the few blacks who had the distinction of serving in the House both before and after his terms in the Senate.[10]

Pierre C. Landry of Ascension was another popular leader from south Louisiana. He was a freeborn, self-educated native Louisianian who lived in Donaldsonville, a town in which he had formerly served as assessor, justice of the peace, police juror, and mayor. This thirty-one-year-old former Union soldier had also been a successful planter. Like Allain, Landry served in the House both before and after his senatorial term. After leaving politics, Landry, a Mason, turned to religion and was ordained a minister of the Methodist Espiscopal Church in 1880. He remained affiliated with this church for fifty years before joining the Missionary Baptist Church. Before his death in 1920, Landry had married twice and was the father of fourteen children. He was extremely active in community affairs, serving as a member of the governing boards of the New Orleans University, Flint Medical College, and Gilbert's Seminary. His connection with the New Orleans City Board of Health entitled him to perform marriage ceremonies. At his death, he was said to "have preached to more people of his race than any other man in his state."[11]

Representative Robert F. Guichard of Saint Bernard Parish

10. Simmons, *Men of Mark*, 208–12; Chicago *Evening News*, June 2, 1880, quoted in *Weekly Louisianian*, June 5, 1880, April 30, 1881, March 18, 1882; *Louisianian Weekly*, February 19, 1949; New Orleans *Daily Picayune*, January 28, 1874, quoting the New Orleans *Bee*; Mrs. Frederic R. Swigart of Galveston, Tex., to the author, May 10, 1974; Tax Assessment Rolls, 1873, West Baton Rouge Parish courthouse, Port Allen, La.; Tax Assessment Rolls, 1870s, 1880s, 1890s, Iberville Parish courthouse, Plaquemine, La.; Blassingame, *Black New Orleans*, 73, 193.

11. Sidney A. Marchand, *The Story of Ascension Parish* (Donaldsonville: Sidney A. Marchand, 1931), 130, 172, 182; New Orleans *Weekly Pelican*, January 31, 1880, January 15, 29, 1887; New Orleans *Daily Picayune*, June 7, 1868; interview, Lillian Landry Dunn, daughter of legislator Landry, November 2, December 7, 1972, August 7, 1974, New Orleans; New Orleans *Times-Picayune*, December 24, 1921. Former governor Warmoth spoke at Landry's funeral. Landry deposited money in the Freedmen's Savings and Trust Company, including money for two of his children, Palmeston, age 11, and Oscar, age 13. Register of Signatures of Depositors, Freedmen's Savings and Trust Company, 1865–74, RG, 101, NA; see also State of Louisiana, *Record of Commissions, 1868–1874*, State Archives and Records, Baton Rouge, p. 269, hereinafter cited as *Records of Commissions* with appropriate date.

was also a well-educated free man of color. Receiving his education abroad between 1858 and 1865, he had acted as the secretary of the campaign committee for the Republicans while serving as an employee in the post office. After his one term in the House, he served in the Senate for almost a decade. Representative J. Ross Stewart of Tensas Parish had been a slave, and a Union army officer. After his service in the Seventy-third United States Infantry, a unit organized at General Butler's request, Lieutenant Stewart was mustered out in Alabama, where he entered politics. He joined Pinchback on a speaking tour in 1865 and later was appointed by Collector Kellogg to a watchman post in the Customhouse. After a creditable term at this job, Stewart joined the firm of Pinchback and Antoine, Cotton Brokers, as an agent in Tensas, where he located as a planter and schoolteacher. Governor Warmoth who saw great promise in Stewart, appointed him a member of the police jury and later as inspector of weights and measures. This position, as well as his ability as a speaker, caused the voters of Tensas to elect him to the House by a large majority.[12]

E. C. Hill of Ouachita was also a former slave. Born in bondage in Mississippi in 1839, he was brought to Louisiana in 1852. A mechanic and carpenter, he had served on the city council for four years before his election to the House. Representative Hill was a quiet and dutiful legislator.[13]

Milton Jones, a planter, was one of Pointe Coupee's Representatives in 1872. He had lived in the parish since 1859. Jones was able to read and write but did not consider himself a scholar. He was treasurer of the school board and served for six years in the House.[14]

Six of Orleans Parish's twenty-two representatives were

12. *Weekly Louisianian*, February 27, 1875, November 1, 1879; *Senate Reports*, 46th, Cong., 2nd Sess., No. 388, p. 345; Register of Signatures of Depositors, Freedmen's Savings and Trust Company, 1865–1874, RG, 101, NA; Custom House Nomination, New Orleans, June, 1869–May, 1870, Box 110, RG 56, NA.
13. *Weekly Louisianian*, February 20, 1875.
14. *Senate Reports*, 46th Cong., 1st–2nd Sess. No. 388, pp. 906, 908, 911.

black in the session of 1872. These six members were serving their first term. Andrew J. Dumont had been the most politically active of the new members. Born in New Orleans in 1854, he was considered a creole by fellow representatives. His education was obtained in Mexico during a stay in the Southwest. A Master Mason and a man of exceptional organizational ability, he was later chairman of the Republican party State Central Executive Committee for over four years. In this position and later as senator, Dumont traveled often for the party and spoke in Louisiana and elsewhere. After his terms in the legislature he was appointed deputy collector of Customs of New Orleans; later, he became an officer in the United States Navy and left the political battlefield. Dumont possessed considerable wealth as a result of his distillery business. He filed a bond for forty-thousand-dollars with Joubert and Weber Securities in early 1881. Later he organized a baseball team for young boys in New Orleans.[15]

The other new Representatives from Orleans Parish served only one term. Aristide Dejoie was a free man of color born in New Orleans. He was a leading merchant on Canal Street and a family man. Later, he served as Tax Assessor for the sixth district of New Orleans. L. S. Rodriguez had served in the Constitutional Convention of 1868 and was "an hereditary freedman"; Thornton Butler, of the Fourth District, entered the legislature on January 22, 1874, after a long-contested election dispute. George Paris was a quadroon, well educated, and polished in manner. He was married, and he spent his sum-

15. *Weekly Louisianian*, 1872–1882 *passim*; *Proceedings of the A. F. & A. M. for Louisiana, 1894–1901* (New Orleans: Paragon Book Print, 1894). This bound volume is in the possession of Dr. John G. Lewis, master mason, Baton Rouge, who kindly permitted this writer to use the proceedings. *Weekly Louisianian*, November 1, 1879; January 31, February 21, December 25, 1880, January 15, May 7, 14, 18, 1881, July 2, 1882; *Senate Reports*, 46th Cong., 1st–2nd Sess., No. 388, pp. 488, 491. He cancelled an earlier bond effort in 1875. Dumont to William P. Kellogg, May 31, 1875, in Kellogg Papers; Tax Register, 1870, Orleans Parish, New Orleans City Library. Dumont was listed as owning $400 worth of real estate.

mers in Pass Christian, Mississippi; later he served on the Louisiana State Board of Assessors. A close friend of Pinchback, Representative Paris served only one term. George Devezin also served one term as representative from the Third District.[16]

Most of the remaining eleven new black representatives came from southern parishes. Victor Rochon and L. A. Martinet of St. Martin Parish were interested in education and attended Straight University law school when the legislature was not in session. Rochon was a thirty-year-old native of St. Martinville. He was employed as a mercantile clerk. He later served as president of the parish board, postmaster of St. Martinville, and for a brief time in the Customhouses as a clerk. Frederick Marie of Terrebonne was a former sheriff and sugar planter; Natchitoches' Henry Raby served for two terms; L. A. Snaer of Iberia was a wealthy sugar planter and former parish assessor and tax collector; St. Mary Parish's Issac Sutton served two terms in the House before moving to the Senate. Sutton was born and reared in St. Mary Parish and lived at Faretown. But the former city councilman and justice of the peace, J. W. Armistead represented West Felicinana for only one term. William Murrell, Jr., of Madison was only twenty-six years old when elected. He was born a slave in Georgia. After fighting in the Civil War, he moved to Delta (Madison Parish), became a property owner, edited the Madison *Vindicator*, and was a colonel in the Louisiana State National Guard. After Reconstruction, he lived in Washington, D.C., where he edited the Baltimore *Vindicator*; then he moved to New Jersey in 1883 and established the *Trum-*

16. Interview, C. C. Dejoie, Jr., grandson of Legislator Dejoie, February 24, 1973, August 27, 1974, New Orleans; St. James *Sentinel*, March 14, 1875; Dejoie was later secretary of the Cosmopolitan Insurance Association in New Orleans in 1882. C. C. Antoine Scrapbook; *House Journal, 1874*, p. 63; New Orleans *Daily Picayune*, January 11, 1874, January 25, 1875. Paris killed the assistant secretary of state, William Weeks, in self-defense in early January, 1875. See also, New Orleans *Republican*, January 26, 1875.

pet. In 1890, he occupied a position in the Department of Interior.[17] Another former slave, John Wiggins, represented De Soto Parish in 1872 before his death on January 2, 1874. He was praised because of his service in the House. Allain eulogized him with these comments: "His moral life was blameless, and, even while in that sad condition [slavery] he was regarded by all who knew him as a most remarkable man for the blameless purity of his life." His entire career, according to Allain, "offers a striking commentary on the reckless base assertations of those who falsely assert that the colored man is incapable of intellectual culture." East Baton Rouge's Augustus Williams was a man of some property who came to that parish in 1859. Later he was manager of the *Grand Era* newspaper and continued to acquire property.[18] Arthur Antoine of St. Mary, Richard Simms of St. Landry, William H. Keyes of Terrebonne, and James Lawes of East Feliciana were the other new members.

Three of the black representatives elected in 1872 had served previously in the legislature during the 1868–1870 session. They were John Gair of East Feliciana, William Murrell of Lafourche, and Milton Morris of Ascension. Six other members were reelected from the 1870–1872 session. These included: Henry

17. Reverend E. M. Cravath, D.D., field secretary of the American Missionary Association Class Roll for the Law Department of Straight University, June 1, 1874, Box 59; Louisiana files, Amistad Research Center. Dr. Martinet was later a newspaper editor and founder of the New Orleans *Daily Crusader*; he was also one of the leading black Orleanians in fighting the rise of segregation in New Orleans, see Desdunes, *Our People and Our History*, 141–47; New Orleans *Daily Crusader*, July 19, 1890; Custom House Nomination, New Orleans, June, 1875–July, 1877, RG 56, NA; Register of Signatures, Freedmen's Savings and Trust Company, 1865–74, RG 101, NA; *Senate Reports*, 46th Cong., 1st–2nd Sess., No. 693, Pt. 2, pp. 512, 517, 533–36; New Orleans *Daily Picayune*, January 11, 1874; *House Journal, 1871*, p. 7, says he was a doorkeeper in the legislative halls. I. Garland Penn, *The Afro-American Press and Its Editors* (Springfield, Mass.: Willey & Co., 1891), 139–40; New Orleans *Republican*, January 13, March 4, 1874.

18. Allain's eulogy in *House Journal, 1874*, p. 25; New Orleans *Republican*, January 10, 1874; *House Miscellaneous Documents*, 44th Cong., 2nd Sess., No. 34, Pt. 2, pp. 60–61. Williams paid taxes amounting to $25.50 in 1872 on property valued at $1,400. His holdings increased until by 1876 he had acquired property and furniture valued at $1,695. See Tax Assessment Rolls, East Baton Rouge Parish, 1872, 1873, 1874, 1875, 1876.

Demas of St. John, Harry Mahoney of Plaquemines, Cain Sartain of Carroll, Adolphe Tureaud of St. James, George Washington of Concordia, and the moderately wealthy Joshua P. Wilson of East Baton Rouge.

In contrast to the House, there was an increase in black membership in the Senate in 1872. Twelve out of the thirty-six senators were blacks. Four senators had served one term in the House. These included Raiford Blunt, the minister from Rapides; East Baton Rouge's J. Henri Burch, a northern-born black; William Harper, the former slave from Caddo; and T. B. Stamps, a businessman from Jefferson Parish. Five of the senators were returning from the previous sessions: Curtis Pollard, James H. Ingraham, George Y. Kelso, A. E. Barber, and Edward Butler.

Three of the senators were new and serving their first terms. They were Jules A. Masicot, Thomas A. Cage, and Emile Detiege. Senator Masicot had served, however, in the constitutional convention. His senatorial election was contested before he was seated.[19]

The remarkable Thomas A. Cage of Houma was the new senator from Terrebonne Parish. Born a slave in Terrebonne in 1845, he became free with the arrival of Union soldiers. He traveled in the North during the war and there acquired the rudiments of an education. Returning to Louisiana in 1869, he engaged in farming and politics. An untiring worker, Cage was immediately successful in local politics. He was elected justice of the peace and the won the office of tax collector. His competency in the latter post earned him respect from his constituents who elected him to a senatorial seat in 1872. A man of fair economic means, he stood high within the Republican party and

19. *House Executive Documents*, 39th Cong., 2nd Sess., No. 68, pp. 215–16; petition to Kellogg, April 30, 1875, in Kellogg Papers; New Orleans *Times*, April 21, 26, May 15, 1868; *Senate Journal, Extra Session, 1872*, pp. 6, 16 for the contested election. In 1880 Masicot owned $2,500 worth of real estate: Tax Ledger, 1880, Orleans Parish, L-P, New Orleans Public Library; Register of Taxes, A-K, Due and Eligible 1880 (New Orleans, 1880) has his home assessed at $200; *Record of Commissions*, 1868–69, p. 551.

often kept his power through awards of patronage from Governor Kellogg. He later became a popular sheriff in Terrebonne, serving until the mid 1880s. Although his poor health eventually limited his political involvement, he remained active in the Republican party until the late 1890s.[20]

St. Martin's senator, Emile Detiege, was a member of a family who had been jewelers and craftsmen in New Orleans for many years. Educated in New Orleans at Lefoulon's French Institute, he had learned the family trade at the age of thirteen. Offering his service to the Unon army, Detiege organized a battalion of black troops, First Regiment, Corps d'Afrique, and was mustered in as a first lieutenant, Company C, Seventy-third United States Colored Infantry in August, 1862; he later resigned because of prejudice. After the war, he canvassed, in the Teche parishes at the risk of his life. He succeeded in organizing the black voters, however, and was elected to the Senate in 1868. Believing that he was ineligible because of his youth, he declined to serve; he helped to choose another candidate, Alexander François. When elected in 1872, Detiege felt more capable of serving and as a senator was often outspoken in his demands. His right to the seat was contested, and he was not seated until January 31, 1874.[21]

The number of blacks elected to the executive branch of the government increased in the election of 1872. C. C. Antoine of Caddo was elected lieutenant governor. The forty-year-old well-educated William G. Brown was chosen as state superintendent of education. He was a native of Trenton, New Jersey, and had lived in Washington, D. C., and Demerara, Ja-

20. *Weekly Louisianian*, August 2, 1872; petition to Kellogg, April, 1873; Cage to Kellogg, April 30, 1875. In this letter he named the clerk for Supervision of Registration; May 29, July 1, 1875; January 14, April 23, 1876, all in Kellogg Papers; *Weekly Pelican*, February 5, April 9, 1887; Uzee, "Republican Politics in Louisiana, 1877–1900," p. 154; *Record of Commissions, 1868–74*, pp. 17, 396–97.

21. Detiege to Kellogg, April 21, 23, 1875, in Kellogg Papers. His belief in justice for blacks was reflected in his desire to organize a Corp of the Grand Army of the Republic in St. Martinville to protect blacks. See Detiege to Warmoth, January 30, 1868, in Warmoth Papers; Military Service Records, RG 94, NA; *Senate Journal, 1874*, pp. 31–33; New Orleans *Republican*, January 27, 30, 1874.

maica. He was the former editor of the *Louisianian* and also a Master Mason. Pierre G. Deslonde of Iberville was elected secretary of state. The wealthy Iberville planter Antoine Dubuclet was elected state treasurer.[22]

One black won election to the national government. P. B. S. Pinchback was chosen by the state legislature as representative-at-large to the Forty-third Congress and also as United States senator. His claim to the representive seat was rejected by Congress, and his opponent, George Sheridan, was seated. Pinchback's claim to a senatorial seat was based on the fact that the Kellogg legislature elected him to a six-year term on January 14, 1873. His seat was not contested at first, but on the scheduled day of the beginning of his term, March 1, 1873, the McEnery legislature elected William L. McMillen to the same post. When both men presented their credentials in December, 1873, a long debate ensued lasting until mid-January, 1874. McEnery's supporters claimed irregularities in Pinchback's election, and the matter was referred to the Committee on Privileges and Elections. The case dragged on until December, 1875, when McMillen withdrew his claim. Pinchback, however, was denied admission. Finally, in 1876, the Committee on Privileges and Elections recommended compensation to Pinchback equal to the mileage of a senator from the beginning of the term. This amounted to $16,096.90; but Pinchback would have preferred the seat.[23]

22. Dubuclet served as state treasurer throughout Reconstruction. His administration was without scandal or corruption, and when the ill-fated Democratic coup d'etat of September occurred, Dubuclet was the only officeholder permitted to remain in office; New Orleans *Tribune*, January 29, 1869; New Orleans *Republican*, September 6, 19, November 6, 7, 1874; April 30, 1875; Dunbar-Nelson, "People of Color in Louisiana, Part II," 76–78; Desdunes, *Our People and Our History*, 74–75; Tax Assessment Roll, 1876, Iberville Parish courthouse, Plaquemine, La. For Brown see New Orleans *Times-Democrat*, May 15, 1883; New Orleans *Republican*, October 11, 1874.

23. Grosz, "P. B. S. Pinchback," 60–79; *Senate Journal, 1873*, pp. 62, 65; *1874*, pp. 4, 17; *1874*, p. 20, *House Journal, 1873*; *1874*; *1875*, p. 18. In most cases black state legislators offered these resolutions granting recognition; New Orleans *Republican*, New Orleans *Times*, New Orleans *Daily Picayune*, January–February, 1873–1876 *passim*; P. B. S. Pinchback Papers, Box 1, Moorland-Spingarn Research Center, Howard

At the extra session in December, 1872, varied programs were introduced by black and white legislators. Many of these proposals were to thwart Warmoth's powers. Several resolutions to appoint a committee to obtain the names of members meeting in the McEnery legislature were also adopted.[24]

To ensure its legitimacy, the legislature went through the formality of counting the votes in the recent election and declaring Kellogg to be governor. Warmoth's last hope to regain control was taken away with the abolition of the Eighth District Court and the creation of a superior district court for Orleans Parish.[25]

Other legislative proposals were of a general reform nature. These included acts to prevent the careless use of firearms, to integrate the Seminary of Learning and Military Science at Baton Rouge (now Louisiana State University), to investigate imprisonment of minors in the state penitentiary, to create offices of road and canal inspectors, to regulate agencies of insurance companies, and to enforce the land provision of the constitution. Also proposed were the appropriation bill and a number of relief acts.[26]

Many of these programs were enacted in the extra session, but others were carried into the regular session. Representative Murrell of Lafourche secured passage of a bill to suppress riot-

University Archives, Washington, D.C., contains his many speeches, and the proceedings. The black senator from Mississippi in Congress, Blanche K. Bruce, spoke for Pinchback's admission. John Hope Franklin (ed.), *Reminiscences of an Active Life: The Autobiography of John R. Lynch* (Chicago: The University of Chicago Press, 1970), 121.

24. *Senate Journal, Extra Session, 1872*, pp. 12, 14–15; *House Journal, Extra Session, 1872*, pp. 15, 17, 19, 30; *Weekly Louisianian*, January 4, 1873.

25. *House Journal, Extra Session, 1872*, pp. 7, 8, 9. This occurred in a joint session. Kellogg was declared to have 72,890 votes to McEnery's 55,249; Antoine was listed as receiving 70,127 to Penn's 57,568. *Senate Journal, Extra Session, 1872*, pp. 10, 12–13, 15; Lerone Bennett, Jr., *Black Power U.S.A.: The Human Side of Reconstruction, 1867–1877* (Chicago: Johnson Publishing Co. 1967), 263–65; New Orleans *Daily Picayune*, January 3, 5–9, 1873. Lonn, *Reconstruction*, 212–11.

26. *Senate Journal, Extra Session, 1872*, pp. 14, 26, 32, 34, 37, 43; *House Journal, Extra Session, 1872*, pp. 12, 17, 26, 27–8, 29, 32, 39, 40–41, 56. Cain Sartain introduced the appropriation bill in the House.

ous and unlawful assemblies; it was aimed at the recent violence that accompanied the November election. In the Senate, Ingraham promoted it.[27]

The hostile feeling of the rival factions continued until the regular session convened on January 6. According to Professor Lonn, the regular session began a few minutes after the extra session adjourned because of the fear that Warmoth might take possession of the statehouse. Most of the same statehouse officials were continued in positions from the extra session. Troops were on hand; several legislators from the Warmoth legislature shifted over to the Kellogg camp; and on January 13 Kellogg was able to give his inaugural address. At the same time, John McEnery was inaugurated as governor by the Democratic faction. This dual governorship continued throughout the session, but only the work of the Kellogg body stands on the statute books.[28]

Ten days after the 1873 session was convened, the House committee assignments were announced. Of the twenty-eight standing committees, blacks were chairman of eleven. However, they had a majority vote on only three. These were the seven-man committees on Corporation (Demas) and Federal Relations (Raby); and the eight-member Committee on Charitable and Public Institutions (Devezin). The other committees chaired by blacks included the committees on State Indebtedness (Rodriguez), Claims (Young), Militia (Paris), Internal Improvement (Stewart), Public Printing (Dumont), Parochial Affairs (Snaer), State Library (Wilson), and Public Buildings

---

27. *Acts*, 1872, pp. 44, 45; Ingraham also pushed for an investigation of the late election. His resolution to urge the federal government to return to the old United States Mint building to the state for possible use as a statehouse was ordered. The resolution was carried into the regular session where it passed in both houses. *Acts of 1872*, pp. 44, 45; New Orleans *Republican*, January 1, 5, 24, 1873; *Senate Journal, Extra Session, 1872*, pp. 10, 25, 38, 39; *Senate Journal, 1873*, pp. 73, 89; *House Journal, 1873*, pp. 73, 89.

28. Lonn, *Reconstruction*, 217, 221, 224–28. In the 1873 session, resolutions were adopted to report on the rival (McEnery) sessions held in Odd Fellows Hall, *Senate Journal, 1873*, pp. 71–72, 79, 83, 85, 99; New Orleans *Daily Picayune*, January 11, 12, 13, 1873; New Orleans *Republican*, January 12, 14, 1873.

(Mahoney). Two other committees that were not chaired by blacks but had black majorities were the seven-member Committee on Elections, and the eight-man Committee on Education. The important seven-man committees on Judiciary, Ways and Means and on Registration had only two blacks each. One seven-man committee—Bank and Banking—had only one black. Four six-member committees were composed of two blacks and four whites. They included the committees on Unfinished Business, Emigration, Pensions, and Constitution. Most special committees had at least one black. The five-man committee to investigate the character of vouchers and warrants held by members was composed of one black and four whites; whereas, the five-man committee to investigate the records of the last General Assembly to ascertain which acts had become law without the governor's signature was made up of two blacks and three whites.[29]

In the Senate, the black members had more significant committee assignments. Eleven of the twenty-five standing committees had black chairmen, and six of the eleven had a black majority. The committees of the latter class included those on Pensions (Masicot), Claims (Butler), Metropolitan Police (Stamps), Libraries (Harper), Health and Quarantine (Barber), and Agriculture, Commerce and Manufactures (Blunt). Three four-member committees with black chairman were evenly divided; they were the committees on Corporation and Parochial Affairs (Kelso), Elections and Qualifications (Ingraham), and Parks and Public Buildings (Cage). Committees chaired by blacks, but having white majorities, included the seven-man Committee on Enrollment and Engrossment (Burch); and five-member Committee on Banks and Banking (Ingraham). Other committees varied in black membership. The five-man committees on Judiciary and on Election and Registration were composed of one black; the four-man Committee on Finance had two blacks; the three-man Committee on Retrenchment and Reform

29. *House Journal, 1873*, pp. 74–75, 85, 88, 89, 223.

had only one black; as well as the four-man Committee on Railroads and Internal Improvement. Blacks composed a majority but were not chairmen of the five-man committees on Public Lands and Levees, and Penitentiary; also, the three-man Committee on Charitable Institutions. The seven-members on the Committee on Education had three blacks and four whites; and the five-man Committee on Auditing and Supervising the Expenses of the Senate had two blacks and three whites. Black senators were also conspicuously present on special committees created by the Senate. Senator Kelso was named to the two-man committee to examine books and accounts of the state auditor. James H. Ingraham was also on a similar two-man committee to examine the books, accounts, vouchers, and other official documents of the state treasurer. The special two-member committee to examine the securities deposited by banks and banking companies listed Senator J. Henri Burch as a member.[30]

The 1874 House legislative[31] session listed an increase of black chairmen to fourteen, and to more powerful committees. Of the fourteen standing committees with black chairmen, five had a black majority vote. The committees with black chairmen included: Appropriation (Allain), Emigration (Lawes), State Library (Dejoie), Charitable Institutions (Devezin), Metropolitan Police Board (Devezin), Contingent Expenses (Young), Unfinished Business (Murrell of Madison), Penitentiary (Augustus Williams), to examine whether banking games were tolerated in Orleans Parish (Snaer), Agriculture (Stewart), Claims (Mahoney), Enrollment (Gair), Corporations (Demas), and Contingent Expenses (Young). The last five had a majority of black members. Four seven-member committees had only two blacks:

---

30. *Senate Journal, 1873*, pp. 70–71, 74.
31. The black membership in the House remained almost the same except for the addition of Thronton Butler (Orleans) and the death of John Wiggins, De Soto Parish. Other cases were decided by the House, but the race of the members involved cannot be determined by this writer, *House Journal, 1874*, pp. 19, 20–21, 23–24, 25, 27, 33–34, 50, 58, 63, 96, 105, 111, 195–96, 153, 180.

Judiciary, Registration, Health and Quarantine, and Constitution; three other seven-member committees had only one black: Address, Public and Private Lands, and Militia. Other standing committees varied in black composition. The six-man Committee on Rules had two blacks.

The composition of special committees listed a greater number of black members. Six of the eight special committees were headed by blacks; and three of the six had a majority; these three included the special committees to examine the books of the Committee on Contingent Expenses for the year 1873 (a committee of only black members chaired by Guichard), to investigate the Slaughterhouse Company (Connaughton), and to investigate the outstanding vouchers of 1871, 1872, and 1873 (Demas). The other special committees chaired by blacks were to investigate whether the public school funds had been diverted (Allain) relative to Article 117,[32] and to "wait on the Chamber of Commerce" (Devezin). The other three-member special committees to investigate the affairs of the Carondelet Canal Company and to report on coal oil explosions had one black each.[33]

The Senate standing committees had fewer black chairmen than in the House. Of the twenty-six committees appointed, seven were chaired by Negro senators. Four of the seven— Metropolitan Police (Masicot),[34] Parks and Public Buildings (Cage), Enrollment and Engrossment (Ingraham), and the Penitentiary Committee (Burch)—had a black majority vote. The five-member Metropolitan Police Committee consisted of four blacks to one white, and the seven-member Committee on

32. Representative Sartain had proposed such a committee to enforce the constitutional stipulation that no person could hold more than one elective office. *House Journal, 1874*, p. 10.

33. *Ibid.*, 48–49, 69, 78, 104, 111, 125, 145, 147, 258. The all-black special committee to examine the books and accounts of the Contingent Expense Committee for the 1872 and 1873 session reported the books to be in a "business like manner . . . and correct."

34. Jules A. Masicot was serving his first term in 1874 because of the contested election following the November, 1872, election. Other contested elections were discussed. *Senate Journal, 1874*, pp. 17, 19, 15–31, 33, 39, 49, 65, 95; New Orleans *Daily Picayune*, January 30, 31, 1873.

Enrollment and Engrossment had a five-to-two majority. The other three committees headed by blacks—Corporation and Parochial Affairs (Kelso), Contested Elections (Stamps), and Apportionment (Barber)—did not have a black majority; however, the four-member committees on Contested Elections and Appointment were evenly divided. For the first time the four-member Judiciary Committee was also evenly divided. Eight five-man committees had a makeup of three whites to two blacks—they included the committees on Claims, Election and Registration, Drainage, Canals and Inland Navigation, Health and Quarantine, Railroads and Internal Improvements, Auditing and Supervising the Expenses of the Senate, and Charitable Institutions. Blacks comprised one-third of the three-member committees on Militia, Agriculture, Commerce and Manufacturers, Federal Relations, and Libraries; one-fourth of the four-member committees on Finance and Reform and on Retrenchment. Only one black served on each of the five-man committees on Pensions, and Printing. The seven-member Committee on Education had three blacks, but the five men on the Committee on Public Lands and Levees were all white. The only special committee appointed by the Senate was the four-member Committee on Pledges and 10 percent bonds issued after the first of January, 1873. It listed only one black member.[35]

During the first two years of the Kellogg administration, most legislators agreed that the most urgent need of the state was financial reform. The governor had promised such reform in his campaign, and it was thought that fulfillment of his pledge would win approval from the many anti-Republican forces in the state. The black legislators, along with their white allies, proposed legislation designed to bring reform; one of the first creations of the assembly was a Committee on Retrenchment and Reform. Representative David Young's bill to appoint a special committee to have all vouchers brought forward for examination and

35. *Senate Journal, 1873*. pp. 70–71, 74.

registration finally won approval in both houses. Young also offered a resolution to have the books of the Committee on Contingent Expenses deposited with the Committee on Outstanding Vouchers, but it was not adopted. Representative Tureaud of St. James proposed a resolution that was adopted instructing the Finance Committee to draft and report a revenue bill before February 3. This would permit members sufficient time to examine the bill.[36]

Many of these resolutions were good, but the desire for aid seemed always to cause the appropriation bill to exceed expectations. The appropriation for the General Assembly of 1873 was placed at $270,000; later, an increment of $95,000 was appropriated for payment of outstanding vouchers and warrants. In other matters of expenditures, the effort to have committees investigate the vouchers and books of the Contingent Expense Committee failed; however, the desire to authorize the funding of the New Orleans floating debt passed. Senator Ingraham's bill to prohibit the payment of interest on bonds issued by the state to corporations that failed to comply with the contract did not reach a committee. Senator Butler urged a measure to reduce the debt of Louisiana by repealing the four-mill levee tax of the Louisiana Levee Company. However, the bill died in the Committee on Lands and Levees.[37]

Efforts to limit contingent expenses were rendered vain when bills had to be enacted to pay extra clerks or pay a per diem and mileage expenses to legislators contesting election. R. I. Guichard unsuccessfully sponsored a bill to reduce the cost of criminal and civil justice in Orleans Parish by providing fixed salaries for officers. Other measures advocated but never approved included fixing the salaries of judges of superior courts and an appropriation for paying superior judges.[38]

36. *House Journal, 1873*, pp. 67, 68, 69–70, 84, 89; *Acts of 1873*, No. 50, pp. 103–105.
37. *House Journal, 1873*, pp. 192–93, 205, 236, 248; *Senate Journal, 1873*, pp. 66, 71, 142–44, 204, 205–208.
38. *Senate Journal, 1873*, pp. 95, 97, 98–99, 126, 136, 144, 192, 210; *House Journal*,

Formation by whites of the Tax Resisting Association also hindered improvement of Louisiana's financial crisis. Organized during Warmoth's term in May, 1872, to resist collection of taxes and to test the Republican taxes in the federal courts, the association now directed its efforts against Governor Kellogg. The Democratic legislature of McEnery forbade the payment of taxes to the Republican administration. Many bills were offered to induce payment of taxes. Senator Allain called for a bill to relieve taxpayers by remitting the penalties if paid within ninety days. When a tax bill was finally passed near the end of the session, it was much harsher. It provided for rigid enforcement of the collection of taxes and the seizure and sale of property of delinquent taxpayers. Both houses adopted the bill, but popular opinion was so much against it that a relief measure remitting all penalties was passed. Other tax relief measures for parishes were asked for by legislators; most were for hometowns and for some families.[39]

In addition to being concerned about finances, blacks demonstrated a continuing interest in education. The entire black membership of the Senate and a majority of blacks in the House supported an act to provide additional regulations for the board of directors of the New Orleans public schools. Senator Barber advocated a House bill to improve the public schools of the cities and of the parish of Orleans. Senator Burch of East Baton Rouge emerged as a friend of Louisiana State University (the former military seminary). He introduced and supported a measure to

---

1873, pp. 73, 170, 180, 192; New Orleans *Republican*, February 15, 1873. Ingraham thought the work of the judges of the superior court was sufficiently important for a raise in salary.

39. John E. Gonzales, "William Pitt Kellogg: Reconstruction Governor of Louisiana," *Louisiana Historical Quarterly*, XXIX (April, 1946), 420–21; St. James *Sentinel*, April 3, 9, 1873, urged citizens not to participate in the resistance schemes; New Orleans *Republican*, January 25, March 4, 5, 1873; Franklin, *Reconstruction*, 145; *Senate Journal, 1873*, pp. 75, 76, 128, 155–56, 160, 234; *House Journal, 1873*, pp. 73, 177, 212, 225, 226. The governor later enlisted the support of the militia to aid collection. An act against tax collectors defaulting in reporting was also advocated. Joe Gray Taylor, *Louisiana Reconstructed, 1863–1877* (Baton Rouge: Louisiana State University Press, 1974), 274–76.

grant money to repair buildings at the institution. Senator Ingraham urged a measure incorporating the New Orleans University, which was adopted by both houses. Representative Gair offered a bill in the house for relief to the state librarian through an appropriation of $350,000.[40]

Black members were determined to uphold the Metropolitan Police force which was viewed as a supportive agency of the state government. Representative Murrell of Lafourche urged a measure to provide for compensation for salary losses incurred by policemen during the fiscal year 1870–1871. John Gair of East Feliciana introduced the measure, which later became Act No. 37, authorizing the Metropolitan Police to become part of the state militia, and authorizing the force to be increased when on military duty to three full regiments. Senator Barber presented Gair's bill in the Senate. Barber also encouraged a measure providing for full and prompt payment for the Metropolitan Police force.[41]

The changing of the Metropolitan Police Board in New Orleans was closely related to efforts to change the city charter. Representative Dejoie pushed for an act to reorganize the city council of New Orleans. The measure was adopted in both houses but was vetoed by the governor. Senator Burch was more successful in his effort to secure corporation privileges for the city of Baton Rouge. His bill was passed in February.[42]

Other local reforms advocated by blacks consisted of acts

40. *House Journal, 1873*, pp. 74, 105, 123, 164, 207, 240; *Senate Journal, 1873*, pp. 127, 128–29, 132, 137, 138, 144, 156–57, 165–66; Walter L. Fleming, *Louisiana State University, 1860–1896* (Baton Rouge: Louisiana State University Press, 1936), 194. Ingraham felt this measure was important since the University admitted students "irrespective of race or color." New Orleans *Republican*, February 16, 1873. Several blacks opposed appropriations to the Agricultural College because of its segregation policy. David F. Boyd to W. F. Sanford, March 14, 1874, in David Boyd Letters.

41. *House Journal, 1873*, pp. 144, 162, 185–86, 195, 197, 212; *Senate Journal, 1873*, pp. 50, 54, 115, 123, 153, 71, 173, 193, 207; *Acts of 1873*, No. 37, pp. 76–77. Ingraham promoted an amendment to the bill giving the Board of Police commissioner the power to remove inefficient officers thirty days after passage.

42. *Senate Journal, 1873*, pp. 16 (for veto), 55–56, 118; *House Journal, 1873*, pp. 162, 165, 231; *Acts of 1873*, No. 110, bound with *Acts of 1874*, pp. 11–25. Apparently this act did not serve the desired purpose as it was repealed by Burch's effort in 1874. See *Senate Journal, 1874*, pp. 44, 90; *House Journal, 1874*, pp. 230–31.

incorporating towns, granting police juries more power and fixing their fees, and removing laws prohibiting admission of blacks to local institutions. Representative Victor Rochon of St. Martin succeeded in pushing through the House a bill to incorporate the town of St. Martinville, but his bill failed in the Senate. He was successful in changing a statute dating back to 1858 that permitted only whites to operate a Catholic church in St. Martinville. Rochon promoted a bill that would repeal this act and permit blacks to incorporate a Roman Catholic church. Senator T. B. Stamps was responsible for an act incorporating the town of Kenner. Introduced on the second day of the session, the bill was referred to the Committee of Corporation which reported it unfavorably almost a month later. Stamps refused to have the unfavorable report accepted in the Senate. At his request, the bill was made the special order for the day two weeks later and was adopted. In the House, it easily won approval. Other acts provided for the incorporation of social, political, and benevolent organizations. Representative Rodriguez promoted the incorporation of the Jerusalem Mutual Benevolent Association of New Orleans. Henry Demas championed the incorporation of the St. Mary Benevolent Association of St. Charles. Senator Ingraham offered bills incorporating the Oscar J. Dunn Monumental Association of Louisiana, and the Louisiana Working Men's Homestead Association, although his measures did not receive House approval until the next year.[43]

Several bills were proposed to give police juries power to issue bonds. Representatives Demas, Murrell (Madison), Sartain, Marie, and Senator Butler offered bills to give their respective parish police juries more power. Most of the proposals received only one reading and others died in committees.[44]

In this session numerous internal improvement bills were

43. *House Journal, 1873*, pp. 81, 90, 94, 134, 140, 162, 165, 192, 193, 198, 202, 205, 213; *Senate Journal, 1873*, pp. 55, 99, 117, 120, 125, 126, 136, 171, 196, 209; *Acts of 1873*, No. 77, p. 141; *Acts of 1858*, No. 293, pp. 207–209; *Acts of 1873*, No. 71, pp. 71, 126–32; No. 57, p. 115; *House Journal, 1874*, pp. 77, 82.

44. *House Journal, 1873*, pp. 68, 78, 99, 108, 169, 195, 233, 240; *Senate Journal, 1873*, p. 56.

offered, ranging in scope from canal construction to incorporation of more railroads. Blacks were usually in support of most measures, but they were also insistent on punishing previous incorporators who had failed to live up to their charters. Representative J. Ross Stewart of Tensas was one of the most vigorous supporters of abolishing programs that had proved to be failures; he called for an act to declare the charter of the Mississippi and Mexican Gulf Ship Canal Company forfeited; he further urged the return of the bonds endorsed by the state. Late in the session, the Committee on Canals and Drainage issued a report calling the company's action a "monstrous outrage and criminal" and regretting that there was not enough time to complete its report on this "swindle." Another Republican representative offered a resolution to authorize the attorney general to immediately bring suit on behalf of the state against the Mississippi and Mexican Gulf Ship Canal Company. The resolution passed the House by a large majority on the last day of the 1873 session. It appeared in the Senate but no action was taken. [45]

To prevent other drainage companies from causing New Orleans "serious financial" difficulties, Stewart promoted a resolution authorizing the Canals and Drainage Committee to examine the work performed by drainage companies and to check the accounts of the New Orleans City Council. This resolution included the Mississippi and Mexican Gulf Ship Canal Company. Upon adoption, the committee was given the power to send for "persons and papers." [46]

Black legislators were equally vigilant in scrutinizing the charter of new companies. When the Louisiana Levee Company bill was adopted in the House, Representatives Allain and Gair and others issued a protest over its attempted hurried passage since the provisions were not read section by section; they were also suspicious of the "purity of motive" of the sponsors. In the Senate, a majority of the blacks voted against suspension of the

45. *House Journal, 1873*, pp. 76, 203–204; *Senate Journal, 1873*, p. 210.
46. *House Journal, 1873*, pp. 89, 127.

rules until the bill was completely read. Senator Ingraham tabled an amendment offered by one of the Democrats providing that parishes not subject to inundation or benefiting directly by the erection of levees should be taxed to support levees. Thus improved, the bill passed the Senate.[47]

Railroad legislation continued to interest black legislators. Representative Dejoie of Orleans promoted an act to incorporate the Carrollton and Kennerville Railroad Company. The House favored the bill, but it did not pass the third reading in the Senate until the last day. It was carried into the next legislative session where it won senatorial approval almost one year later. An act to incorporate the Louisiana Central Railroad Company won the approval of both houses but under protest, since several members claimed that the charter required a greater amount of state revenue than was necessary. Some blacks demanded investigation of the practices of already chartered roads, especially the New Orleans, Mobile and Texas Railroad. All efforts to pass investigation bills failed.[48]

Blacks maintained a continuing watch on proposed laws governing workers on plantations. When a Democratic Representative, F. M. Grant of Morehouse, introduced an act allowing planters certain advantages in work contracts and penalties to laborers for noncompliance, blacks let it pass as an apparently harmless protective measure. Two days later, however, Representative Tureaud of St. James had the bill returned from the

47. *Ibid.*, 171, 172, 174, 196; *Senate Journal, 1873*, pp. 141, 157, 158, 160–61; New Orleans *Republican*, February 20, 21, 1873.

48. *House Journal, 1873*, pp. 180, 202, 230; *Senate Journal, 1873*, p. 210; *Senate Journal, 1874*. See March 5, 1874 session. *House Journal, 1873*, pp. 63, 67, 85, 90–91, 108–109, 113–14, 118, 201; *Senate Journal, 1873*, pp. 71, 78, 82, 109, 113, 115, 117, 120, 135, 156, 161–62, 164; *Acts of 1874*, No. 111. The chairman of the Senate Railroad Committee resigned during the heated debate over the bill. An expert was then hired to advise on railroad matters. During the December, 1872, extra session and the current session, Ingraham urged an act creating the office of inspector of roads and canals, but this bill died in the Railroad Committee. *Senate Journal, Extra Session, 1872*, p. 43. Black legislators urged the enforcement of the provision of the thirteenth article (civil rights) of the constitution in chartering railroads. To prevent competition with free labor, the railroads were restrained from hiring convicts for construction and maintenance of the road. New Orleans *Republican*, January 29, February 1, 5, 9, 1873.

Senate and asked for a reconsideration of the adoption vote. Representative Gair ordered that the bill be printed and made the special order for the next day. This disclosure revealed that the bill established a lien system on ensuing crops by permitting planters and workers to secure advance supplies; such mortgages and privileges were to be listed in the recorder's office. However, violators of these provisions were charged with misdemeanor and upon conviction were charged not less than a hundred dollars. Blacks, believing that the system would not be helpful to freed labor, were able to get the measure postponed indefinitely.

In the next legislative session, Representative Grant offered the proposal again. When it came up for a vote, only one black urged indefinite postponement, and it was easily passed. Because of the economic depression of 1873, the pledging of crops provided the only means of securing supplies, since the Senate passed a similar bill enabling planters, merchants, traders, and others to pledge and pawn cotton, sugar, and other agricultural products for supplies.[49]

Blacks still evinced apprehension that the whites would resort to force to recover control. Near the end of the session a resolution was passed by both houses asking the president to guarantee protection from domestic violence because "evil disposed persons are forming combinations to disturb public peace." Senator Kelso promoted an act making parishes liable for damage done by mobs or secret societies, but the bill died in the Committee on Judiciary. Black legislators continually insisted that the militia must be made more efficient. Particularly active in this area was Senator Barber, chairman of the Committee on Militia. The law making the Metropolitan Police part of the militia finally won approval in both houses.[50]

49. *House Journal, 1873*, pp. 138, 209, 211–12, 216–17; *1874*, pp. 32, 41, 108, 109; New Orleans *Republican*, March 2, 1873, February 5, 27, 28, 1874; *Senate Journal, 1874*, pp. 238, 263; Senator Young favored a bill to give merchants a lien, and physicians a lien to five dollars. The bill failed.

50. *Senate Journal, 1873*, pp. 79, 95, 119, 134, 145, 200, 205, 207, 230; *House Journal, 1873*, pp. 207, 227, 228; *Acts of 1873*, No. 37.

An attempt to repeal the monopoly of the Slaughterhouse Company, chartered in 1869, brought a split in black votes. A special committee appointed to investigate the chartering act demanded its repeal or modification; the committee found that the company was a "thoroughly equipped monopoly." Senator Butler, who chaired the special committee, offered an act to repeal and modify the act creating the company. When the bill eventually came up for a vote, Senators Ingraham and Burch moved for indefinite postponement, and the repeal effort was killed. Another monopoly coming under black attack was the Louisiana Lottery Company. Representative Demas proposed a constitutional amendment to repeal its charter; his measure was referred to the Committee on constitution and was not reported. Later Senator Butler unsuccessfully urged an act to revoke and annul the Lottery charter; another legislator also pushed a repeal measure, but all efforts at repeal failed.[51]

On occasion, blacks promoted measures that had international connotations. Senator Burch of East Baton Rouge offered a joint resolution asking Congress to assist in the suppression of slavery in Cuba. The bill passed its first reading and was placed on the calendar; four days later, Burch called it up for the second time, spoke at length on its merits, and secured its adoption. In the House, Representative Snaer of Iberia championed the resolution. He amended the bill to include a provision that the legislatures of the former slave states (southern) be invited to adopt this resolution. The resolution was, on Representative Demas' motion, referred to a house committee of three (Demas, Snaer, and Carey). Later it won unanimous approval. Representative David Young introduced a bill to permit American citizens who had studied in the legal institutions of France, Germany, or England and had been admitted to the superior courts of these countries to practice in the courts of Louisiana. The bill won easy adoption and was signed by the governor.[52]

51. *Senate Journal, 1873*, pp. 75, 90–93, 95, 97, 126, 136; New Orleans *Republican*, January 3, 11, 21, 1873; *House Journal*, 1873, pp. 62, 78, 82, 187.
52. *Senate Journal, 1873*, pp. 73, 75, 80, 113, 116, 118; *House Journal, 1873*, pp. 94,

A civil rights bill was also included in the legislation of the session. Offered during the December extra session by Representative Cain Sartain, the bill was read twice and buried in the Judiciary Committee. During the first week of the regular session, Sartain had the bill withdrawn and made the special order for January 15. The bill did not reappear. One month later in the Senate, Barber introduced a similar bill; it was read twice and reported to the Judiciary committee which reported favorably. It finally passed the Senate on February 24. The House adopted the Senate civil rights bill three days afterward by a fifty-six to one vote. It required all common carriers (including those crossing state lines), innkeepers, and managers of places of public amusement to afford equal accomodation to all citizens without regard to race or color.[53]

The political strife between the factions did not end when the session adjourned. The congressional committee investigating the 1872 election rendered a majority report favorable to neither government. To solve the impasse, the committee proposed the holding of a new election under federal authority. Four of the seven senators—Mathew H. Carpenter of Wisconsin, John A. Logan of Illinois, James L. Alcorn of Mississippi, and Henry B. Anthony of Rhode Island—devised this plan. The other three members—Lyman Trumbull of Illinois, Oliver Morton of Indiana, and Carl Schurz of Missouri—dissented for various reasons. Since Congress adjourned without taking action on the situation, the president was able to continue his recognition of the Kellogg government.[54]

127, 129, 135, 137, 146, 173; *Acts of 1873*, No. 29, p. 66, Joint Resolution No. 37, pp. 63–64; Burch received acclamation from Cuba, and was given the title of "general Representative of the Republique of Cuba Abroad." Several mass meetings were held in New Orleans in support of the resolution, New Orleans *Republican*, February 5, 7, 8, 11, 13, 1873.

53. *House Journal, Extra Session, 1872*, pp. 40, 44; *Senate Journal, 1873*, pp. 132, 140, 149–50; *House Journal, 1873*, pp. 191–92, 194; *Acts of 1873*, No. 84, pp. 156–57; Gonzales, "Kellogg," 484. This act was never tested in the courts, but the Democratic press was very critical of it. See Fischer, "The Segregation Struggle in Louisiana," 89–90.

54. *Senate Reports*, 42nd Cong., 3rd Sess., No. 457, pp. i–lxxx; Grosz, "P. B. S.

The unsettled conditions in the state led white conservatives in New Orleans to propose a political union with blacks. "The situation that produced the movement, then, was compounded of political and racial elements, but the strongest one was economic in nature," writes Professor T. Harry Williams. "The men who would sponsor the movement were almost without exception conscious of race and racial difference, but under the strain of economic distress they acted to remove race as an issue in politics."[55]

General P. T. G. Beauregard, former Confederate general, was the nominal head of the movement. It included the leading white businessmen and merchants of New Orleans and the wealthy aristocracy of the "creole Negroes." A committee of fifty from each race developed the plan.

The "appeal" of the unificationists was the offer of social, political, and economic equality for blacks in return for black votes to overthrow the carpetbag rule. Reactions were mixed. New Orleans and south Louisiana were generally favorable toward unification, but the movement was not agreeable to the state "north of Baton Rouge." After an initial June 16 meeting, a mass meeting was held on July 15 in Exposition Hall. Of the five speakers, three were black; Representative (later Senator) T. T. Allain, Senator J. Henri Burch, and James Lewis, administrator of improvements in the New Orleans City Council. Allain praised the effort generally and urged economic reform; but Burch and Lewis were more cautious. They recalled that violence had gone unpunished in the recent Colfax riot (April 13) in which over fifty-nine blacks were killed and many wounded. Burch declared that the hostility of the whites had "forfeited entirely the confidence of the colored people of this state." If

---

Pinchback," 55–56; Senator Morton was the only member of the congressional committee in favor of the Kellogg government. See Lonn, *Reconstruction*, 230–45; New Orleans *Republican*, February 14, 28, 1873.

55. T. Harry Williams, *Romance and Realism in Southern Politics* (Athens: University of Georgia Press, 1961), 30. See also T. Harry Williams, "The Louisiana Unification Movement of 1873," *Journal of Southern History*, XI (August, 1945), 350–51.

blacks were allowed to vote freely, Burch continued, they would elect a biracial government without white aid.[56] Moreover, since Governor Kellogg had recently signed the civil rights bill into law the blacks were already assured of these protections. Lewis also emphasized that the blacks had little to gain from unification. He maintained that blacks could unite with whites only when their full civil and political rights were recognized. Until prerequisites were conceded, blacks would hold back from union.

The burden of failure has been placed on the shoulders of blacks. Nevertheless, the precongressional and postcongressional periods in history have proved Burch's assertion correct. If these "conditional" pledges called for by blacks caused the failure, then perhaps the movement was doomed to failure almost from the start. Many blacks felt that the unificationists gave only words. They were skeptical of whites who, at the very time of making the promises, refused to recognize the constitution governing the state. Governor Warmoth had proved to be distasteful to many blacks; but Governor Kellogg seemed to be more sincere. Perhaps, they felt that one bird in the hand was worth three in the bush. Besides, unification only had the approval of a faction—less than 5 percent—of the whites; and Beauregard, one of its leading architects, was absent at the crucial meeting. How could blacks, surmissed many leaders, base their hopes on such illusions? More important, the planter-business class would never have made the financial concessions necessary to supply the social services promised blacks in the platform of the unificationists. Such services could only be obtained by high taxes, and curtailment of taxes was the objective of the movement.[57]

56. *House Reports*, 43rd Cong., 2nd Sess., No. 261, Pt. I, pp. 13–19; Manie W. Johnson, "The Colfax Riot of April, 1873," *Louisiana Historical Quarterly*, XIII (July, 1930), 411–19; The trial of the instigators ended in a mistrial. New Orleans *Republican*, February 26, March 17, 1874; New Orleans *Times*, July 16, 1873; Vincent J. C. Marsala, "The Louisiana Unification Movement of 1873" (M. A. thesis, Louisiana State University, 1962), 56–62.

57. T. Harry Williams, "An Analysis of Some Reconstruction Attitudes," *Journal of Southern History*, XII (November, 1946), 482–85; Marsala, "The Louisiana Unifica-

Governor Kellogg opposed the Unification scheme. He felt that it was a threat to Republicanism in Louisiana. The Colfax riot, together with violence in St. Martin Parish and the attempted assassination of the governor, reinforced his views. Moreover, with the May 22 proclamation of President Grant, recognizing the Republican regime, the governor could be more adamant in opposing white offers of cooperation.

After an extensive northern tour during the summer to drum up northern capital for Louisiana, Kellogg returned more assured of his position. He addressed the State Colored Men's Convention in New Orleans on November 18 and called for their support to carry out measures to better the state, emphasizing that Louisana was "on trial" before the nation. When Congress convened in December, the Louisiana question was again debated for a few months and finally tabled on April 28, 1874.[58]

When the 1874 session opened, Governor Kellogg addressed the assembly and made a number of proposals. He spoke for a program of internal improvements and financial reform, relief from heavy taxation, and the fixing of fees of sheriffs and coroners. The theme of his message was the return of peace and prosperity to the state. Such an outcome was possible only if internal hostilities against the Republican government ceased. Five weeks later he outlined many of these programs in a message sent to both houses of the assembly. His specific proposals concerned the limitation of taxes and the more efficient collection of revenue in New Orleans.[59]

The passage of an effective taxation program was a troublesome task. Several black legislators proposed schemes for acquiring tax revenues. Senator Butler urged that oysteries be taxed and fisheries regulated in the state, but the measure never

---

tion Movement," 69–75; Walter Prichard (ed.), "The Origins and Activities of the White League in New Orleans (Reminiscenses of a Participant in the Movement)," *Louisiana Historical Quarterly*, XXIII (April, 1940), 531–32.

58. Gonzales, "Kellogg," 421–27.

59. *Senate Journal, 1874*, pp. 4–14; *House Journal, 1874*, pp. 5–12, 138–39 (February 13, 1874); New Orleans *Times*, January 6, 1874.

received committee approval. Representative David Young promoted an act to give a reward of 5 to 10 percent deduction on all license taxes, paid during the first two months of the year; the bill received no action. Senator Ingraham offered a bill to remit all penalities against delinquent taxpayers if taxes were paid within sixty days of the passage of the bill; the bill died in the Judiciary Committee. Representative Allain promoted a similar bill in the House, and the Judiciary Committee presented two reports on the bill. The majority report was favorable; the minority report of the committee was unfavorable. Because of the importance of taxation, both reports were made the special order for the same afternoon. The minority report was unfavorable for two reasons: first, the members felt that remitting a penalty was an injustice to prompt taxpayers; secondly, such a law would encourage nonpayment of current taxes. The minority report was overwhelmingly adopted and the bill was defeated.[60]

Equally as pressing as the problem of collecting taxes was the difficulty of assessing property values fairly. Representative Demas promoted an act to "insure equitable assessment of property real and personal in the state by admitting testimony as to the actual market value in suits to enforce collection"; the bill did not appear in the Senate. Murrell urged a similar act but with compensation for overvaluations previously made; the bill was postponed indefinitely near the end of the session. Senator Barber called for a law to provide a single assessment of property in the parish of Orleans for state and city taxation by a board of state and city assessors; it did not get beyond a first reading. Buried in committee was a proposal by Senator Burch to correct errors in assessment of property for taxes. Many other assess-

60. Senator Butler promoted a similar bill that would have stopped suits by the state in attempting to collect back taxes. The bill did not return from the Judiciary Committee. *House Journal, 1874*, pp. 21, 81, 86, 89, 188. Requests for relief from parish, town, and city taxes were numerous. *Ibid.*, 85, 102, 103, 124, 150, 152, 153, 190; *Senate Journal, 1874*, pp. 18, 19, 20, 21, 41, 45, 46, 55, 61, 78, 86, 89, 209–10, 234–69. A bill for postponement of tax collection in New Orleans passed both houses.

ment and tax-collection bills were offered but did not pass. Several taxation reform measures were passed. The methods of collecting taxes were improved, and assessment cost was reduced with the substitution of a quadrennial revision. The latter plan saved New Orleans $250,000 every four years.[61]

Along with taxes and assessment, other tax-related measures were considered. A bill setting the number and salaries of tax assessors and collectors was adopted. Their responsibilities were increased, which caused a decrease in the number of clerks required in the auditor's office. Later, one of the four constitutional amendments proposed in this session limited the state debt to $15 million and the taxation rate to twelve and one-half mills per thousand dollars.[62]

Three other economic measures passed in this session were intended to effect a reduction in expenditures. One of them endorsed the funding system previously considered by the legislature to settle the state debt and to consolidate existing bonds. The second stipulated that annual expenses must be adjusted to revenues. The third limited the debt of New Orleans. Blacks supported the amendment and other measures to effect the economy. As example Senator Thomas Cage promoted an act that created a board of commissioners to examine the outstanding indebtedness of Terrebonne Parish. Representative Demas urged a resolution to have a special committee appointed to examine all outstanding vouchers or warrants issued by the House since 1870 and to advertise the same in the city newspapers. The resolution was adopted.[63]

Although blacks often supported economy measures, they just as often proposed bills that increased expenditures. Usually

61. A bill imposing a penalty on delinquent taxpayers in New Orleans was adopted. Lonn, *Reconstruction*, 249. An act providing for the sale of delinquent taxpayers property was approved by both houses. *Senate Journal, 1874*, pp. 23, 114, 182, 185, 186, 192, 193, 208, 251, 270; *House Journal, 1874*, pp. 23, 55, 78, 125, 126, 167–68, 232, 249–50.

62. *Senate Journal, 1874*, pp. 37, 229, 262, 265; *House Journal, 1874*, pp. 58, 245, 259, 260.

63. *Senate Journal, 1874*, pp. 35, 44, 124, 129, 148–49; *House Journal, 1874*, p. 177; *Acts of 1874*, No. 74, pp, 124–25.

they introduced these bills to satisfy the social needs of their constituents and tacked them onto the appropriation bill. For instance, the appropriation bill of 1874 was burdened by items such as the $20,000 for the erection of a charity hospital in the town of Shreveport; it also included appropriation for the militia. Other items in the bill were small; $300 for H. O. Hive for serving as a guide on the Red River, Grant Parish expedition; and similar amounts to individuals who furnished supplies to the militia. On the other hand, the payment for mileage and per diem of the members saw a great decrease over the past years. The act for 1874 provided $65,000 for House members and $25,000 for senators. This act was adopted early in the session.[64]

Another issue debated extensively was the funding bill. Black legislators supported this scheme and had offered such a plan before the governor's program on funding was passed. Senator T. B. Stamps introduced and secured passage of a bill providing for funding of the public debt of the state, including all legal and valid bonds. In the House, Representative Dejoie, of New Orleans, called up the bill but it did not receive the approval of the Committee on Ways and Means. Nevertheless, the constitutional amendment recommended by Governor Kellogg endorsing a funding bill and the act for consolidation of bonds passed both houses.[65]

At this time, local governments seeking to increase their revenues hit on the device of extending their corporation limits. Usually, blacks supported these measures. In the 1874 session Representative Issac Sutton of St. Mary introduced an act to enlarge the corporate limits of Franklin. The bill

64. New Orleans *Republican*, January 28, 30, February 3, 1874; *Acts of 1874*, No. 32, p. 67, No. 59, pp. 99–108. Other appropriation bills of the session were designed to cover loans from previous loss incurred by members because of nonpayment of warrants. *House Journal, 1874*, 20–21, 40–41, 161–62, 255–56; *Senate Journal, 1874*, 49, 121, 255, 258–62.

65. *Senate Journal, 1874*, pp. 21, 36–37, 74. The bill passed 24–0 in the Senate. New Orleans *Times*, January 20, 1874, Representative Gair thought the bill was important to help keep schools open. Lonn, *Reconstruction*, 249; *House Journal, 1874*, pp. 34, 47, 54, 55–56. The final funding bill was similar to Stamps's bill that died in the House Ways and Means Committee.

passed the House in the last week of January and was sent to the Senate for approval. There it encountered opposition inspired by the planters and the property holders of the town. In a petition presented by a friendly senator, they opposed the extension of the corporate limits because of the added taxation that such a law would cause. The Senate dismissed the petition near the end of the session and the bill was adopted. Representative Murrell of Lafourche promoted a similar bill to extend the corporation of Thibodaux in 1873, but the act was vetoed; in the 1874 session, Murrell had the bill passed over the veto. In the upper House, Senator Barber of New Orleans vigorously supported a measure to extend the limits of New Orleans and to annex Carrollton. In support of the bill, Senators Barber and Burch presented petitions containing over three hundred names urging this act. The bill eventually passed both houses.[66]

The recurring issue of whether to charter a company that would rival the Louisiana Lottery Company again found black legislators divided. The divisions arose when Representative Arthur Antoine of St. Mary introduced a bill "to create a revenue; to provide for the disposition thereof, and to incorporate the New Orleans Lottery Company." The bill provided that the company must have a capital of $1 million divided into one thousand shares and that it must pay the state $40,000 annually for the benefit of public schools and charitable institutions. The bill passed its third reading but was later killed when the House voted to adjourn. When two other bills were offered and passed, giving the existing company the rights to operate in Louisiana, Henry Demas as chairman of the Committee on Corporation reported favorably on the bills and ordered them to their third reading. In the Senate, Senator Blunt attempted to get these measures postponed indefinitely but was unsuccessful. Both became law.[67]

66. *House Journal, 1874*, pp. 28, 46, 86, 109, 172–73, 230–31, 267. Nordhoff, *The Cotton States in the Spring and Summer of 1875*, p. 62, was critical of incorporations. *Senate Journal, 1874*, pp. 106, 120, 196–98, 230.
67. Two days later, on February 27, after the bill did not come up for a final vote,

Parish and district courts were also subjects of much interest to black legislators. Senator Thomas Cage of Terrebonne Parish championed a bill to fix the term of the district court in the fifteenth district; after winning Senate approval, the bill died in the House Judiciary Committee. Representative Demas introduced a bill to prevent unauthorized persons from practicing in the Louisiana courts. The bill was printed but no action was taken. Senator Blunt promoted a bill, written by the white radical, Senator W. Twitchell, fixing the limits of the Seventeenth District Court, and setting a time for holding court in the parishes of the district. The Senate easily concurred in the House amendments. Representative Dejoie promoted an act conferring criminal jurisdiction upon the Seventh Judicial Court of Orleans Parish and regulating its fees. Senator Ingraham urged a similar bill establishing a criminal district court for Orleans Parish. The act also established the organization for such a court. Another proposal of Ingraham was aimed at expediting the trials in the supreme court at New Orleans. Other legislation called for investigation of several district courts whose judges were charged with irregularities in performing their duties. The criminal sheriff and clerk of the First District Court had retained prisoners at the expense of the city; the judge was found negligent and had brought charges against the city without "strict correctness." The report recommended a bill regulating the compensation of criminal sheriffs and limiting the fees of clerks. Senator Jules A. Masicot, the former criminal sheriff of Orleans Parish, headed the investigative committee.[68]

---

resolution was offered arraigning Representative John Gair of East Feliciana for seizing the roll book. Apparently, Gair felt the bill was being engrossed before its second reading. The resolution was not adopted. *House Journal, 1874*, 41, 68–69, 97, 196, 197–99, 202, 215; *Senate Journal, 1874*, 84, 85; Alwes, "The History of the Louisiana State Lottery," 980–81. Representative Demas apparently had united with prolottery forces by 1874. In the 1873 session he offered legislation to repeal the charter by submitting a constitutional amendment to the people. The bill died in the Committee on Constitution after its second reading. *House Journal, 1873*, 63, 82; Nordhoff, *The Cotton States*, 60.

68. *Senate Journal, 1874*, pp. 19, 40, 55, 61, 67, 83, 89, 99, 124, 143, 167, 169, 174,

The condition of the penitentiary and the use of the convict lease system was an issue often discussed by black legislators. Senator Cage, chairman of the Committee on Parks and Public Buildings, found the building at the penitentiary almost deserted; according to his report to the Senate in 1874, the convicts had been leased out to work on many projects. Most black legislators saw this practice as undesirable because of the competition it provided to free labor. Moreover, they were concerned about the treatment of convicts most of whom were black. But apparently some blacks favored the lease system. Certainly Representative Cain Sartain of Carroll had constituents who liked it. In early January he presented a petition from "colored men, renters and farmers in the Parish" opposing legislation to prevent employment of convicts in the cotton field. The petitioners favored using convicts outside the walls to help serve as deterrent to crimes. Generally, however, blacks supported legislation requiring better treatment of convicts. They also advocated measures looking to a more humane treatment of prisoners. Representative Ward introduced a measure in the house to prevent "the incarceration of petty offenders"; the bill was printed but the Penitentiary Committee (two blacks and five whites) reported it unfavorably. Senator Burch was one of the most ardent critics of the penitentiary. On February 3 he gave notice of three bills he planned to introduce concerning the condition of this institution; one would abolish flogging and other extreme punishment; a second, better defined the "board of control;" a third created the office of inspector for the penitentiary. Neither one of the bills was actually introduced because Burch decided on a more comprehensive plan. He introduced a bill recommending a code of prison reform and discipline for the penitentiary. His plan called for separation of prisoners according to their crime; a series of reforms designed to check on lodging, food, and clothing of the inmates; and improvement of

178, 186–87, 200, 201, 267; *House Journal, 1876,* 77, 118, 173, 185, 186–87, 227, 228. Many other bills were introduced by other black and white legislators.

the quality of matrons, teachers, and the treatment of prisoners confined for life. The bill was read twice and referred to the five-man Committee on Penitentiary headed by Burch; the committee issued a favorable report. The bill again reappeared near the end of the session and was not passed as Burch was unable to muster adequate support.[69]

In 1875 blacks rendered their effort to improve prison conditions. Senator Stamps of Jefferson introduced, in early February, an act to prohibit the lessees of the penitentiary from employing convicts outside the walls. The bill was read twice and referred to the Committee on Penitentiary (again headed by Burch). This committee was uncertain as to whether the bill conflicted with sections of the revised statutes (2855, 2862, and portions of 2866) and hence urged the Judiciary Committee to check the bill. The committee reported the bill favorably, and the Senate then adopted it. The House approved the bill on March 2, and it was promulgated by the governor on March 31. The act provided a penalty of five thousand dollars for violations and abrogation of the lease.[70]

Blacks made a determined effort to amend the act of 1869 establishing the Bureau of Immigration. Led by Representatives Guichard and Gair, they secured passage of a measure reorganizing the bureau and requiring it to supervise the landing of immigrants. The bill entrusted enforcement to the chief of the bureau and several commissioners of immigration. Captains of ships had to report to the bureau the number of their passengers, their age, and their mental status. A penalty of one hundred

69. *House Journal, 1874*, pp. 72, 73, 173, 184–85. Ward introduced another measure to prevent abuses in the penitentiary; but it never came up for a vote. New Orleans *Republican*, January 29, February 14, 17, 1874; Mark T. Carleton, "The Politics of the Convict Lease System in Louisiana, 1868–1901," *Louisiana History*, VIII (Winter, 1967), 10–11; *Senate Journal, 1874*, pp. 103, 145, 228, 250–51, 257.

70. The Penitentiary Committee said it had considered the same matter in 1873 and had called the lessee (S. L. James and Company) before it; apparently, the lessees had convinced the committee of the harmlessness of their practice of employment. *Senate Journal, 1875*, 69, 85–86, 110, 116; *House Journal, 1874*, p. 133; *Acts of 1874*, No. 22, p. 54; Carleton, *Politics and Punishment*, 23–24; New Orleans *Republican*, February 13, 15, 17, 24, 1874, for comments on the condition of convicts.

dollars was inflicted for each passenger not reported, the money to go to the New Orleans Charity Hospital. The chief of the bureau had the responsibility to register all immigrants and aid them in securing homesteads.[71]

New election and registration laws were strongly favored by black legislators. Senator Ingraham authored the election law that amended sections of the 1872 law. In the House, Representative Gair pushed the bill through just before the session ended. This revision of the election law gave the supervisors more power at the polls and during elections. The bill was vetoed by the governor, but it passed over his veto in the next session. Ingraham and Gair teamed up again in promoting an act providing for "the revision and correction of the lists of voters of the state." The law gave the governor the power to appoint, with the consent of the Senate, a state registrar of voters, who held office for two years; the other sections established his salary and assistants. The law also empowered parish supervisors of registration to review the list of voters before local elections, adding the names of newly qualified electors. Obviously, blacks were greatly alarmed over the approaching November election.[72]

Blacks continued to support educational reform. A House bill to reorganize the public schools of New Orleans was pushed in the Senate by Ingraham. Representative Allain amended the law so that future school board appointments would represent the city at large. The reorganization of the board was promulgated in April. The establishment of the Agricultural and Mechanical College was also promoted, and the union of the state university and agriculture college urged. Senator Blunt wrote a bill to relieve Leland University from taxation. Another law abolished unnecessary city board directors and provided textbooks.[73]

71. *House Journal, 1874*, pp. 141, 142, 192, 246; *Senate Journal, 1874*, p. 270; *Acts of 1874*, No. 154, pp. 271–76; New Orleans *Republican*, February 27, 1874.

72. *Senate Journal*, 1874, pp. 38, 40, 245, 249; *House Journal, 1874*, p. 249; *Senate Journal, 1875*, pp. 122–23; *Acts of 1875* No. 155, pp. 5–9.

73. New Orleans *Times*, April 23, 1874. A House amendment to prevent members of the legislature from serving as school board members caused a split in the black Representatives' vote, and the motion was tabled. *House Journal, 1874*, pp. 18, 123,

Black legislators were not vindictive toward white educational aspirations. When a Senate bill, offered by Democrats, to require parents and guardians of children to give them a choice of public or private schools came up for a vote, a majority of the black senators supported it. Senator Burch favored the bill because it would make the future generation "good citizens," who would be able to protect themselves against "unprincipled men, who are always ready to defraud the uneducated." The bill passed the Senate but did not appear in the House. Senator Burch was also a champion of legislation to aid the struggling Louisiana State University. He promoted a resolution appointing a subcommittee to investigate the condition of the university and a joint resolution authorizing the payment of university law department instructors. Burch also presented petitions from the city of Baton Rouge urging funds for the university, and a "memorial" from President David F. Boyd asking for relief of the school's $90,647 debt. As if this were not enough, Burch pushed through the legislature the 1876 act uniting the university and the Agricultural and Mechanical College. The university community showed little gratitude for the black legislators or the black community and remained segregated; moreover, when Burch was forced out of Baton Rouge by white "regulators" only the president, David F. Boyd, expressed objections.[74]

Conditions at public institutions for the unfortunate were always of concern to black legislators. The destitution and indebtedness of the existing public charitable institutions were shocking. The surgeon of the Shreveport charity hospital re-

149–50, 175–76, 248–49, 260, 266–67; *Senate Journal, 1874*, pp. 201, 239, 273; New Orleans *Republican*, January 22, 31, February 7, 1874.

74. *Senate Journal, 1874*, pp. 75, 91, 103–104, 129–30, 142, 145, 151–56, 236; *Senate Journal, 1875*, pp. 12, 23; *Senate Journal, 1876*, pp. 79, 117, 136, 185, 214–15, 267, 270; *House Journal, 1876*, p. 322. (Guichard promoted the union of the University and A & M College in the House). The Baton Rouge city council plea for the location was presented to the legislature by Burch. D. F. Boyd to W. L. Sanford, December 23, 1871, March 14, 1874, in David F. Boyd Letters; Germaine A. Reed, "David Boyd: Southern Educator" (Ph.D. dissertation, Louisiana State University, 1970), II, 381–84. New Orleans *Republican*, January 22, February 3, 5, March 1, 3, 1874.

ported the tremendous demands made on the facilities of that institution. Two years after its establishment in 1866, the city government could not afford the financial burden. From November, 1868, to January 1, 1872, the hospital had been called on to accomodate 29,020 indigent sick in the infirmary. During that period the state had furnished $20,000 and the parish $10,000. From January 1, 1872, to January 1, 1874, the hospital had accomodated 32,000 sick persons (both immigrants and indigent) but had not received state aid. A black senator, William Harper, immediately promoted a bill appropriating $20,000 for the hospital. Other institutions were in need of assistance. The report of the Committee on Charitable Institutions indicated a similar crisis at the insane asylum at Jackson; the indebtedness for the asylum in 1873 amounted to $15,624. In a report by the House Committee on Public Buildings, the cost to repair the asylum and other institutions was estimated at $254,000. The Asylum for the Deaf and Blind and the statehouse at Baton Rouge (the latter had been damaged by a fire), and the penitentiary also needed repairs.[75]

The city of Baton Rouge needed a charity hospital, and Representative Augustus Williams presented the petition of Doctor J. W. Dupree asking for such an institution. Several days after the petition was read, Senator Burch introduced a bill to establish a hospital in Baton Rouge. Earlier, the Committee on Charitable Institutions reported that the existing charitable facilities in Baton Rouge, for males and females, were in deplorable condition. The Deaf and Dumb Institution, which was also the quarters for the State Seminary, was in debt for over $8,000

75. *Senate Journal, 1874*, p. 262; *Acts of 1874*, No. 59, p. 107. Another legislator also promoted an act to relieve the hospital. See New Orleans *Republican*, January 27, February 8, 27, March 4, 1874, for critical comments on the condition of the insane asylum. The building at Jackson needed a new roof; the existing roof provided "no protection against rain, and well nigh the whole interior is saturated with water after heavy rains." The state penitentiary needed a new floor. An itemized account of $254,000 indicated a division of: $200,000 for the repair of the statehouse; $50,000 for the insane asylum; $1,000 for deaf and blind asylum; and $3,000 for the penitentiary. *House Journal, 1874*, pp. 133–34; 155–56, 216, 218, 221–27, 229.

as of April, 1873. The bill establishing a charity hospital was approved by both houses and signed by the governor.[76]

In addition to supporting state charitable institutions, black legislators supported reforms for their local constituents. Most of their demands, in fact, were for incorporation of benevolent associations and similar societies. Many of the associations cared for the sick and aided in burying members. Others were established to purchase land, build churches, and provide schools. Some of them represented business ventures, such as insurance companies. Relief bills to pay for services rendered or aid widows or the destitute were also numerous. Representative Henry Raby wrote a bill establishing a poorhouse in Natchitoches Parish; Senator Blunt promoted the measure in the upper House.[77]

Other demands for local legislation took the form of internal improvements for home parishes and for consumer protection measures. Blacks led in supporting a bill to regulate private markets. The act was designed to prevent the sale of rotten meats and to enforce sanitary regulations. It would abolish some markets and provide strict regulations of others. Supporters of the measure claimed that these private markets sold cheaper meat than the public markets. The measure was vetoed by the governor but passed over his veto.[78]

In this session blacks continued to urge legislation to maintain the Metropolitan Police District, whose force was still considered necessary to the survival of Republican rule. The legisla-

76. *House Journal 1874*, pp. 97–98, 223; *Senate Journal, 1874*, pp. 55, 57, 144, 179; *Acts of 1874*, No. 137, pp. 248–49.

77. *House Journal, 1874*, pp. 21, 24, 28, 33, 40, 46, 59, 66–67, 74, 80, 92–93, 96, 103, 106, 117, 126, 129, 140, 163, 187, 192, 253, etc.; see *Acts of 1874*, Nos. 13, 21, 39, 47, 48, 77, 81, 82, 89, 95, 97, 98, 102, 103, 116, 152, 153, 154; *Senate Journal, 1874*, pp. 18, 20, 50–51 106, 116, 124, 174, 223, 234.

78. *House Journal, 1874*, pp. 69, 70–71, 77, 201–202, 208, 212–13; *Senate Journal, 1874*, pp. 214–15. Several blacks had supported a similar bill in 1873. See *House Journal, 1873*, p. 139. Later, in 1875 and 1876 Representative Cain Sartain attempted to get the act repealed. *House Journal, Extra Session, 1875*, pp. 25, 53; *House Journal, 1876*, p. 32. Both efforts failed. New Orleans *Republican*, January 23, February 3, 19, 26, 27, 1874; New Orleans *Daily Picayune*, January 24, 1874; Gonzales, "Kellogg," 476–77.

tion offered was designed to make the police force less expensive and more efficient. Senator Ingraham again took the lead in proposing necessary legislation. On February 4 he introduced a bill to amend and reenact sections fifteen and twenty-seven of the acts of 1868 and 1869 and to change the fiscal year of the Board to begin in January and end in December. Section fifteen was changed to permit the Board of Police Commissioners to select a treasurer annually, instead of allowing him to serve an unspecified time period; section twenty-seven was amended to authorize the towns and parishes in the police district to levy a special tax to maintain the force, in the place of their "estimated and apportioned" share of taxes. The proposal passed the Senate nine days later. In the lower House, Representative David Young guided the bill through with several amendments added.[79]

Three days after the Senate had approved the bill, and while it was in the House, Senator Ingraham offered another bill to amend sections six and ten of the 1869 Metropolitan Police District Act. These changes greatly reduced the expenses of the Metropolitan Police. The amended sections reduced the number of personnnel and patrolmen. The bill won the approval of both houses near the end of the session. Other legislation to improve the Metropolitan Police was attempted. Senator Masicot proposed a measure to refund the force $20,000 for the salaries paid to members in 1873. The bill died in the Finance Committee. A bill to make the Metropolitan Police checks issued by the district receivable for all city taxes due prior to 1874 was advocated by Senator Harper. The bill never received a hearing.[80]

At the same time, blacks moved to make the militia less costly to the state. Senator Barber introduced a bill to provide payment for the militia when it was called out to suppress riots or public disturbances. The parish police jury of the area where the trou-

79. *Senate Journal, 1874*, pp. 106, 110–11, 126, 145–46, 177; *House Journal, 1874*, pp. 162–63; *Acts of 1874*, No. 33, pp. 68–72.

80. *Senate Journal, 1874*, pp. 58, 61, 157–58, 202, 251–52; *House Journal, 1874*, 232–33; *Acts of 1874*, No. 60, pp. 108–109.

ble occurred would assess the cost and levy a tax for the money. The bill passed the Senate a little over a week after it was introduced. In the House a majority of the blacks supported it, and it became law in late February. However, for some reason, the governor did not sign the bill until August.[81] Its enactment was prophetic of the turbulence that would mark the November election.

81. *Senate Journal, 1874*, pp. 71, 100–101, 177; *House Journal, 1874*, pp. 178–79. The black representatives from a portion of the southwestern parishes and from St. Bernard (Guichard, Martinet, Rochon, and Snaer) opposed the bill probably because they felt that the taxes to support the measure could not be obtained. *Acts of 1875*, No. 156, pp. 16–17.

CHAPTER VIII

Modest Gains and Decline, 1874–1876

Louisiana was an armed camp during the spring and summer of 1874. Because the conservatives felt that the election of 1872 had been a fraud and that the Kellog government was a ursurpation, they were determined to carry the November election. The instrument used to ensure a conservative victory was the White League, an organization through which a white man's party could be organized by dividing the races on the color line.[1]

The initial move toward this militant white unity began with the establishment in Alexandria (Rapides Parish) of the *Caucasian* newspaper on March 28, 1874.[2] After the first White League was organized at Opelousas (St. Landry Parish) in late April, 1874, the movement quickly spread throughout the state. De Soto Parish took the lead in north Louisiana, and all conservative whites were enlisted. The organization cut across class lines; the poorer whites were generally the tools of the wealthy and professional class of whites.[3] Courthouses and town halls

---

1. New Orleans *Republican*, September 9, 1874.
2. "Condition of the South," *House Reports*, 43th Cong., 2nd Sess., No. 261. p. 508. The White Leaguers were a substitute for another militant group formed at the outset of Congressional Reconstruction in Louisiana, seven years earlier, the Knights of the White Camellia. See Allie B. W. Webb, "Organization and Activities of the Knights of the White Camellia in Louisiana, 1867–1869," *Proceedings of the Louisiana Academy of Sciences*, XVII (March, 1954), 117.
3. Windham, "Methods and Mechanisms Used to Restore White Supremacy in Louisiana," 47–57. See John Ellis, Judge of Fourth District Court of New Orleans, to Tom Ellis, July 3, 1874 quoted in *ibid.*, 54. *House Reports*, 42nd Cong., 2nd Sess., No. 261, pp. 247–54 *passim*; H. Oscar Lestage, Jr., "The White League and Its Participation

were used by many organizers as conference rooms for the formation of these terrorist organizations. One of the most traditional historians of Louisiana Reconstruction, Professor Ella Lonn, found no evidence of a similar organization among blacks. For public consumption, whites claimed that they were organizing merely to defend themselves against "black leaguers." [4] The New Orleans *Bulletin* served as the official organ of the White League, but other conservative newspapers quickly joined. [5] The organization gave the impression of using persuasion to win black voters, but if this did not succeed, force was to be the order.

Tactics used by the conservative organizations were numerous. Social ostracism of white Kellogg appointees was one; others included economic suppression, denial of work, threats of physical abuse, loss of homes, and even murder. The partisan testimony of both political factions indicates that an overt commitment, violent if necessary, was designed to sweep the conservatives into office.

The white leaguers were successful in forcing many Republican officeholders from power. In Natchitoches, the parish and district judges, police jury, and tax collectors resigned and fled the state. At Coushatta in Red River Parish, on August 30, the sheriff, tax collector, state representative, and two other officeholders were killed because whites alleged that plots of "overt acts" were to be committed by blacks under these officeholders' direction. The governor offered a five-thousand-dollar reward for evidence leading to the arrest and conviction of the murderers, but they remained free. Similar murders and outrages went unpunished in nearly every parish of the state.

in the Reconstruction Riots," in *Louisiana Historical Quarterly*, XVII (July, 1935), 643–50; New Orleans *Republican*, September 1, 3, 4, 5, 13, 1874; Ernest Russ Williams, Jr., "The Florida Parish Ellises and Louisiana Politics, 1820–1918" (Ph.D. dissertation, University of Southern Mississippi, 1969), 133–34.

　　4. Lonn, *Reconstruction*, 254; New Orleans *Republican*, September 5, 1874, quoting the Minden *Democrat*; September 6, 1874, quoting the Baton Rouge *Advocate*; October 31, 1874; New Orleans *Weekly Louisianian* February 13, 1875.

　　5. *House Reports*, 43rd Cong., 2nd Sess., No. 261, p. 247; Lestage, "The White League," 647–48.

Finally, additional Federal troops were sent into the state, but the army was inadequate to sustain order.[6] On September 14 a large armed conservative force led by General F. N. Odgen, claiming that police had seized arms destined for (White Leagues) private citizens, forcibly took possession of the state officials. The Metropolitan Police was called to protect state property. In the battle that followed, forty-four city policemen and approximately twelve of the insurgents were killed. Governor Kellogg and state officials retreated to the Customhouse, and the triumphant insurgents proclaimed D. B. Penn as governor.

The president intervened on the side of Governor Kellogg. In a proclamation on September 15 he ordered the lawlessness to cease, and those responsible for it to disperse. United States troops were mobilized, and twenty-seven companies were stationed in New Orleans. General Emory was instructed to suppress the insurrection and to restore Governor Kellogg to power. By the nineteenth he had succeeded.[7]

A month earlier, both political factions had held conventions to endorse candidates for the congressional posts and treasurer. The Republicans met in Baton Rouge for four days, August 5–9, and experienced internal strife. The blacks wanted a more biracial party and an equal distribution of offices between blacks and whites. Lieutenant Governor C. C. Antoine, who was favored for chairman by most black delegates, did not receive this office which went instead to Representative David Young. Sufficient unity prevailed to enable nominations to be made and to endorse the Kellogg government, the proposed constitutional amendments, and the Civil Rights bill before Congress. Resolutions denouncing the recent violence and calling for a fair election were also adopted.[8]

6. Lestage, "The White League," 649–82; Lonn, *Reconstruction,* 255–61, 264–66; New Orleans *Republican*, September 1, 3, 1874; Attakapas *Sentinel*, June 4, 1874.

7. *House Reports*, 43rd Cong., 3rd Sess., No. 261, pp. 798–835; New Orleans *Republican*, September 15, 16, 17, 18, 19, 20, 1874; Stuart Omer Landry, *The Battle of Liberty Place: The Overthrow of Carpetbag Rule in New Orleans, September 14, 1874* (New Orleans: Pelican Publishing Co., 1955), *passim*.

8. Campbell, "The Political Life of Louisiana Negroes, 1865–1890," 182–83; a large anti-Kellogg rally was later held on October 18, 1874, by blacks to denounce the manner

The Democrats, who convened in Baton Rouge on August 24, also experienced dissension. However, they were united by the cry that all conservatives must support the fight against usurpation. A denunciation of the Republican programs was encouraged: the constitutional amendment, the pending National Civil Rights bill, and the election laws. The preamble of the party best summarized their theme: "We, the White People of Louisiana." The convention then proceeded to nominate white candidates.[9]

The approaching election brought an increase in the violent activities of the White Leaguers. Intimidations, economic and political proscription of black laborers, riots, and the publication of names of white and black Republicans by conservative newspapers were only a few of the devices used. The merchants of Shreveport signed a pact not to "advance supplies or money to any planter who will give employment or rent land to any laborers who vote the radical ticket in the coming election." White women were encouraged not to hire servants whose husbands were affiliated with the Radical party. On election day armed bands of whites gathered at the voting polls.[10]

In this hostile atmosphere the election was held. The results, according to the conservatives, had gained for them a majority of twenty-nine in the lower House. However, the Returning Board threw out many of the Democratic victories certified by local officials as having been gained by fraud or intimidation, and proclaimed a narrow Republican majority in the lower chamber. Apparently the Republicans were going to be able to hold on to power for two more years. The large Democratic vote revealed that the whites would not concede credit to Kellogg and his party

in which the governor had dismissed James H. Ingraham as clerk of the First District Court, and Felix C. Antoine as recorder of births and deaths, New Orleans *Daily Picayune*, October 28, 1874.

9. Lonn, *Reconstruction,* 262–63; *House Reports*, 43rd Cong., 2nd Sess., No. 261, p. 1038; New Orleans *Republican*, September 9, 1874.

10. *House Reports*, 43rd Cong., 2nd Sess., No. 261, pp. 314, 753, 756. For Kellogg's comments on tax reforms of his administration, see p. 1034; Windham, "Methods and Mechanisms," x–xii, 60–98.

for enacting financial reform and effecting a substantial reduction in the tax rate. Regardless of what the Republicans had done or might do, they were going to be judged by white Louisiana on the basis of race. Nationally, the results of the election of 1874 were "epoch making in the history of reconstruction after the War." The Democrats gained control of the House of Representatives and had a near majority in the Senate. These results meant an inevitable demise of the Radical policy in the South.[11]

As in the previous election, the 1874 returns were subject to dispute. Each party claimed victory and charged the other with fraud, and only the presence of Federal troops kept the peace. In his annual message to Congress in early December, 1874, President Grant noted the chaotic situation in Louisiana and urged a special committee to investigate the alleged fraud in the election. The House accordingly ordered the Speaker to appoint a special seven-man committee headed by George F. Hoar of Massachusetts. From this committee a subcommittee was sent to New Orleans; it consisted of William Phelps of New Jersey, Charles Foster of Ohio (both Republicans), and a New York Democrat, Clarkson N. Potter. At the same time the president sent General Philip H. Sheridan to New Orleans to evaluate the situation. When the legislature convened, the Democrats by trickery took control of the House, ejected the Republican claimant, and organized the chamber. This procedure outraged Sheridan, who issued a statement urging Grant to treat the Democratic legislators and White Leaguers as "banditti." With Sheridan's approval, Federal troops entered the legislature and expelled sufficient Democratic members to restore the Republicans majority in the lower House. While these events were occurring, the subcommittee was taking evidence, and preparing to issue its report.[12]

The subcommittee's findings disappointed the president's ex-

11. William A. Dunning, *Reconstruction: Political and Economic, 1865–1877* (New York: Harper and Brothers, 1907), 251.

12. New Orleans *Republican*, January 6, 9, 12, 1875; Lonn, *Reconstruction*, 292–305.

pectation. The report issued on January 15 found no intimidation in the election. It stated that "the people of the State of Louisiana did fairly have a free, peacable and full registration and election, in which a clear Conservative majority was elected to the lower house of the legislature." The report found no basis for Repbulican charges of White League violence.[13]

The report was shocking to Republicans. Instead of settling the problem, it reopened it and carried the threat of continued strife that might effect the party's national chances in 1876. In a move to counter the effect of the report, the full special committee was dispatched to New Orleans. William A. Wheeler of New York, William P. Frye of Maine, and Samuel Marshall of Illinois came down on January 22, 1875, conducted an investigation, and issued a report in February. This report concluded that the election of 1874 "was neither full, free, nor fair." It further found intimidation of blacks rampant in areas where White Leagues were active. But the committee also concluded that no power could reconstitute the House except the chamber itself. Obviously an adjustment would have to be devised that was acceptable to both sides, and Congressman Wheeler provided such an adjustment. In essence, the plan of conciliation consisted of three parts: claimants to House seats would abide by the decision of the committee, which awarded a majority to the Democrats; Democratic senators elected in 1874 would return to the Kellogg legislature, and the legislature would not disturb or attempt to impeach the present state government. The Republicans accepted the terms of the adjustment immediately, but the conservatives grudgingly consented in caucus on February 24 by a thirty-four to thirty-three vote. The adjustment was later consummated in the extra session in mid-April.[14]

13. *House Reports*, 43rd Cong., 2nd Sess., No. 261, pp. 5, 6; New Orleans *Republican*, January 3, 5, 6, 7, 16, 19, 24, 1875.

14. James T. Otten, "The Wheeler Adjustment in Louisiana: National Republicans Begin to Reappraise Their Reconstruction Policy," *Louisiana History*, XIII (Fall, 1972), 360–62; Gonzales, "William Pitt Kellogg, Reconstruction Governor of Louisiana," 444–46; Lonn, *Reconstruction*, 362–64; New Orleans *Republican*, January 23, 24, February 6, 9, 17, 23, 25, 26, March 3, 24, 1875; New Orleans *Daily Picayune*, January 22, 23, 24, 26, February 3, 7, 8, March 24, 1875.

While the problem was being resolved, the legislature convened on January 4. As a result of the election, the black membership of the House had decreased to twenty-nine and with the establishment of the Wheeler adjustment in April, it shrank to nineteen. In the Senate there was an increase in black members; fifteen blacks presented themselves at the beginning of the session and only one was unseated. The November election also produced the only black to serve Louisiana in Congress, Charles E. Nash, elected from the Sixth District. Born in New Orleans in May, 1844, Nash received a limited education and was working as a bricklayer when he enlisted in the Union army in 1863. He lost a leg during the storming of Fort Blakely in Alabama—the last infantry battle of the Civil War—and was honorably discharged with the rank of first sergeant. As a Republican representative to the Forty-fourth Congress, he served on the committees on education and labor. Before and after his one term in Congress, he served in several other occupations; night inspector of customs for Louisiana and postmaster at Washington, Louisiana. A man who was not very well known by the rank and file of the party, Nash died in New Orleans on June 13, 1913.[15]

In the state legislature, eight of the twenty-nine black representatives were serving their first term in the House. One of the new members was a thirty-year-old former slave, Vincent Dickerson, from St. James Parish. Born in Markville, Tennessee, in 1847, he remained in slavery until he escaped behind Union lines into Louisiana. In late 1862 he enlisted under General Benjamin Butler in the First Mississippi Black Regiment and served for only four months before he was captured by Confederate forces and imprisoned in Houston, Texas. At the end of the war, he returned to Louisiana and became a prominent

15. See Appendices E and G, herein. "Rebuilding the Waste Places after War," *Negro History Bulletin*, I (April, 1938), 3–4; Samuel D. Smith, *The Negro in Congress, 1870–1901* (Chapel Hill: University of North Carolina Press, 1940), 88–89; *Weekly Louisianian*, September 26, November 7, 1874; Charles E. Nash to James S. Casey, August, 1869, Customhouse Nominations, Louisiana, New Orleans: June, 1869–May, 1870, Box 110, RG 56, NA. Nash served as "night inspector" in the Customhouse; J. H. Moseley, *Sixty Years in Congress and Twenty-eight Out* (New York: Vantage Press, 1960), 58–59.

businessman. He established a grocery store, raised cattle, and was vice-president of the Republican Executive Committee for his parish and served on the school board. Later he closed his grocery business and began to raise rice. During his term in the legislature most of his business transactions were performed by his clerk.[16]

Another former slave, F. R. Wright, represented Terrebonne Parish in the 1874 legislature. Born in St. Charles Parish on March 5, 1849, he had attached himself to a Union army camp, where he learned to read. Active in local politics, Wright was appointed by Governor Warmoth as recorder of St. Charles Parish at the age of twenty-two. The next year he moved to Terrebonne Parish, established a business, and served as deputy sheriff for two years. He was also tax collector for one year before his short term in the legislature.[17] Representative Wright would be one of the Republican representatives to lose his seat because of the Wheeler adjustment.

J. J. Johnson was yet another former slave elected in 1874, but he had his service terminated by the Wheeler adjustment. He represented De Soto Parish where he had lived since 1857. He had been taken from New Orleans by his master to De Soto. An able man, he learned to read and write after emancipation and was looked to by local blacks for political leadership in Mansfield. He was reelected in November, 1876, but with the inauguration of the Nicholls regime he retired from politics.[18]

The other four new members came from Plaquemines, Orleans, Rapides, East Feliciana, and Assumption parishes. Alfred Étienne Milon, forty-three, had lived in Plaquemines Parish for thirty-three years. He had served in Company C, Eighty-first

16. *Senate Reports*, 46th Cong., 1st–2nd Sess., No. 693, Pt. I, p. 744; *Weekly Louisianian*, February 27, 1875; St. James *Sentinel*, March 26, November 19, 1873, June 17, 1874, May 22, 1875; State of Louisiana, *Official Journal of the Proceedings of the House of Representatives of the General Assembly, 1890* (Baton Rouge, 1890), last page.

17. *Weekly Louisianian*, February 27, 1875; *House Journal, 1875*, p. 6; Wright was appointed as a police juror in Terrebonne Parish in July, 1875. Thomas A. Cage to William P. Kellogg, July 1, 1875, in William P. Kellogg Papers.

18. *House Reports*, 43rd Cong., 2nd Sess., No. 261, pp. 352–57; *Senate Reports*, 46th Cong., 1st–2nd Sess., No. 693, Pt. I, p. 68.

Regiment, United States Colored Volunteers, as an orderly sergeant. A former school board director, Milon served two terms in the legislature, one of these terms being after the Democrats had returned to power.[19] John Baptiste Jourdain of Orleans Parish, a thirty-two-year-old former Union army recruiter and lieutenant, was a married free man of color.[20] J. Shiby Davidson of Iberville, a property holder in Bayou Goula, had one of the longest careers among blacks in Louisiana politics. A former justice of the peace, Representative Davidson served in the House for two terms and was then elected to the Senate. He was refused his senatorial seat, but four years later he returned to the lower House to serve an additional six years. In all, he served approximately ten years in public office.[21] The former sheriff of East Feliciana, Robert R. Ray, served one term. Robert Poindexter of Assumption has served previously in the Constitutional Convention of 1868 and in the Senate. He was in his early forties. Representative Poindexter also lost his seat in April, 1875, because of the Wheeler adjustment.[22]

W. John DeLacy, representative from Rapides Parish, met a similar fate. A native of the parish and a former two-term sheriff, the twenty-four-year-old DeLacy lost his seat in April, 1875. However, he was reelected in 1876 and then cooperated with the Nicholls Democratic administration.[23] Because of the Com-

---

19. *Senate Reports*, 46th Cong., 1st–2nd Sess., No. 693, Pt. 1, pp. 799–801.

20. Jourdain was listed as owning $400 worth of real estate in Orleans Parish in 1871. He committed suicide in April, 1888. He had served as inspector of flour in the Customhouse. *House Reports*, 39th Cong., 2nd Sess., No. 16, pp. 102–103, 105, 204, 208–209; *Register of Taxes, 1871*, Orleans Parish, A–L, New Orleans Public Library; Civil War Pension Files, Records of the Veterans Administration, RG 15, NA; New Orleans *Daily Picayune* August 2, 4, 1868.

21. *Senate Journal*, 45–48, 55–56; *Weekly Louisianian*, December 14, 1878, February 21, 1880. After he was rejected from his senatorial seat in 1880, he later received a commission and qualified as United States warehousekeeper, and later joined the Stalwart Republican ranks; *Revision of Assessment Roll for Iberville Parish, 1878;* and *Tax Assessment Rolls, Iberville Parish, 1880, 1901*. All are in the parish courthouse at Plaquemine. *House Journal, 1890*, last page.

22. *House Journal, Extra Session, 1875*, p. 6.

23. *Senate Reports*, 46th Cong., 1st–2nd Sess., No. 693, Pt. I, p. 144; DeLacy accepted money to desert the Republican legislature after 1876, *ibid.*, 196–97; *Record of Commissions, 1868–69*, p. 29; *Record of Commissions, 1868–74*, pp. 552–53.

promise five other black Representatives would also lose their seats after only one year. They were William Crawford and Joseph Connaughton of Rapides, Victor Rochon and L. A. Martinet of St. Martin and Frederick Marie of Terrebonne.[24] The other fifteen black representatives had served previously and would complete the current term.

Of the fifteen black senators, nine were completing terms to which they had been elected in 1872; they were Blunt, Burch, Cage, Detiege, Harper, Kelso, Masicot, Pollard, and Stamps. Six of them were new, but four of these had previously served in the House. They were T. T. Allain, wealthy planter from Iberville, Andrew J. Dumont, a creole from Orleans who had been educated in Mexico; Pierre Landry, a former mayor of Donaldsonville, and David Young, the former slave from Vidalia (Concordia Parish).

Two of the senators were newcomers to the legislature. They were Jacques A. Gla of East Carroll and Oscar Crozier of Lafourche. Senator Gla was one of the most influential blacks in northeast Louisiana. Originally from New Orleans, he was a descendant of "an old creole family." After the war he moved to Alexandria and later settled in Carroll Parish, engaging in planting and horseraising and in local politics.[25] As a school board member, he instituted lawsuits against past Republican officials who squandered school money, and he encouraged the state superintendent of education to retain T. Morris Chester, a black man, as superintendent of education of the Fifth Division. Senator Gla performed many taks for the Republican party in his district. He advised the governor on appointments; as president of the parish executive committee, he often made speaking tours into Mississippi.[26] Senator Gla remained in politics after

24. *House Journal, Extra Session, 1875*, p. 6; New Orleans *Republican*, April 15, 17, 18, 1875; New Orleans *Daily Picayune*, April 16, 1875.

25. *Weekly Louisianian*, July 24, 1875, November 5, 1881; Wilson, *Black Phalanx*, 176; Civil War Pension Files, Records of the Veterans Administration, RG 15, NA. Gla was married and possessed property in East Carroll.

26. Gla to William G. Brown, July 7, 1876, in Kellogg Papers; *House Reports*, 43rd

the restoration of the Democrats to power. Toward the end of the Kellogg regime, he became disillusioned with the Republicans, thinking they had not fulfilled their promises to blacks. His faith in the party was slightly revitalized when he was selected to head a delegation of black Republicans that conferred with President James A. Garfield in April, 1881. Later that year he was appointed as surveyor general of Louisiana.[27]

Oscar Crozier had a short legislative career. A thirty-one-year-old sugar planter when elected, the former city Alderman possessed substantial wealth and was able to hire ten laborers on his plantation located near Thibodaux. After he was unseated in the extra session, Crozier returned to Lafourche where he was elected tax collector and remained active in politics for another decade.[28]

In this session blacks in the House suffered from their decreased membership. Fewer blacks were on important committees than in previous sessions. No blacks were initially appointed to the committees on Contingent Expenses, Judiciary, and Appropriation; but midway into the session, Robert F. Guichard secured a spot on the latter committee. Twelve of the thirty-three standing committees had black chairmen but only six of this number had a majority of blacks. The committees headed by blacks and with a majority of black members included: Immigration (Raby), Public Lands (Connaughton), Enrollment (Demas), Federal Relations (Sartain), Charitable and Public Institutions (Ray), and Registration (Murrell). Two 4-member committees chaired by blacks had an even number of black and white members: Public Health and Quarantine

Cong., 2nd Sess., No. 261, pp. 240–41. See letter from Pinchback, n.d., in Archives of Negro History, Claver Building, New Orleans; Gla to Antoine, August 11, 16, 20, 1875; September 1, 12, 25, 1875, in Kellogg Papers.

27. *Weekly Louisianian*, October 18, November 1, 29, 1879; January 31, May 22, June 12, 1880; March 5, 9, 19, 26, April 16, May 28, November 5, December 3, 1881; Carroll *Conservative*, November 30, 1878; Carroll *Watchman*, May 27, June 17, 1875.

28. *House Miscellaneous Documents*, 44th Cong., 2nd Sess., No. 34, Pt. V, pp. 92–93; *Weekly Louisianian*, April 3, 1880; *Record of Commissions, 1868–74*, pp. 9, 18, 397.

(Wright) and Claims (Stewart), and the eight-man Committee on Parochial Affairs (Snaer). The other three committees headed by blacks were Public Printing (Marie), Claims (Stewart), and Pensions (Davidson). Blacks were a majority on the committees on Corporations, Internal Improvement, Railroads, Canals and Drainage, and Charitable Institutions. The six-member committees on Retrenchment and Reform, Elections and Qualifications, and Militia were composed of two blacks and four whites. The four-man committees on Public Lands and Levees and Banks and Banking were evenly divided. Only one black served on the five-man Committee on Constitution, the six-man Committee on Ways and Means, and the four-member Committee on Penitentiary. Three Negroes were on the eight-man Committee on State Library and three on the seven-man Committee on Rules. Two blacks served on the same numbered Committee on Public Buildings and two served on the five-man Committee on Education.[29]

In the Senate, blacks played a more significant role on committees. Over half the standing committees appointed had black chairmen. Fourteen of the twenty-seven announced committees were headed by blacks: twelve of the fourteen had a majority of black votes. These included the three-man committees on Militia (Detiege), Federal Relations (Landry), Libraries (Blunt); the five-man committees on Claims (Stamps), Penitentiary (Burch), Parks and Public Buildings (Cage), Pensions (Crozier), Drainage, Canals, and Inland Navigation (Harper), and Election (Allain), the seven-member Committee on Enrollment and Engrossment (Masicot), and the four-man committees on Charitable Institutions (Kelso), and Metropolitan Police (Dumont). The two committees headed by blacks with a white majority were the committees on Apportionment (Pollard), and Retrenchment and Reform (Young). Other committees with black mem-

29. *House Journal, 1875*, p. 11, 27–28, 30, 33, 37–38, 46, 56, 70, 131, 142. Several special committees were urged but not approved. Two special five-man committees were appointed, however. The committee to investigate loan offices, with one black, and the committee on the appropriation bill which included two black members.

bership were the Judiciary, Finance, Agriculture, Commerce, and Manufacture; five committees were evenly divided—Public Education, Printing, Public Lands and Levees, Health and Quarantine, and Banks and Banking. The other three committees with a black majority were Railroads and Internal Improvement, Elections, and Registration.[30]

Blacks were also assigned to the Senate special committees. No black was chairman of a special committee, but the two 4-member committees to examine the books and accounts of the state treasurer and the treasurer's and auditor's books and accounts were evenly divided in membership. A special three-man committee on political persecution and outrage had a majority of black members. The three-man special committee to investigate the Board of Levee Commissioners and the Louisiana Levee Company had only one black. The five-man committee to investigate the Crescent City Live Stock Company was composed of two blacks and three whites.[31]

On occasion a committee was called on to investigate fellow legislators. Such an experience fell to the Committee on Retrenchment and Reform. One of the members, J. B. Jourdain, offered a resolution directing the committee to investigate the books of the Committee on Contingent Expenses for 1874. In the course of the inquiry, the committee asked the previous chairman of the Contingent Expense Committee, David Young, to turn over the books, vouchers, and accounts for the 1874 year. Senator Young told them that the books were in Vidalia and could not be produced at the current session. The committee returned to the House and asked for further instructions. Because the session was nearing an end, no instructions were issued and no report was made.[32] However, Young came under additional criticism from the Assembly for allegedly misusing school funds while on the Concordia Parish school board. A

30. *Senate Journal, 1874*, pp. 30–31.
31. *Senate Journal, 1875*, pp. 14, 17, 28, 34, 48–49, 61. Other committees were asked for but not approved.
32. *House Journal, 1875*, pp. 34, 41, 96.

resolution authorizing a three-man committee to investigate this matter was adopted in the House, but in the upper chamber black senators moved quickly to table the resolution. Young was saved by a narrow vote.[33]

In the 1875 session blacks continued to advocate educational bills that would benefit both races. Senator Kelso of Rapides authored a bill to amend and carry into effect an act of 1874 providing for the reception and use of public lands by the United States to the Agricultural and Mechanical College. As a member of the Board, Kelso was the caretaker for the bill. Introduced on January 28, Kelso pushed the bill to final passage on February 26. The House adopted the measure on March 2, and Governor Kellogg signed it into law twenty days later. This act facilitated the union of the state university and the Agricultural and Mechanical College the next year. Senator Burch still watched over the welfare of the state university. State Superintendent William G. Brown was a constant advocate of universal education. His message urged the legislature not to "abstain from an alienation of the now extremely limited sum devoted to public education." Another measure urged by black legislators would have abolished the offices of divisions superintendent and provided other methods of performing their duties. At least three separate proposals to effect this change were offered, but all died in the Committee on Education. A measure consolidating the schools of Tensas Parish into one district did win approval in both houses.[34]

As in previous sessions, blacks pushed legislation to protect laborers. Robert Poindexter, who as a senator in 1868 had championed labor bills, now as a representative returned to the attack. During the second week of the session, he introduced a bill to secure laborers the first privileged lien on crops of cotton, sugar, or other agricultural products raised by them in whole or in part.

---

33. *Senate Journal, 1875*, pp. 79, 81. Senator Young was absent during the proceedings.

34. *Ibid.*, 48, 128, 136, 137, 158–59; *Acts of 1875*, No. 20, pp. 50–52; New Orleans *Republican*, February 14, 1875; *House Journal, 1875*, pp. 13, 19, 59–60, 63, 114, 133, 135.

The bill received two readings and was referred to the Judiciary Committee; two weeks later an unfavorable report was issued, and the bill was postponed indefinitely. Ascension Parish's Pierre Landry, gave notice of a similar bill for the protection of laborers on plantations throughout the state, but for some reason he failed to introduce his bill. Representative Dickerson proposed a bill to recover payment for laborers who had worked on the St. James Parish levees during the high waters of the preceding year, but his measure was buried in the Committee on Lands and Levees.[35]

As had been the case in previous legislatures and would be the case in future legislatures, the appropriation bill received more consideration than other measures. Introduced into the House on January 12 by Cain Sartain, it won approval in two weeks. The Senate approved the bill a week later. The bill was vetoed by the governor because it proposed $185,000 for mileage and per diem compensation, a sum that Kellogg thought was excessive. The house then amended the bill to provide only $158,000 for mileage and per diem. Thus changed, the measure was approved by the governor. Some items in the bill although criticized as extravagant, were not unduly costly. The bill to illuminate the assembly with gas was $500. Salaries and expenses of clerks and officials were substantial but lower than in previous years.[36]

The state's financial problem was complicated by many requests from localities for exemption from taxes or relief compensation for taxes already paid. Senator Allain continued to advocate a remittance of penalties for delinquent taxpayers providing they paid their taxes within ninety days; the bill died in the Judiciary Committee. Senator Crozier urged an act to exempt taxpayers in the town of Thibodaux and another act to relieve

35. *House Journal, 1875*, pp. 28, 29, 44, 50; *Senate Journal, 1875*, p. 27.

36. *House Journal, 1875*, pp. 19, 26, 31, 32, 78, 79, 84, 85, 96, 98, 109, 113–14, 124, 134, 136, 144, 147. Later the Speaker and lieutenant governor said that the bill as ratified in the House and signed by the governor was different. The measure could not be revoked after it was signed. A violent debate erupted during the House Session. New Orleans *Republican*, February 18, March 31, April 1, 2, 4, 1875. *Senate Journal, 1875*, pp. 96, 98, 99–100, 104, 148, 166, 167, 169, 172.

taxpayers on the overflowed lands in the parishes of Lafourche, Assumption, and Terrebonne. Senators Young and Blunt opposed such relief; Young remarked that even though his plantation in Concordia was annually subject to overflowing waters, he did not think the state could afford to lose the revenue. Other relief measures were still urged, however. Senator Burch urged help for taxpayers in Baton Rouge. Senator Kelso promoted a relief bill for taxpayers wrongfully assessed. Representative Milon championed a measure similar to Allain's for delinquent taxpayers in Plaquemines Parish, and Representative Snaer introduced an identical bill in the House a week after the Senate Judiciary Committee received Allain's proposal. The Snaer bill was reported unfavorably by the House Judiciary Committee and postponed indefinitely. Senators Blunt, Gla, Demas, and others asked for similar relief plans, but all failed. Other legislators proposed bills to eliminate the tax collector's office and to assign this function to the sheriffs; William Murrell asked for a bill to make the tax collector's office elective. These also failed.[37]

Governor Kellogg vetoed several proposed bills dealing with tax collection and parish indebtedness. One was an act to provide for more efficient collection of taxes; the House passed the bill over the veto but the Senate sustained the veto. A proposed plan authorizing parishes to fund their outstanding indebtedness and limiting parish taxation received the veto of the governor, which was sustained.

Directly related to tax legislation was the issue of property assessment. Representative Murrell urged an act to assess property according to its value, and to repeal overvaluations previously made. The bill was not reported back from the Judiciary Committee. However, a measure providing for equitable assessment of property in New Orleans and defining the

---

37. New Orleans *Republican*, February 12, 1876; *Senate Journal, 1875*, pp. 11–12, 14, 28, 48, 57, 67, 102, 135, 141; *House Journal, 1875*, 22, 25, 63, 143.

duties of the state assessors was adopted by both houses.[38]

Blacks generally supported measures to provide protection to consumers and to regulate the practices of business. Senator Young promoted by request an act to prevent the adulteration of milk; the bill received a favorable report but was postponed on the last day of the session. Senator Stamps proposed measures designed to prevent fraudulent insurance companies from operating in the state. He gave notice of an act proposing the creation of the office of superintendent of insurance but then failed to introduce it. Three weeks later, however, Stamps introduced an act to provide for the appointment of a state insurance inspector, which was lost in committee. Finally he suggested a bill establishing an insurance inspection department, which would be empowered to publish insurance regulations and to establish penalties for violations. This bill came up for a vote four times after the Committee on Agriculture and Commerce gave it a favorable report; it was finally postponed indefinitely two days before the session ended.[39]

Blacks manifested interest in preventing lawlessness that escaped the notice of Reconstruction historians. Their efforts failed because of the disinterest of white legislators. Senator Blunt promoted a measure to punish persons guilty of discharging firearms in any city or town. It passed the Senate, but was not reported out of the House Judiciary Committee after two readings. Senator Young urged a similar bill; it proposed to empower the magistrates of Orleans Parish to issue warrants of arrest on Sundays for law breakers; it died in the Senate Judiciary Com-

---

38. *Senate Journal, 1875*, pp. 170–71, 175; *House Journal, 1875*, pp. 92, 126, 135, 139–40; New Orleans *Republican*, March 4, 1875.

39. *Senate Journal, 1875*, pp. 42, 48, 60, 92, 94, 107, 143, 148, 157; New Orleans *Republican*, March 3, 1875; For a discussion of the black legislators' attempt to enact a "blue law," see, Charles Vincent, "Louisiana's Black Legislators and Their Efforts to Pass a Blue Law during Reconstruction," *Journal of Black Studies*, VI (1976), forthcoming. Stamps felt the measure would better protect the small propertyholders; Young opposed the measure, because it created a new governmental office with an added expense. New Orleans *Republican*, January 29, February 19, 1875.

mittee. Other related measures were to prohibit cruelty to animals and prevent the kidnapping of children. Senator Kelso promoted two animal protective measures; one was to incorporate the Louisiana Society for the Prevention of Cruelty to Animals, and a similar measure prescribing penalties for violations. Both measures failed; the former was indefinitely postponed near the end of the session, and no action was taken on the latter proposal after the Judiciary Committee reported favorably. Senator Blunt promoted a general and somewhat vague act to protect human beings from abuse and cruelty; it prohibited the practice of servitude and had a clause to protect minor girls against seduction. The bill was read twice and reported to the Judiciary Committee which did not issue a report.[40]

The changing of parish boundaries was a matter of concern to some blacks. Their probable motive was to prevent safe districts from being absorbed by doubtful ones. Coming in for particular notice was St. Bernard Parish. Thus in January, Representative Guichard introduced a bill to define the limits of the parish; it passed the House on February 18. In the Senate, Masicot of New Orleans championed the House bill. The measure won the Senate's approval the same day it appeared in the Senate. Other black legislators were unsuccessful with similar bills. Senator Gla was unable to win approval of his bill to divide the parish of Carroll into police jury wards; likewise, Senator Cage failed to get a hearing on an act to change the boundaries of Assumption Parish; Representative Snaer's proposal to change the limits of the parishes of St. Martin and Iberia did not receive a hearing; another bill proposed creating the parish of Algiers was authored by Senator Dumont, but it did not reappear after the January 11 session.[41]

As a part of their effort to improve local government, blacks

40. *Senate Journal, 1875*, pp. 16, 37, 39, 42, 44–45, 65, 86, 93, 107, 148, 157; *House Journal, 1875*, p. 109. The Society for the Prevention of Cruelty to Animals had been chartered in 1874. See critical comments on the charter in Nordhoff, *The Cotton States*, 61; *Senate Journal, 1876*, pp. 38, 42.

41. *Senate Journal, 1875*, pp. 14, 91, 102, 136; *House Journal, 1875*, pp. 13, 21, 22, 65, 90; *Acts of 1875*, No. 23, pp. 54–55.

attempted to amend previous acts incorporating towns. Senator Allain promoted an act to amend the incorporation law of the town of Plaquemine (Iberville Parish). When the bill was amended by white legislators to exempt the town from taxation, Allain opposed the bill along with a majority of the black senators, but the bill was approved by one vote. In the House it was approved and passed on the same day it appeared. Representative Snaer authored a bill that was approved by both houses amending the third section of an (1843) act incorporating the town of St. Martinville. It became a law without the governor's signature. It stipulated that qualified electors had to live in the town two months preceding the election of local officials. Many other bills to amend city incorporation acts, and to amend statutes in general were introduced but were not passed.[42]

The introduction of an act reducing the cost of public printing was one of the highlights of the session. Henry Demas of St. John wrote the initial bill. Presented to the House on the second day of the session, the bill sought to establish an official journal at New Orleans and to repeal the existing printing law. The bill was passed by the House on February 20, and it won Senate approval within a week.[43] It greatly reduced the expense of official printing and established the official publication closer to the seat of government.

The session of 1875 had produced only a moderate and modest legislative program. Some of the legislation introduced by blacks had been forward looking, but most of their bills failed. More obvious was that their accomplishments in the direction of reform went unappreciated in the rising social turmoil gripping the state. An extra session would meet almost immediately, and in it black legislators would face their final test, a test to survive.

---

42. *Acts of 1875*, No. 4, p. 25; *House Journal, 1875*, pp. 39, 40, 45, 67, 83, 107, 110, 125; *Senate Journal, 1875*, pp. 46, 52, 57, 64, 68, 94, 96, 99, 103, 115–16, 156.

43. *House Journal, 1875*, pp. 11, 39, 47, 53, 97; *Senate Journal, 1875*, p. 139; *Acts of 1875*, No. 3, p. 102. While this act was under debate, Representative Wright of Terrebonne sought a resolution to lease out the printing to the lowest bidder; it was referred to the Committee on Printing.

CHAPTER IX

The
Battle for
Survival

Approximately six weeks after the first session of the regular term ended, an extra session was convened. Kellogg's proclamation announcing the session was issued in late March, and the session was scheduled to open on April 14 for ten days. The call stipulated the subjects upon which the legislature was to act: to ratify the political adjustment, to reduce taxes, to try to solve the revenue difficulties of the state, and to regulate port charges and the Board of Trade in the Crescent City.[1]

Some whites and most black Republicans were opposed to calling the session and consummating the adjustment, which would cause nine black representatives and one black senator to lose their seats. Pinchback, who was still fighting for a seat in Congress, opposed the adjustment because it would "denationalize" the Louisiana case. However, the national Republican leaders, including President Grant wanted the situation settled, and the state leaders were persuaded that the adjustment probably would bring peace. Both parties, after caucusing, decided to accept the compromise. On April 15, the Committee on Privilege and Elections presented a joint resolution allocating the contested seats and recommending "recognition of the Kellogg government." The House accepted the resolution by an

1. *Senate Journal, Extra Session, April 14, 1875*, pp. 3, 9–12; New Orleans *Republican*, March 26, April 14, 1875.

eighty-nine to eighteen vote and the Senate passed it by a vote of twenty-seven to three.[2]

The adjustment was not an ideal solution but it enabled the legislature to organize itself and at least attempt to consider some of the problems afflicting the state. However, continued bickering between the Democrats or conservatives and the Republican parties permitted very little time for legislative matters.[3] Most of the legislation that was enacted was passed on the last two days of the session.

Blacks offered legislation embracing a variety of subjects and often minor subjects. Representative Henry Demas introduced two separate bills designed to protect the game and useful birds in the state. One of the proposals reached its second reading but did not reappear because the end-of-the session rush killed it. Senator David Young's proposal to enact a law to release persons from any official bond they may have signed for sheriffs if the courts were given a thirty-day notice was referred to the Judiciary Committee and did not reappear. Senator Blunt promoted an act requiring better qualifications of persons presenting themselves before the examination bar for admittance to the Supreme Court; it received the same fate as Young's bill.[4]

Other legislative proposals dealt with more important themes. Senator Dumont of Orleans Parish (Algiers) sought an act to reduce the taxes the city of New Orleans levied to maintain the

2. *House Journal, April 14, 1875*, pp. 6, 7. *Senate Journal, Extra Session, 1875*, pp. 17, 20; Lonn, *Reconstruction in Louisiana*, 373–75; New Orleans *Republican*, April 13, 15, 16, 17, 18, 1875; New Orleans *Daily Picayune*, April 16–18, 1875. The *Picayune* quoted black Representative Robert Poindexter as saying, "He resigned his seat to the man who used to own him." April 16, 1875.

3. Lonn, *Reconstruction*, 376–77; impeachment of the Auditor of Public Accounts, Charles Clinton, took up much of the extra session time, *Senate Journal, Extra Session, 1875*, pp. 33, 41, 44–47, 57, 59; *House Journal, Extra Session, 1875*, pp. 20, 27, 24–25, 59–60. All on pp. 27, 29, of the latter journal for the ousting of the four Republicans returned by the Returning Board. They were given per diem expenses, pp. 41, 48; New Orleans *Daily Picayune*, April 16, 1875; New Orleans *Republican*, April 18, 24, 1875.

4. *House Journal, 1875*, pp. 38, 47. Demas also sought a statute to prohibit the selling and purchasing of mocking birds or pop birds outside the city of New Orleans. *Ibid.*, 21; *Senate Journal, 1875*, pp. 15, 18, 21, 29.

Metropolitan Police. After being amended, the bill passed the Senate on April 23 and the House on the last day of the session. The remitting of tax penalties and interest on taxes paid on lands that had overflowed in 1874 was a successful proposal championed by Senator Young. The penalties and interest were remitted if the principal of the taxes was paid before December 1, 1875. Other tax relief proposals were designed to bring relief to delinquent taxpayers, reduce the outstanding indebtedness of the state, and provide for seizure of property of delinquent taxpayers.[5]

Attempts by blacks to secure internal improvements for their districts usually failed. Senator Cage, after being unable in the regular session to get a congressional appropriation of $50,000 to clean Bayou Terrebonne, tried in the extra session to secure $20,000 from the state. His bill disappeared in Committee. Senator Allain promoted a petition for repair of levees from the people of Grosse Tete and Maringouin, and Senator Burch championed a request for reimbursement for money spent on levee repairs from the city of Baton Rouge. Both measures failed.[6]

Equally unsuccessful were black efforts to enlarge the powers of police juries. Representative Milon wrote a measure that passed the House authorizing the police jury of Plaquemines Parish to issue bonds. Since the House approved the measure on the last day of the session, the Senate did not receive the bill for action. Vincent Dickerson, St. James representative, promoted a similar measure authorizing the police jury of his parish to bond the floating indebtedness, but probably because of lack of support he did not introduce the measure.[7]

One black legislator was interested in bringing new industry to the state. Senator Dumont wrote a bill to encourage the manufacture of cotton and woolen goods. Introduced on the third

5. *Senate Journal, Extra Session, 1875*, pp. 14, 18, 22, 34, 35, 36, 54; *House Journal, Extra Session, 1875*, pp. 43, 52, 54, 63; *Acts of Extra Session, 1875*, No. 7, p. 106 (in rear of volume containing *Acts of 1875*).

6. *Senate Journal, Extra Session 1875*, pp. 5, 15, 29, 52, 138.

7. *House Journal, Extra Session, 1875*, pp. 21, 48, 57.

day of the session, the bill provided that mills making such goods would be relieved of certain state, parish, and municipal taxes. The measure was approved by the Agricultural Committee and won the Senate's approval on April 23. The House voted favorably on the last day of the session.[8] Democrats naturally did not know that he was advocating a program that white legislators in the twentieth century would seize on as their own. His measure was one of the few accomplishments of blacks in the session.

The legislative sessions—both regular and extra of 1875—had not accomplished the reforms urged by the governor. Reform was obviously impossible if the strife in the state continued, and this strife gave every indication of becoming bitter. Shortly after the extra session adjourned, a faction of conservatives began to organize to overthrow the Wheeler adjustment. They held a convention in August and then in December, elected delegates to another convention scheduled for early January. Their demand was for an investigation into the election of 1872.[9]

The January convention denounced the Kellogg administration and called for specific reforms—abolition of the useless offices, tax reduction, and elimination of monopolies. It also pledged support for the national Democratic party and sent a memorial to Congress condemning the Wheeler adjustment.[10]

The Republicans were forced on the defensive. Governor Kellogg, returning from a trip to the North seeking business for the state, found that his supporters were fearful that the conservatives were preparing to resort to violence. In East Feliciana Parish the Republican sheriff had been shot and a "reign of terror" was in effect. While the governor attempted to cope with this situation, violence also flared in East Baton Rouge, West Feliciana, and Natchitoches parishes. In this atmosphere the

8. *Senate Journal, Extra Session, 1875*, pp. 17, 22, 48, 49; *House Journal, Extra Session, 1875*, pp. 52–53, 56.

9. New Orleans *Daily Democrat*, December 21, 1875; E. Merton Coulter, *The South During Reconstruction, 1865–1877* (Baton Rouge: Louisiana State University, 1947), 353.

10. New Orleans *Daily Democrat*, January 5, 6, 7, 8, 14, 1876; Lonn, *Reconstruction*, 380–85.

Republicans met in caucus to plan their strategy.[11] Apparently the only commitment made was to continue to support the Kellogg administration.

When the legislative session convened on January 3, the outlook for action to improve the state's economic plight remained doubtful. With the House dominated by the conservatives and the Senate by the Republicans, the legislative process was almost stagnant. Republicans seemed to sense that their rule was nearing an end, and blacks had to watch almost helplessly as their power basis was eroded.

The House committee assignments were the most evident example of the decline of black influence. Their membership on standing committees was the smallest during the entire Reconstruction period. No committee had a black chairman; and no committee had a majority of black votes. Five committees—Judiciary, Public Education, Appropriations, Public Printing, and Contingent Expenses—had no black members. Although ten committees had memberships ranging from five to eleven members, these committees included only one black legislator. Two blacks served on the seven-man committees on Canal and Drainage, Penitentiary, and Claims; one black on the seven-man committees on Corporation, Banks and Banking, Railroads, Pensions, Health and Quarantine, and Registration; one black on the five-man committee on Public and Private Land Claims, and one on the nine-man Committee on Militia. Blacks were on other committees but were never a majority. Two of the six members on the Elections and Qualification Committee were blacks, as well as two of nine members on the Parochial Affairs Committee. The committees with the most blacks were the nine-member committees on Public Buildings and Charitable and Public Institutions, which had three blacks.[12]

In the Senate, blacks retained their positions on standing

11. Gonzales, "William Pitt Kellogg," 448–51; New Orleans *Republican*, January 8, 15, 20, 21, 22, 25, 28, 1876.

12. *House Journal, 1876*, pp. 33, 47.

committees. Their assignments equaled those held in the 1875 session. Twelve of the twenty-six standing committees were chaired by blacks; five of the twelve had a majority of black members. These included the committees on Militia (Detiege), Enrollment and Engrossment (Masicot), Libraries (Gla), Metropolitan Police (Dumont), and Elections (Allain). The other committees chaired by blacks but with a white majority in membership were: Claims (Stamps), Penitentiary (Burch), Charitable Institutions (Kelso), Parks and Public Buildings (Cage), Pensions (Blunt), Drainage, Canals and Navigation (Harper), and Elections and Registration (Landry). Although not chaired by blacks, the seven-member committees on Corporations and Parochial Affairs, and Public Education had black majorities. In fact every committee, except the Retrenchment and Reform Committee had black members; on this committee the black members assigned declined to serve giving no reason for their action. The seven-member committees on Apportionment and Banks and Banking consisted of three blacks and four whites. Other committee ratios varied in black membership: two of seven on the Judiciary Committee, one of seven on the Finance Committee, two of four on the Agricultural Committee, two of the six on the Committee on Printing, two of five on the Auditing and Supervising the Expenses of the Senate Committee; two of nine on the Public Lands and Levees Committee; two of seven on the Health and Quarantine Committee, and two of seven on the Committee on Railroads.[13]

Although the session was often racked by debates, several reform measures were passed. The appropriation bill was cut, and the contingent expenses were reduced to $175,000 and per diem.[14] The governor's salary was also limited to $6,000 per annum. Another effort was made to eliminate the functions of the tax collectors and to assign their duties to the sheriffs of the

13. *Senate Journal, 1876*, pp. 39–40; two blacks were also assigned to the seven-member Federal Relations Committee, but one declined. *Ibid.*, 40.

14. *House Journal, 1876*, 335; *Senate Journal, 1876*, pp. 235, 253.

parishes, who would have a fixed salary. Representative Sartain introduced a bill to effect this change, but it did not reappear from the Judiciary Committee.[15]

In attempting to secure relief for their districts blacks usually were frustrated. Senator David Young wanted a law allowing Concordia Parish to settle its funded debt by levying a tax; the Finance Committee never reported on the bill. Senator Detiege's proposal to restrict mortgage and tax privileges to property taxes received similar action from the Judiciary Committee. Senator Dumont sought a relief bill for the taxpayers of the city of New Orleans, which provided for the payment of one-third of the interest of the bonded debt of the city. The bill was calendared for a third reading but never reappeared.[16]

Legislation designed to alter the operation of local offices proved more successful. Representative Milon of Plaquemines Parish promoted an act that repealed a law of the previous session and authorized the police jury of the parish to issue bonds and provide for their redemption. In the Senate, Dumont guided the bill to passage. It eliminated the danger of a rising parish debt. Senator William Harper of Caddo wrote three bills to improve local government in his parish. The first act, incorporating the town of Greenwood, was introduced in mid-February and passed a week later. It provided that Greenwood was entitled to a town council composed of a mayor, two administrators, and a marshal; all were to be elected every two years at the general election. Harper's second act established a board to audit outstanding obligations against Caddo Parish. This responsibility was given to the president of the police jury, the mayor, and three appointed citizens. They were to audit all outstanding indebtedness occurring prior to January 1, 1876, and to pay the valid claims.[17] His third act was designed to reduce the expenses of the city government of Shreveport by lowering

15. *House Journal, 1876*, pp. 76, 78. Senators Young and Blunt thought the tax collector could be kept, but favored a reduction of the collector's salary, New Orleans *Republican*, February 9, 1876.

16. *Senate Journal, 1876*, pp. 61, 96, 213.

17. *Ibid.*, pp. 163, 164, 212, 214, 272; *House Journal, 1876*, pp. 169, 275; *Acts of*

the salaries of certain city officials; among them were the mayor, the city attorney, and the city physician. According to the act, the mayor was to receive a yearly salary of $600, and the city attorney and physician were limited to $300. Other legislators sought bills to satisfy their local constituencies. Senator Dumont urged a bill to provide a common council to administer the affairs of New Orleans. The bill easily passed the Senate but received only one reading in the House. Senator Allain's proposal to provide better security on street railroad cars in New Orleans by employing conductors was referred to the Railroad Committee. The bill would have required the roads to employ on each car one person to drive and another person to collect fares and would have limited the passenger load to twenty-five persons. The Railroad Committee took no action on the bill.[18]

Senator Kelso won passage of a bill of vital importance to his home parish of Rapides. In almost every session since 1868, Kelso had introduced a bill to provide for restoration of public records lost in the burning of the courthouse in Alexandria in May, 1864. Now at last he succeeded. His act provided that persons who wanted to establish deeds, mortgages, or judgments lost by the fire could do so by applying at the district judge's office in writing and describing the contents of the lost document.[19]

Blacks continued to promote acts providing for incorporation of benevolent societies and associations, towns, and corporations. Senator Harper introduced a measure incorporating the Hebrew Lion Congregation of Shreveport. Harper also offered bills to incorporate the Saint James Methodist Episcopal Church Association of Shreveport. Burch sought incorporation of the

---

1876, No. 59, p. 91, No. 69, pp. 110–11; Act No. 80, pp. 124–125. This act had been promoted by Senator Edward Butler in the 1874 session and had increased the parish debt. Nordhoff, *The Cotton States*, 51; *House Journal, 1876*, p. 332.

18. *Senate Journal, 1876*, pp. 53, 58, 203, 216–17, 236; *House Journal, 1876*, pp. 311, 320, 324; *Acts of 1876*, No. 83, pp. 28–29; Senators Burch and Stamps approved of the measure because it would help prevent accidents. New Orleans *Republican*, February 11, 17, 1876; The *Republican* was critical of the measure.

19. *Senate Journal, 1876*, 260, 268, 270; *House Journal, 1876*, 330; *Acts of 1876*, No. 82, pp. 126–28.

Catholic Mutual Benevolent Aid Association. Demas proposed charters for three societies in New Orleans—the Demoiselles Sinceres Mutual and Benevolent Association, the Saint Helene Benevolent and Mutual Aid Association and the L'Equate Benevolent and Mutual Aid Association. Senator Gla pushed for incorporation of the town of Lake Providence in East Carroll Parish, and Representative Murrell wished to incorporate the town of Delta in Madison Parish. Some of the proposals passed, but most of them failed. Somewhat more successful were black efforts to secure charters for corporations they favored. Senator Burch secured passage of an act to incorporate the Merchant's Exchange of New Orleans. Senator Young introduced a bill to incorporate the Vidalia and Lake Concordia Railway and Steamboat Company; the House referred the bill to the Corporation Committee and it never reappeared. Senator Cage steered to enactment a House bill incorporating the Protector Fire Company No. Two of Thibodaux.[20]

Internal improvements were still high on the black legislative programs. Senator Dumont was author an act authorizing the governor to appoint a roadmaster who was to collect tolls and establish tollgates on the road passing between New Orleans and the English Turn in Plaquemines Parish (right bank). Representative Milon secured House approval. The sponsors explained that the road would aid planters and other persons having business in New Orleans. Other blacks proposed measures to repair roads and streets in Pointe Coupee and in the city of New Orleans, and to clear bayous in Terrebonne and Ascension parishes and to improve False River. Construction of more public roads and bridges in West Baton Rouge Parish was a demand of Senator Allain, but the House refused to concur with him.[21]

20. *Senate Journal, 1876*, 42, 55, 73–74, 133, 143, 168–69, 195–96, 218, 224, 271; *House Journal, 1876*, pp. 32, 50, 77, 80, 113, 125, 129, 258, 265, 271, 297, 298, 331. The last two requests were indefinitely postponed.

21. *Senate Journal, 1876*, pp. 142–43, 147, 163, 203, 268; *House Journal, 1876*, pp. 106, 219, 228, 231, 236, 318, 326–27, 333.

An act to extend the limits of the Second Judicial District was of great interest to black legislators from Orleans Parish. Introduced by Senator Stamps, the measure sought, in addition to extending the limits, to fix the term of court, to provide clerks, and to alter the jurisdiction of the Sixth and Seventh Municipal districts. After passage in the Senate, the act passed the House on March 2 with no black opposition in a fifty-three to thirty vote. The governor signed the measure into law approximately two weeks later.[22]

Probably the most controversial bill of the session was the election law bill. Offered by conservatives in the House who were anxious to eliminate the Returning Board, the bill was designed to invest the responsibility of counting votes to the secretary of state. However, when the Republican-controlled Senate passed a substitute measure to maintain the five-man board (three appointed by the governor and two by the House), the conservatives immediately labeled the action as a violation of the Wheeler adjustment. The House refused to consent to the Senate amendment and sent the bill back to the Senate with this provision struck out. The issue was a stalemate, since neither side was willing to submit the issue to a conference committee, and the bill died.[23]

The election bill issue had placed a great strain on the adjustment, but open repudiation did not come until the Democrats attempted to impeach Governor Kellogg near the end of the session. The effort came after a seven-member House investigative committee claimed that the State Treasurer Dubuclet had stolen nearly $200,000. Moreover, the committee, dominated by Democrats, accused the governor of being more guilty than the treasurer and recommended the impeachment of both to the House. At the instigation of Democratic leaders, a resolution of

22. *Senate Journal, 1876*, pp. 212, 23, 270; *House Journal, 1876*, pp. 330, 332; *Acts of 1876*, No. 45, pp. 86–87.

23. New Orleans *Republican*, January 6, 23, 29, February 4, 19, 1876; New Orleans *Daily Democrat*, February 5, 9, 1876, for critical comments; *House Journal, 1876*, p. 224.

impeachment of Kellogg for "divers high crimes and misdemeanors in office" was adopted by sixty-one to forty-five
vote, with all the black members voting in the negative. Moving
quickly, the House committee presented the accusation to the
Senate, which became a court to receive the case. On the following day, however, the Senate adopted a resolution of acquittal,
claiming the House had failed to present specific charges. Then
the Senate adjourned *sine die* in an attempt to kill the movement.
Later, a committee exonerated Treasurer Dubuclet of any
wrongdoing.

On the next day the House presented specific charges against
Kellogg. The governor denied the charges in a message to the
(already adjourned) Senate, and the House, realizing that no
action against the governor was possible, had to content itself by
adopting a resolution declaring the Senate's action "partisan and
arbitrary" and referring the matter to the people.[24]

In the meantime, the governor issued a call for an extra
session of the Senate to meet immediately after the regular
session, from March 2 through 12. When the Senate met, the
Democratic senators attempted to declare the governor without
authority to call such a session, but the motion was ruled out of
order. Little was accomplished in the Senate session. The hiring
of additional sergeants-at-arms and the calling of frequent executive sessions were about the only business transacted. On the
last day the question of choosing a successor to Pinchback as
United States senator was briefly brought up, but no action was
taken.[25]

24. *House Journal, 1876*, pp. 307–308, 310–11, 324–25; *Senate Journal, 1876*, pp.
255–57, 280–81; see near the end of Senate *Journal* for proceedings, 289–95; Senator
Detiege was the only black to vote against the acquittal motion in the Senate, *Journal*,
257; New Orleans *Daily Democrat*, February 12, 16, March 1, 3, 1876; New Orleans
Republican, February 27, 29, March 1, 2, 3, 9, 1876; Gonzales, "Kellogg," 454–59; For
Treasurer Dubuclet, see Dunbar-Nelson, "People of Color in Louisiana," 76–77.

25. *Senate Journal, Extra Session, 1876*, pp. 283–87. Lieutenant Governor Antoine
received $160 salary as president of the Senate. See Certificate on p. 69, in The Honorable
C. C. Antoine Scrapbook; Lonn, *Reconstruction*, 398–99; New Orleans *Republican*,
March 7, 9, 1876; New Orleans *Daily Democrat*, March 8, 9, 1876.

The attempted impeachment was a prelude to the approaching election in 1876. The conservatives were determined to regain control of the state's government and to use whatever means were necessary for victory. In the parishes of East Feliciana and East Baton Rouge, they were resorting to open terror. Horrifying to Republicans was the murder of John Gair of East Feliciana a popular black former legislator. Resolutions were offered in the Senate to send a committee of five to investigate his death, but the measure failed to win approval. Letters were presented in both houses describing the self-styled "regulators," a militant white organization in these parishes, but these too failed to elicit action. Other terroristic incidents occurred in Coushatta where several Republicans were killed, and also in Ouachita Parish.[26]

The Democrats finally denied the charges of violence and claimed they were employing normal political activity. Organized early in the year, the Democratic campaign consisted of four phases: formation of clubs, registration of voters, mass meetings with speeches and barbecues, and acts of violence.[27]

Conventions were held by both factions in preparation for the November election. The Republicans met in New Orleans on May 30 and 31 to select delegates to the national convention. More blacks than whites were present, and the convention elected four men, two blacks and two whites: Pinchback, W. G. Brown, S. B. Packard, and Kellogg. Almost a month later the Republicans reconvened to nominate candidates for state offices. As in previous conventions, factionalism split the party. The factional lineup pitted the Kellogg-Packard group against a

26. *House Journal, 1876*, pp. 94–95, 110; *Senate Journal, 1876*, pp. 37, 45–46; New Orleans *Daily Picayune*, October 20, 21, 1874; *House Miscellaneous Documents*, 45th Cong., 3rd Sess., No. 31, pp. 3, 91, 93, 554–55; *House Miscellaneous Documents*, 44th Cong., 2nd Sess., No, 34, Pt. VI, pp. 113, 116, 278, 299; B. W. Marston to William P. Kellogg, May 1, 1875, in Kellogg Papers.

27. Fanny Z. Lovell Bone, "Louisiana in the Disputed Election of 1876," in *Louisiana Historical Quarterly*, XIV (October, 1931), 552; New Orleans *Daily Democrat*, January 5, 6, 14, September 3, 4, 28, 29, October 1–29, 1876, *passim*; Fayette Copeland, "The New Orleans Press and Reconstruction," *Louisiana Historical Quarterly*, XXX (January, 1947), 247–49.

Warmoth-Pinchback combination, the latter now having re-united.[28]

The proceedings of the convention were almost riotous, according to hostile accounts, but on the sixth day the body settled down to decide on a ticket headed by Marshal S. B. Packard for governor and Caesar C. Antoine for lieutenant governor. William G. Brown was nominated for superintendent of education, Emile Honoré for secretary of state, George B. Johnson for auditor, William Hunt for attorney general, and Pinchback was reelected chairman of the central committee.[29]

The Democrats convened on July 24 in Baton Rouge to nominate candidates. Their only serious division was over which of several candiates for governor could make the best race. On the third day the convention agreed on Francis T. Nicholls, a former Confederate general as the gubernatorial candidate. Louis A. Wiltz, who had aspired to top spot, was selected for lieutenant governor. The other candidates were N. H. Odgen for attorney general, W. E. Strong for secretary of state, A. Jumel for auditor, and R. M. Lusher for superintendent of education.[30]

The election passed off quietly, but as was becoming the pattern in Louisiana elections, the results were disputed, and both sides claimed victory. The governor moved quickly and attempted to invalidate the returns from five parishes[31] that had a Democratic majority because of violence. He claimed that "bulldozing" activities had prevented a fair election in these parishes. President Grant then urged several prominent Republicans to go to New Orleans to examine the counting. Not to be outdone, the National Democratic Committee asked several prominent Democrats to go also to New Orleans. In all, more than twenty Democrats came.

28. P. B. S. Pinchback to Henry C. Warmoth, May 6, 1876, in Warmoth Papers.

29. Lonn, *Reconstruction*, 401–408; New Orleans *Republican*, September 3, 1876; New Orleans *Daily Democrat*, September 23, 24, 28, 1876.

30. Lonn, *Reconstruction*, 408–11.

31. The Republican Returning Board excluded the parishes of East Baton Rouge, East and West Feliciana, Ouachita, and Morehouse.

Since these congressional members were sent as private citizens to witness the canvass, the actual canvass was performed by the Returning Board. Composed of Republican members, the board returned a verdict favorable to the Republican candidates. The members of the board included James M. Wells, a former governor; Thomas C. Anderson, a white legislator; Louis M. Kenner, a black barroom operator; and Gadane Cassanave, a black undertaker. The Democrats considered the board as corrupt and were extremely hostile toward it.[32]

The decision of the Returning Board was not final, however. The election of 1876 transcended local importance, since the national election was also in doubt. Along with Louisiana, the electoral votes from Florida and South Carolina were disputed. Three separate investigations of the Louisiana situation resulted. A resolution was adopted in both branches of Congress instructing the committees on elections to proceed to these three southern states to investigate the recent election. Conflicting reports were turned in by these agencies. Dominated by Republicans, the Senate Committee organized its headquarters in New Orleans and conducted its investigation without leaving the city; the majority report concluded that white terrorism against blacks had carried the state for the Democrats. The House committee, with a Democratic majority, reached a contrary conclusion; blacks had supported the Democrats because of discontent with the Republican administration's failure to deliver on promises of schools, jobs and political offices.[33]

In the statewide election both sides produced evidence of victory. The Democrats claimed that Samuel J. Tilden, their presidential candidate had defeated his Republican rival, Rutherford B. Hayes by a vote of 83,817 to 76,178. They further

32. *House Miscellaneous Documents*, 44th Cong., 2nd Sess., No. 34, Pt. VI, pp. 42, 85, 184, 227; Marguerite T. Leach, "The Aftermath of Reconstruction in Louisiana," *Louisiana Historical Quarterly*, XXXII (1949), 637–40. The vacancy caused by the resignation of one board member, Oscar Arroyo, was left unfilled.

33. Tunnell, "The Negro, the Republican Party, and the Election," 112–13; New Orleans *Daily Democrat*, September 24, 28, 1876.

contended that Nicholls had received 81,505 votes and Packard only 76,067, and that Nicholls had a majority in thirty-one of fifty-seven parishes. On the other hand, the Republicans claimed they had won. The Packard or Republican legislature certified the following returns as received from the secretary of state: for governor, Packard 74,624, Nicholls 71,198; for lieutenant governor Antoine 71,198 to L. A. Wiltz's 71,093.[34] Both sides inaugurated their gubernatorial candidates and established their legislature, and Louisiana again had dual governments.

The outcome was not going to be determined in Louisiana but in Washington, and the fate of the Republican government and therefore of Louisiana blacks rested with the national Republicans. It soon became evident that the national leaders were unwilling to support southern Republicans and blacks. They preferred to make sufficient concessions to southern Democrats to ensure the election of a Republican president. And so, the "bargain" of 1877 was struck, which secured the inauguration of Hayes. The Democrats were rewarded with "two cabinet posts, local control of southern states, appropriations for internal improvement and the passage of the Texas Pacific Railroad bill.[35]

The blueprint of this "bargain" had developed through the electoral commission, created by Congress, to pass on all disputed votes. The commission was composed of eight Republicans and seven Democrats and by a partisan vote of eight to seven it decided every disputed vote for Hayes. Congress accepted the final verdict of the agency on March 2. The Hayes administration completed the arrangements by withdrawing Federal troops on April 24, 1877. The Republican administration in Louisiana collapsed as the Democrats took control. Most of

34. Bone, "Disputed Election," *Louisiana Historical Quarterly*, XV (January, 1932), 114–15; (April, 1932), 234–36; Garnie W. McGinty, *Louisiana Redeemed: The Overthrow of Carpetbag Rule, 1876–1880* (New Orleans: Pelican Publishing Company, 1941), 86–94.

35. C. Vann Woodward, *Reunion and Reaction: The Compromise of 1877 and the End of Reconstruction* (Boston: Little, Brown and Co., 1951), 208.

the Republican legislators who had convened in the statehouse joined the Nicholls assembly, meeting in Odd Fellows Hall. Rewards for abandoning the Packard legislature amounting to $250,000 were liberally extended by the notorious Louisiana Lottery Company.[36]

By 1877 the national Republican party had abandoned southern blacks. It no longer needed their votes to sustain its power. Not only were the blacks left without national support, but many of their leaders had been driven from politics by intimidation or despair. Senator George Y. Kelso of Rapides was forced to flee to Arkansas. East Feliciana's John Gair had been killed. In Natchitoches Parish, Raiford Blunt, Henry Raby, and John Lewis, received constant threats of violence and had to cease their political activity. Senator William Harper of Caddo returned to his grocery business. Curtis Pollard, former senator from Madison Parish, left the state in 1879. J. Henri Burch was forced out of East Baton Rouge by regulators. T. B. Stamps of Jefferson Parish departed the legislature in 1876 to devote full time to his business. One black legislator, Robert Poindexter of Assumption, joined the Democrats. He had become disenchanted with the Republicans because of their failure to establish enough public schools.[37] Senator Jacques Gla of East Carroll Parish also joined the Democrats, charging Republicans with "betrayal of the confidence" blacks had placed in them. Although some blacks remained in the Republican party and in politics, the majority realized that an era was coming to an end.

36. Alwes, "The History of the Louisiana State Lottery Company," 997–98.

37. Rayford W. Logan, *The Betrayal of the Negro: From Rutherford B. Hayes to Woodrow Wilson* (London: Collier-MacMillan, Ltd., 1969), 23–47; Stanley P. Hirshson, *Farewell to the Bloody Shirt: Northern Republicans and Southern Negroes, 1877–1893* (Chicago: Quadrangle Books, Inc., 1968), 29–31; *Senate Reports*, 42nd Cong., 3rd Sess., No. 457, p. 778; "Condition of the South," *House Reports*, 43rd Cong., 2nd Sess., No. 101, Pt. II, p. 45; Allie B. Webb, "A History of Negro Voting in Louisiana, 1877–1906," (Ph.D. dissertation, Louisiana State University, 1962), 43–48; *Senate Reports*, 45th Cong., 3rd Sess., No. 855, pp. 24–26; New Orleans *Daily Democrat*, September 28, October 2, 8, 25, 1876; New Orleans *Republican*, October 19, 20, 1876.

The black newspaper, the *Weekly Louisianian*, summed up the feeling of the race: "Politics as a paying investment has had its day, and we must now look for other avenues and pursuits to build up our fortunes, and to recover in a measure the ground lost in its avocation."[38]

38. Carroll *Conservative*, November 30, 1878; New Orleans *Weekly Louisianian*, September 20, 1879.

Summing up

The Reconstruction era, to a greater degree than most periods in our history, is encrusted with myth that has survived by oral tradition and has been perpetuated in print. A staple item in the myth is that blacks were in the majority in many if not all of the legislatures of the South. Recent research reveals that such was not the case. Only in one state, South Carolina, did blacks have control, and this was for a short time in only one house of the legislature. In other states, including those where they formed a majority of the population, blacks were a minority in the legislature. They were a minority in Louisiana, where the black population slightly outnumbered the white. According to the 1870 United States Census, blacks were a majority in thirty-three of the fifty-three parishes (62 percent) in Louisiana, and were 50.1 percent of the total population.[1] Unlike Mississippi, where, according to Vernon L. Wharton, few black leaders emerged from the free black class, Louisiana's free blacks provided active leadership. Delegates, and later legislators, came from vari-

---

1. The 1860 census shows that thirty-three out of the forty-eight parishes (69 percent) had a black majority. Statewide blacks comprised 49.5 percent. By 1880 the black population majority had increased: thirty-six out of the fifty-eight parishes (62 percent) had a black majority, and statewide, blacks were 51.5 percent of the total population. *Compendium of the Tenth Census* (June 1, 1880) (Washington: Government Printing Office, 1883), Part I, 352–53; Registration figures are more difficult to obtain. The state registrar report indicates, however, that 99,047 blacks and 88,179 whites were registered in 1872; two years later the figures were 90,781 blacks and 76,823 whites. See *Louisiana Legislative Documents* (New Orleans: Republican Office, 1875), table No. 4.

ous occupations—teachers, mercantile class, Union army officers, the ministry, and Freedmen's Bureau agents—similar to the black leadership in South Carolina.[2] During the entire span between 1868 and 1877 in Louisiana only ninety-nine black representatives and twenty-four black senators can be identified. In the post-Reconstruction years, nine blacks served as senators and twenty-one as Representatives. The last black senator left office in 1890 and the last black representatives in 1900.

Again, contrary to the myth, blacks in Louisiana did not win many nonlegislative offices. No black was nominated by the entire Republican party for governor or held that office, although Pinchback claimed it on an acting basis. Two blacks were elected lieutenant governor, and one, Pinchback, succeeded to the position. One black was secretary of state, one was superintendent of education, and one was state treasurer. Nor did Louisiana blacks win elections to the national offices that their voting strength in the Republican party might have won for them. Only one black was selected for the Senate, Pinchback, and he was not admitted. Two blacks claimed seats in the House of Representatives, but only one, Charles E. Nash, was seated, and he served for only one term.

Blacks might have fared better in securing local offices, especially in areas where they outnumbered whites. But even in these localities blacks received few rewards. The writer found but nineteen black sheriffs elected during Reconstruction, 1868–1877, and two black deputy sheriffs. Seventeen of the nineteen sheriffs served for only one term. Two of the seventeen were criminal sheriffs for Orleans Parish, which had criminal and civil officers. Four other blacks were elected sheriff after 1876.

2. Vernon L. Wharton, *The Negro in Mississippi, 1865–1890* (Chapel Hill: University of North Carolina Press, 1947), 172–73; an older study on Mississippi by James W. Garner, *Reconstruction in Mississippi* (New York: Macmillan Company, 1901), 269–70, asserts that many black legislators were former slaves; an excellent study of South Carolina is Thomas Holt, "The Emergence of Negro Political Leadership in South Carolina During Reconstruction" (Ph.D dissertation, Yale University, 1973), 119.

Some of the black sheriffs became legislators either before or after their term as sheriff. These included Representative Frederick Marie of Lafourche (1868–1870), Representative John DeLacy of Rapides (appointed 1868–1870 and elected 1872–1874), Senator George Hamlet of Ouachita (1874–1876), Representative W. H. Keyes of Terrebonne (1870–1872), Representative Emile Honoré of Pointe Coupee (1870–1872), Representative Robert R. Ray of East Feliciana (1872–1874), Representative Robert J. Taylor of West Feliciana (1872–1874), and Senator Jules A. Masicot of Orleans Parish (1868–1870). Three legislators served as sheriff after Reconstruction —Senator Thomas Cage of Terrebonne (1880–1882), Representative Jordan Stewart of Terrebonne (1876–1878), and Representative Cain Sartain of East Carroll. The other blacks who were elected sheriffs during Reconstruction were Amos Sims of Terrebonne (1873–1876), Charles Sauvinet of Orleans Parish (1870–1872), James Franklin (1872–1874) and Oren Steward (1874–1876) of Concordia Parish, H. W. Peck of Madison (1874–1876), and John Webre of St. John (1874–1896). One sheriff of Avoyelles cannot be identified. E. A. Verrett of Iberville was elected sheriff in 1868 but served only until 1869 when he was removed for alleged financial irregularities; another sheriff, Gustave LeBlanc of East Baton Rouge was elected in 1874 but was forced to resign in early 1876.

Other local offices went to blacks sparingly. Thirteen blacks served as parish tax collectors, twelve as parish recorders, twelve as parish assessors, and thirteen as parish coroners. Most of these men held their offices for only one term. Two blacks served as parish judge, J. S. Dula of West Feliciana, and Gustave Dupart of St. Tammany, and only four blacks were elected as mayors—Pierre Landry in Donaldsonville, Israel Jones and M. L. LeBlanc, both of Mandeville, and Gilbert Harrison in Carrollton. Harrison was apparently used to win black votes and later resigned to permit a white man to hold the office. The only local offices in which a large number of blacks were found were those of justice of the peace, constable, and police juror.[3]

Blacks in legislative and other positions have received a low rating in most of the historical accounts of the period. Especially in the older works were the judgments and evaluations of black performance negative, and when not negative, patronizing. Thus a popular view of black legislators is that they held hostile feelings toward whites and wanted to punish them. Actually, the contrary is closer to the truth. Blacks did not attempt to enact vindictive laws designed to deny whites certain privileges. Former Governor Warmoth, who was not always a friend to blacks, stated that there was "great affection" for their former masters.[4] As early as the constitutional convention blacks voiced opposition to the stringent disfranchisement clause and were among the most ardent supporters of the constitutional amendment to repeal the provision. Blacks worked constantly to secure universal education and improved educational facilities, including those for whites. Most were willing to forego enforcement of the integration clause in the constitution if schools were established in black communities. They demanded civil rights laws, but usually they were satisfied to secure the laws and only sparingly attempted to integrate hotels, taverns, or railroads. They asked for laws to protect laborers and plantation workers, but on this issue they won few concessions. Their principal victory was an act that merely proclaimed the workers' right to vote and prohibited planters from interfering with the exercise of the franchise. Blacks who attempted to effect more fundamental reforms met reversals, since on these issues white Republicans deserted their black allies. Black legislators made no serious effort to secure confiscation of land but did try to help blacks purchase land with the constitutional stipulation of the amount of the land purchases. In fact, black legislators eventually consented to the lien crop system, perhaps because they thought

3. Compiled from newspapers, various government reports, and Record of Commissions of the Governors.

4. Warmoth, *War, Politics and Reconstruction*, 266.

this was the only means of obtaining supplies for laborers; perhaps because they innocently believed that white and black planters would treat black workers humanely.

Other demands of blacks were for legislation that later generations would call social welfare and reflected the fact that the legislators represented the poor and unfortunate. Some of their proposals were "modern"; that is, they anticipated future legislators. Blacks also grasped another modern concept, namely that the state could stimulate the economy by extending its credit to corporate interests. Penitentiary reforms and kinder treatment of convicts were not considered important at first, but finally the improvement of prison conditions became the special project of several legislators. Many internal improvement schemes, which would later prove both unprofitable and profitable, were championed by blacks; the readiness of blacks to grant monopolies and underwrite bonds was in many instances exploited by unscrupulous companies operating in the state and led to much of the extravagance that has attracted the attention of the historian of this inflationary period. The vast majority of programs offered and supported by blacks were necessarily expensive. An expanded public school system, social welfare services, enlarged charitable institutions, and other projects cost money. But these projects were legitimate.

Another frequently voiced opinion was that the vast majority of them were ignorant former field hands who had no education or political experience and hence were unfit to particiapte in the democratic process. It is also held that most of them owned little or no property and were contemptuous of property rights. Again, these conclusions are wrong. The writer has been able to established the following facts about the twenty-four black Louisiana senators who served during Reconstruction and the nine who served in the post-Reconstruction period: (1) All of the senators had some educational advantages—five were self-educated former slaves and three were educated abroad. (2) Seven had had military careers and had been officers in the

Union army. (3) Over 25 percent, or nine, of them owned their businesses—including three who had thriving newspapers. (4) Two were schoolteachers. (5) Ten were engaged in farming, and six of these could be considered planters. (6) Eight had served in the House before moving to the Senate, and two were elected to the House both before and after their senatorial tenure. (7) Eight of the men had also served as delegates to the Constitutional Convention of 1868. Additional facts reveal that eight of the senators came from Orleans Parish or the immediate area, that only five were not native-born Louisianians, that only two were publicly charged with fraud, and that no one of them was totally illiterate. In the House, representatives had received some education, were property holders, and had served in many local positions before their tenure in the lower chamber. Forty-eight can be identified as free, only fifteen can be indentified as slaves, and fourteen—counting slaves and free blacks—were found not to be native Louisianians.

It is at last possible to establish accurately the number of blacks serving in the Louisiana legislature. They were, as has been indicated, always a minority. Their largest membership in the Senate was slightly over 40 percent of the total, but this was for a brief period in 1874 before the Wheeler adjustment went into effect; their average membership in the upper house averaged one-third of the total. The percentage of blacks in the House was never over one-third of the total. The largest number of blacks was present in the 1870–1872 session when 37 members out of 120 were blacks. The turnover of black House members as well as white House members was far greater than that of senators; more than one-half served only one term.

Black legislators wrote a significant chapter in Reconstruction and American history. They accomplished some important gains for their race and, it can be said without exaggeration, some gains for the Democratic concept. They appear to have placed the Republican party first and race second. If they failed to achieve all their goals, and they did fail on many fronts, it was not always because of their ineptitude or ignorance. They failed essentially because they could not surmount the opposition of white racism and the somewhat costly extravagance accompanying many legislative acts. But in failing they pointed the way to the future.

Appendix A

BLACK LEADERS IN THE CONSTITUTIONAL CONVENTION OF 1867–1868

DELEGATES	PARISHES
C. C. Antoine	Caddo
Arnold Bertonneau	3rd District Orleans
O. C. Blandin	2nd District Orleans
Emile Bonnefroi	West Baton Rouge
Crane Bonseigneur	1st District Orleans
William Brown	Iberville
Dennis Burrell	St. John the Baptist
William Butler	Livingston (Washington?) St. Helena (St. Tammany?)
R. I. Cromwell	2nd District Orleans
Samuel E. Cuney	Rapides
P. G. Deslonde	Iberville
Auguste Donato, Jr.	St. Landry
Ulgar Dupart	Terrebonne
Gustave Duparte	Washington (St. Helena?)
J. B. Esnard	St. Mary
Louis François	East Baton Rouge
John Gair	East Feliciana
R. G. Gardner	Jefferson
Leopold Guichard	Plaquemines (St. Bernard?)
J. H. Ingraham	Caddo
Robert H. Isabelle	1st District Orleans

DELEGATES	PARISHES
Thomas Isabelle	1st District Orleans
George Y. Kelso	Rapides
Victor M. Lange	East Baton Rouge
Charles Leroy	Natchitoches
J. B? Lewis	DeSoto
Richard Lewis	East Feliciana or West Feliciana?
Theophile Mahier	West Baton Rouge
Frederick Marie	Terrebonne
Thomas M. Martin	Jefferson
Jules A. Masicot	3rd District Orleans
William R. Meadows	Clairborne
Milton Morris	Ascension
Solomon R. Moses	1st District Orleans
William Murrell	Lafourche
Joseph C. Oliver	St. James
John Pierce	Bossier
P. B. S. Pinchback	2nd District Orleans
Robert Poindexter	Assumption
Curtis Pollard	Madison
Fortune Riard	Lafayette
D. D. Riggs	St. Tammany
J. H. A. Roberts	Jefferson
L. A. Rodriguez	1st District Orleans
Sothene L. Snaer	St. Martin
C. A. Thibaut	St. Bernard (or Plaquemines?)
P. F. Valfroit	Ascension
Henderson Williams	Madison and Franklin
David Wilson	1st District Orleans

Appendix B

BLACK MEMBERS OF THE 1868–1870 HOUSE OF REPRESENTATIVES,

NAMES	PARISHES (District)	DATES
Curron J. Adolphe	Orleans (7th)	1868–70–72
Frank Alexander	Orleans (Right Bank)	1868–70
F. C. Antoine	Orleans (3rd)	1868–70–72
*Dennis Burrell	St. John the Baptist	1868–70
*Samuel F. Cuney	Rapides	1868–70
*P. G. Deslonde	Iberville	1868–70
Noah Douglas	St. Landry	October 8, 1868–70
*Ulgar Dupart	Terrebonne	1868–70
*J. B. Esnard	St. Mary	1868–70
*John Gair	East Feliciana	1868–70; 1872–74
Charles Gray	St. James	1868–70
*Jerry Hall	Orleans	1868–70
Gloster Hill	Ascension	1868–70
Emile Honoré	Pointe Coupee	1868–70
Stephen Humphreys	DeSoto	1868–70–72
*Robert H. Isabelle	Orleans (3rd)	1868–70
Robert Lange	East Baton Rouge	1868–70
*Victor M. Lange	East Baton Rouge	1868–70
*Charles Leroy	Natchitoches	1868–70
Harry Lott	Rapides	1868–70–72
*Theophile Mahier	West Baton Rouge	1868–70
Joseph Mansion	Orleans (5th)	1868–70

NAMES	PARISHES (District)	DATES
*Milton Morris	Ascension	1868–70–72
*William Murrell	Lafourche	1868–70; 1872–74
*John Pierce	Bossier	1868–70
M. Raymond	Jefferson	1868–70
William Smith	Pointe Coupee	1868 (Died Oct. 5, 1868)
Moses Sterrett	Caddo	1868–70
Robert Taylor	West Feliciana	1868–70
H. C. Tournier	Pointe Coupee	1868–70–72
George Washington	Assumption	1868–70–72
*Henderson Williams	Madison	1868–70–72
W. C. Williams	East Feliciana	1868–70
Adolphe Tureaud	St. James	1868–70–72–74
David Young	Concordia	1868–70–72–74

*Served in the Constitutional Convention

Appendix C

BLACK MEMBERS OF THE 1870–1872
HOUSE OF REPRESENTATIVES

Names	Parishes (District)	Dates
Curron J. Adolphe	Orleans (7th)	1868–70–72
F. C. Antoine	Orleans (3rd)	1868–70–72
W. E. Barrett	Orleans (3rd)	1870–72
Armand Belot	Orleans (5th)	1870–72
Raiford Blunt	Natchitoches	1870–72
Ben Buchanan	Orleans (Algiers)	1870–Feb. 27, 1871
J. Henri Burch	East Baton Rouge	1870–72
William Crawford	Rapides	1870–72–74, April 15, 1875
Prosper Darinsburg	Pointe Coupee	1870–72
Edgar Davis	Orleans (5th)	1870–72
Henry Demas	St. John the Baptist	1870–72–74
R. G. Gardner	Jefferson	1870–72
William Harper	Caddo	1870–72
Stephen Humphreys	DeSoto	1868–70–72
R. J. M. Kenner	Orleans	1870–72
Harry Lott	Rapides	1868–70–72
Joseph Lott	Rapides	1870–72
Harry Mahoney	Plaquemines	1870–72
Eugene V. Macarty	Orleans (6th)	1870–72
John J. Moore	St. Mary	1870–72
E. C. Morphy	Orleans (5th)	1870–72
Milton Morris	Ascension	1868–70–72

NAMES	PARISHES (District)	DATES
Thomas Murray	Orleans (2nd)	1870–72
John Nelson	Lafourche	1870–72
Anthony Overton	Ouachita	1870–72
J. W. Quinn	Orleans (3rd)	1870–72
Charles W. Ringgold	Orleans (4th)	1870–72
Cain Sartain	Carroll	1870–72–74–76
T. B. Stamps	Jefferson	1870–72
H. C. Tournier	Pointe Coupee	1868–70–72
Adolphe Tureaud	St. James	1868–70–72
George Washington	Concordia	1870–72
George Washington	Assumption	1868–70–72
Henderson Williams	Madison	1868–70–72
Joshau Wilson	East Baton Rouge	1870–72–74
David Young	Concordia	1868–70–72–74

Appendix D

BLACK MEMBERS OF THE 1872–1874
HOUSE OF REPRESENTATIVES

NAMES	PARISHES (District)	DATES
Theophile T. Allain	West Baton Rouge	1872–74
Arthur Antoine	St. Mary	1872–74
J. W. Armistead	West Feliciana	1872–74
Thornton Butler	Orleans (4th)	(Jan. 22,1874)–76
Joseph Connaughton	Rapides	1872–74–April 14, 1875
Aristide Dejoie	Orleans	1872–74
Henry Demas	St. John The Baptist	1870–72–74
George Devezin	Orleans	1870–72–74
Andrew Dumont	Orleans	1872–74
John Gair	East Feliciana	1868–70; 1872–74
R. F. Guichard	St. Bernard	1872–74
E. C. Hill	Ouachita	1872–74–76
Milton Jones	Pointe Coupee	1872–74–76
W. H. Keyes	Terrebonne	1872–74
Pierre Landry	Ascension	1872–74
James Lawes	East Feliciana	1872–74
Harry Mahoney	Plaquemines	1870–72–74
Frederick Marie	Terrebonne	1872–74–April 15, 1875
L. A. Martinet	St. Martin	1872–74
Milton Morris	Ascension	1868–70; 1872–74
William Murrell	Lafourche	1868–70; 1872–74
William Murrell, Jr.	Madison	1872–74–76

NAMES	PARISHES (District)	DATES
George Paris	Orleans	1872–74
Henry Raby	Natchitoches	1872–74–76
Victor Rochon	St. Martin	1872–74–April 20, 1875
L. A. Rodriguez	Orleans	1872–74
Cain Sartain	Carroll	1870–72–74–76
Richard Simms	St. Landry	1872–74
L. A. Snead	Iberia	1872–74
J. Ross Stewart	Tensas	1872–74
Issac Sutton	St. Mary	1872–74
Adolphe Tureaud	St. James	1870–72–74
William Ward	Grant	1872–74
George Washington	Concordia	1870–72–74
John Wiggins	DeSoto	1872–Jan. 9, 1874
Augustus Williams	East Baton Rouge	1872–74
Joshua Wilson	East Baton Rouge	1870–72–74
David Young	Concordia	1870–72–74

Appendix E

BLACK MEMBERS OF THE 1874–1876 HOUSE OF REPRESENTATIVES

NAMES	PARISHES (District)	DATES
J. W. Armistead	West Feliciana	1872–74–76
Thornton Butler	Orleans	1872–74–76
Joseph Connaughton	Rapides	1872–74–April 14, 1875
William Crawford	Rapides	1870–72–74–April 15, 1875
J. S. Davidson	Iberville	1874–76
William J. DeLacy	Rapides	1874–April 15, 1875
Henry Demas	St. John the Baptist	1870–72–74–76
Vincent Dickerson	St. James	1874–76
R. F. Guichard	St. Bernard	1872–74–76
E. C. Hill	Ouachita	1872–74–76
Gloster Hill	Ascension	1868–70; 1874–76
Emile Honoré	Pointe Coupee	1868–70; 1874–76
J. J. Johnson	DeSoto	1874–April 15, 1875
Milton Jones	Pointe Coupee	1868–70; 1874–76
J. B. Jourdain	Orleans (7th)	1874–76
W. H. Keyes	Terrebonne	1872–74–76
Frederick Marie	Terrebonne	1872–74–April 15, 1875
L. A. Martinet	St. Martin	1874–76–April 20, 1875
Alfred Etienne Milon	Plaquemines	1874–76
William Murrell, Jr.	Madison	1872–74–76
Robert Poindexter	Assumption	1874–April 15, 1875

NAMES	PARISHES (District)	DATES
Henry Raby	Natchitoches	1872–74–76
Robert R. Ray	East Feliciana	1874–1876
Victor Rochon	St. Martin	1872–74–April 20, 1875
Cain Sartain	Carroll	1870–72–74–76
L. A. Snaer	Iberia	1872–74–76
J. Ross Stewart	Tensas	1872–74–76
Issac Sutton	St. Mary	1872–74–76
F. R. Wright	Terrebonne	1874–April 15, 1875

Appendix F

NAMES	PARISHES (District)	DATES
Edward Butler	Plaquemines (1st)	1870–72–74
Thomas Cage	Terrebonne (9th)	1872–74–76
Emile Detiege	St. Martin (11th)	(January, 1874)–76
William Harper	Caddo (20th)	1872–74–76
James H. Ingraham	Orleans (3rd)	1870–72–74
George Y. Kelso	Rapides (23rd)	1868–70–72–74
Jules A. Masicot	Orleans (5th)	1872–74–76
Curtis Pollard	Carroll (25th)	1868–70; 1872–74
T. B. Stamps	Jefferson (7th)	1872–74–76

*Served in the Constitutional Convention

Appendix G

BLACK MEMBERS OF THE SENATE OF LOUISIANA, 1874–1876

NAMES	PARISHES (District)	DATES
Theophile T. Allain	West Baton Rouge (14th)	1874–76–78
Raiford Blunt	Natchitoches (19th)	1872–74–76
J. Henri Burch	East Baton Rouge (16th)	1872–74–76
Thomas Cage	Terrebonne (9th)	1872–74–76
Oscar Crozier	Lafourche (9th)	1874–April 18, 1875
Emile Detiege	St. Martin (11th)	(January, 1874–76)
Andrew Dumont	Orleans (Algiers, 6th)	1874–76–78
Jacques Gla	East Carroll (25th)	1874–80
William Harper	Caddo (20th)	1872–74–76
George Y. Kelso	Rapides (18th)	1868–70–72–74–76
Pierre Landry	Ascension (8th)	1874–76–78
Jules A. Masicot	Orleans (5th?)	1872–74–76
Curtis Pollard	East Carroll (25th)	1868–70; 1872–72–76
T. B. Stamps	Jefferson (7th)	1872–74–76
David Young	Concordia (26th)	1874–76–78–80

Bibliography

PRIMARY SOURCES
Manuscripts

DEPARTMENT OF ARCHIVES OF THE LOUISIANA STATE
UNIVERSITY LIBRARY, BATON ROUGE
John P. Breda Papers, 1867–76.
John R. Ficklen Papers, 1840–77.
Benjamin F. Flanders Papers, 1862–65.
Walter L. Fleming Collection, 1867–76.
William Pitt Kellogg Papers, 1869–84.
James G. Taliaferro and Family Papers, 1867–75.

SOUTHERN HISTORICAL COLLECTION, UNIVERSITY OF NORTH
CAROLINA, CHAPEL HILL
Henry Clay Warmoth Papers, 1864–1889.

LIBRARY OF CONGRESS
Nathaniel P. Banks Papers.

NATIONAL ARCHIVES
Carded Military Service Records for U.S. Colored Troops. Records of
the Adjutant General's Office, Civil War. Record Group 94.
Civil War Pension Files, Records of the Veterans Administration.
Record Group 15.
Records of Custom House Nominations: Louisiana. New Orleans,
Bureau of Customs, 1866–77. Record Group 56.

Records of the New Orleans Branch and Shreveport Branch, Freedman's Savings and Trust Company. Record Group 101.

MISCELLANEOUS MANUSCRIPTS

Antoine, C. C., The Honorable, Scrapbook, 1836–1921, Black Heritage Room, Southern University Library, Baton Rouge.

"Appeal in behalf of the Colored People of N[ew] O[rleans] and Offering Their Services," January 20, 1861 (copy from Rebel Archives, War Department Records, National Archives). State Archives and Records Center, Baton Rouge.

Louisiana Files, The American Missionary Association Archives, 1869–1876. Amisted Research Center, Dillard University, New Orleans.

P. B. S. Pinchback Papers, 1874. Archives of Negro History, Claver Building, New Orleans.

P. B. S. Pinchback Papers, 1882–1923. Department of Archives and Rare Books, Howard-Tilton Memorial Library, Tulane University, New Orleans.

P. B. S. Pinchback Papers. Manuscript Division, Moorland-Spingarn Research Center, Howard University, Washington, D.C.

Wills and Succession Papers, 1893–1895. Orleans Parish Court House, New Orleans.

―――. Caddo Parish Courthouse, Shreveport.

Register of Taxes, Orleans Parish, 1870, 1871, 1880. City Archives, New Orleans Public Library.

State of Louisiana. *Record of Commissions, 1868, 1868–74, 1872–76*. State Archives and Records, Baton Rouge.

Tax Assessment Rolls, East Baton Rouge Parish, 1872–1880. Office of Clerk of Court, East Baton Rouge Parish Courthouse Annex, Baton Rouge.

Tax Assessment Rolls, Iberville Parish, 1868–1890, Office of the Clerk of Courts, Plaquemine.

Tax Assessment Rolls, West Baton Rouge Parish, 1860–1878. Office of the Clerk of Courts, Port Allen.

Tax Ledgers, Orleans Parish, 1870, 1880, City Archives, New Orleans Public Library.

United States Census Reports, Ninth (1870).

Official Documents and Publications

FEDERAL

House Executive Documents. 39th Congress, 2nd Session, No. 68.
_____. 42nd Congress, 2nd Session, No. 20.
_____. 42nd Congress, 3rd Session, No. 91.
House Miscellaneous Documents. 41st Congress, 2nd Session, No. 154, Part I; Part II.
_____. 42nd Congress, 2nd Session, No. 211.
_____. 43rd Congress, 2nd Session, No. 21.
_____. 44th Congress, 2nd Session, No. 34, Part I; Part III; Part V; Part VI.
_____. 45th Congress, 3rd Session, No. 31.
House Reports. 43rd Congress, 2nd Session, No. 101, Part II.
_____. 43rd Congress, 2nd Session, No. 261.
Senate Documents. 40th Congress, 1st Session, No. 14.
_____. 44th Congress, 2nd Session, No. 2.
Senate Miscellaneous Documents. 44th Congress, 2nd Session, No. 14.
Senate Reports. 42nd Congress, 34th Session, No. 457.
_____. 45th Congress, 1st–2nd Session, No. 693, Part I; Part II; Part III.
_____. 46th Congress, 2nd Session, No. 388.
Compendium of the Tenth Census (June 1, 1880). Pt. I (Washington: Government Printing Office, 1883).
The War of the Rebellion: A Compilation of the Official Records of the Union and Confederate Armies. Washington: Government Printing Office, 1880–1901.

STATE

Acts Passed by the General Assembly of the State of Louisiana (1868–1870). New Orleans: A. L. Lee, State Printer, 1868–1870.
Acts Passed by the General Assembly of the State of Louisiana (1871–1876). New Orleans: Republican Office, New Orleans, 1871–76.
Civil Code of the State of Louisiana with Statutory Amendments from

1825 to 1866 Inclusive and Reference to the Decisions of the 17th Volume of the Annual Reports, Inclusive, with an Exhaustive Index. New Orleans: B. Bloomfield, and Co., 1867.

Constitution of the State of Louisiana with Amendments. New Orleans: Republican Office, 1875.

Debates of the Senate of the State of Louisiana (1870). New Orleans: A. L. Lee, State Printer, 1870.

Debates of the House of Representatives of the State of Louisiana. (1869–1871). New Orleans: A. L. Lee, State Printer, 1869–71.

Legislative Documents 1871. New Orleans: A. L. Lee, State Printer, 1871.

Louisiana Civil Code: Revision of 1870, Edited with Annotation. Indianapolis: Bobbs-Merrill Co., 1932.

Official Journal of the Proceedings of the Convention for Framing a Constitution for the State of Louisiana (1867–1868). New Orleans, 1868.

Official Journal of the Proceedings of the House of Representatives of the State of Louisiana (1868–1871). New Orleans: A. L. Lee, State Printer, 1868–71.

Official Journal of the Proceedings of the House of Representatives of the State of Louisiana (1872–1876). New Orleans: Republican Office, 1872–76 *(1890,* Baton Rouge).

Official Journal of the Proceedings of the Senate of the State of Louisiana (1869–1871). New Orleans: A. L. Lee, State Printer, 1869–71.

Official Journal of the Proceedings of the Senate of the State of Louisiana (1871–1876). New Orleans: Republican Office, 1871–76. *(1884,* Baton Rouge).

Memoirs, Published Correspondence, or Proceedings and Travel Accounts

Basler, Roy P. ed. *The Collected Works of Abraham Lincoln.* 9 vols. New Brunswick, N.J.: Rutgers University Press, 1953.

Brown, Williams Wells. *The Black Man: His Antecedents, His Genius, and His Achievements.* Savannah: James Symns & Co., 1863

Desdunes, Rodolphe L. *Our People and Our History.* Translated and edited by Sister Dorothea Olga McCants. Baton Rouge: Louisiana State University Press, 1973.

Hepworth, George H. *The Whip, Hoe and Sword; or, The Gulf Department in '63*. Boston: Walker, Wise and Co., 1864.

Nordhoff, Charles. *The Cotton States in the Spring and Summer of 1875*. New York: D. Appleton and Co., 1875.

Personal Memoirs of P. H. Sheridan, General United States Army. 2 Vols. New York: Charles L. Webster and Co., 1888.

Private and Official Correspondence of General Benjamin F. Butler, During the Period of the Civil War, 5 Vols. Norwood, Mass.: The Plimpton Press, 1917.

Proceedings of M.W. Eureka Grand Lodge A.F. & A.M. for Louisiana, 1894 –1922. New Orleans: Paragon Book Print, 1894–22.

Reed, Emily H. *Life of A. P. Dostie: Or the Conflict in New Orleans*. New York: Wm. P. Tomlinson, 1868.

Warmoth, Henry Clay. *War, Politics and Reconstruction: Stormy Days in Louisiana*. New York: Macmillan Co., 1930.

Wilson, Joseph. *Black Phalanx: A History of Negro Soldiers of the United States in Wars of 1775 –1812, 1861 –65*. Hartford: American Publishing Co., 1888.

Wright, Howard C. *Port Hudson: Its History from an Interior Point of View*. St. Francisville, 1863.

City Directories

Edwards' Annual Director of the Inhabitants, Institutions, Incorporated Companies, Manufacturing, Business, Business Firms, etc., etc., in the City of New Orleans for 1870 (St. Louis and New York: Southern Publishing Co., 1870).

Gardner's New Orleans Directory, 1866. New Orleans, 1866.

Gardner's New Orleans Directory, 1867. New Orleans, 1867.

Gardner's and Wharton's New Orleans Directory for the Year 1858: Embracing the City Records, a General Directory of the Citizens and a Business and Firm Directory. New Orleans, 1858.

Gardner's and Wharton's New Orleans Directory for the Year 1866: Embracing the City Records, a General Directory of the Citizens and a Business and Firm Directory. New Orleans, 1866.

Other Primary Sources

Appleton's *Biographical Encyclopedia*. New York: D. Appleton Co., 1889.
"Louisiana." *The American Annual Cyclopedia and Register of Important Events of the Year 1863*. New York: Appleton and Co., 1865.
"Louisiana." *The American Annual Cyclopedia and Register of Important Events of the Year 1864*. New York: Appleton and Co., 1866.
"Louisiana." *The American Annual Cyclopedia and Register of Important Events of the Year 1865*. New York: Appleton and Co., 1866.
"Louisiana." *The American Annual Cyclopedia and Register of Important Events of the Year, 1866*. New York: Appleton and Co., 1867.
31 *Louisiana Annals*, 158.

Newspapers

Alexandria *Louisiana Democrat*, 1867–1869
Attakapas (St. Martinville) *Sentinel*, 1874
Baton Rouge *Daily Capitolian-Advocate*, 1883
Baton Rouge *Tri-Weekly Gazette and Comet*, September–October, 1867
Baton Rouge *Weekly Advocate*, 1870
Black Republican (New Orleans), April–May, 1865
Bossier *Banner*, 1867–1871
Carroll *Conservative*, 1878–1879
Carroll *Record*, 1868–1869
Carroll *Republican*, April–October, 1873
Carroll *Watchman*, 1875–1876
Concordia *Eagle*, 1875–1876
Daily Picayune (New Orleans), 1862–1877
New Orleans *L'Union*, September, 1862–July, 1864
New Orleans *Louisianian*, December, 1870–June, 1882
Natchitoches *Vindicator*, 1875
New York *National Anti-Slavery Standard*, 1863, 1866–1868
New Orleans *Crescent*, 1867–1868
New Orleans *Daily Crusader*, 1890

New Orleans *Democrat*, December, 1875–April, 1877
New Orleans *Republican*, 1870–1877
New Orleans *Times*, 1867–1877
New Orleans *Times-Democrat*, 1883
New Orleans *Times-Picayune*, 1900
New Orleans *Tribune*, July, 1864–February, 1868, March 1870
New Orleans *Weekly Democrat*, October 5, 1878
New Orleans *Weekly Pelican*, 1886–1889
Opelousas *Courier*, 1868
Plaquemines *Protector*, 1887
Richland *Beacon*, January 1, 1876
St. James *Sentinel*, 1873–July, 1875
St. John the Baptist *Meschacebe*, 1868–1875
Thibodaux *Sentinel*, February, 1868–January, 1869
Vidalia *Weekly Herald*, 1870
Weekly Iberville South, 1868–1870

SECONDARY WORKS
Books

Allen, James S. *Reconstruction: The Battle for Democracy, 1865-1876*. New York: International Publishers, 1936
Benedict, Michael Les. *The Impeachment and Trial of Andrew Johnson*. New York: W. W. Norton and Co., 1973
Bennett, Lerone, Jr. *Black Power, U.S.A.: The Human Side of Reconstruction, 1867–1877*. Baltimore: Penguin Books, 1967.
Bragg, Jefferson D. *Louisiana in the Confederacy*. Baton Rouge: Louisiana State University Press, 1941.
Brown, Warren, comp. *Check List of Negro Newspapers in the United States, 1827–1946*. Jefferson City: Lincoln University School of Journalism, 1946.
Capers, Gerald M. *Occupied City: New Orleans Under the Federals, 1862–1865*. Lexington: University of Kentucky Press, 1965.
Carleton, Mark T. *Politics and Punishment: A History of the Louisiana Penal System*. Baton Rouge: Louisiana State University Press, 1971.
Carter, Hodding, *et al*, eds. *The Past as Prelude: New Orleans 1718–1968*. New Orleans: Tulane University Press, 1968.

Caskey, Willie M. *Secession and Restoration in Louisiana*. Baton Rouge: Louisiana State University Press, 1938.

Cornish, Dudley T. *The Sable Arm: Negro Troops in the Union Army, 1861–1865*. New York: W. W. Norton and Co., 1956.

Coulter, E. Merton. *The South During Reconstruction, 1865–1877*. Baton Rouge: Louisiana State University, 1947.

Cox, LaWanda and John H. *Politics, Principle, and Prejudice, 1865–1866: Dilemma of Reconstruction America*. New York: Macmillan Co., 1963.

Cruden, Robert. *The Negro in Reconstruction*. Englewood Cliffs, N.J.: Prentice-Hall, Inc. 1969.

Cunningham, Edward. *The Port Hudson Campaign, 1862–1863*. Baton Rouge: Louisiana State University Press, 1963.

DuBois, W. E. B. *Black Reconstruction in America, 1860–1880*. New York: Harcourt, Brace and Co., 1935.

Dunning, William A. *Reconstruction: Political and Economic, 1865–1877*. New York: Harper Brothers, 1907.

Ficklen, John R. *Reconstruction in Louisiana: Through 1868*. Gloucester, Mass.: Peter Smith Reprints, 1966.

Fleming, Walter L. *Louisiana State University, 1860–1896*. Baton Rouge: Louisiana State University Press, 1936.

Foote, Shelby. *Civil War: A Narrative, Fort Sumter to Perryville*. New York: Random House, 1958.

Franklin, John Hope. *Reconstruction: After the Civil War*. Chicago: The University of Chicago Press, 1961.

_____, ed. *Reminiscences of an Active Life: The Autobiography of John Roy Lynch*. Chicago: The University of Chicago Press, 1970.

Garner, James W. *Reconstruction in Mississippi*. New York: The Macmillan Co., 1901.

Hair, William Ivy. *Bourbonism and Agrarian Protest: Louisiana Politics, 1877–1900*. Baton Rouge: Louisiana State University, 1969.

Harrington, Fred P. *Fighting Politician, Major General N. P. Banks*. Philadelphia: University of Pennsylvania, 1948.

Haskins, James. *Pickney Benton Stewart Pinchback*. New York: Macmillan Co., 1973.

Hirshson, Stanley P. *Farewell to the Bloody Shirt: Northern Republicans and the Southern Negro, 1877–1893*. Chicago: Quadrangle Paperback, 1968.

Landry, Stuart O. *The Battle of Liberty Place: The Overthrow of Carpetbag Rule in New Orleans, September 14, 1876.* New Orleans: Pelican Publishing Company, 1955.

Logan, Rayford W. *The Betrayal of the Negro: From Rutherford B. Hayes to Woodrow Wilson.* London: Collier-Macmillan, Ltd., 1965.

Lonn, Ella. *Reconstruction in Louisiana (after 1868).* Gloucester, Mass.: Peter Smith Reprints, 1967.

Marchand, Sidney A. *The Story of Ascension Parish.* Donaldsonville: Sidney A. Marchand, 1931.

McConnell, Roland C. *Negro Troops of Louisiana: A History of the Battalion of Free Men of Color.* Baton Rouge: Louisiana State University Press, 1968.

McFeeley, William S. *Yankee Stepfather: General O. O. Howard and the Freedmen.* New York: W. W. Norton and Company, 1970.

McGinty, Garnie W. *Louisiana Redeemed: The Overthrow of Carpetbag Rule, 1876–1880.* New Orleans: Pelican Publishing Company, 1941.

McKitrick, Eric L. *Andrew Johnson and Reconstruction.* Chicago: University of Chicago Press, 1960.

McPherson, James M. *The Negro's Civil War: How American Negroes Felt and Acted During the War for the Union.* New York: Vintage Books, 1965.

Mosely, J. H. *Sixty Years in Congress and Twenty-Eight Out.* New York: Vantage Press, 1960.

O'Pry, Maude. *Chronicle of Shreveport.* Shreveport: Journal Printing Co., 1928.

Patrick, Rembert W. *The Reconstruction of the Nation.* New York: Oxford University Press, 1967.

Penn, I. Garland. *The Afro-American Press, and Its Editors.* Springfield, Mass., Willey and Co., 1891.

Perkins, A. E. *Who's Who in Colored Louisiana.* Baton Rouge: Douglas Loan Co., 1930.

Quarles, Benjamin. *Lincoln and the Negro.* New York: Oxford University Press, 1962.

_____. *The Negro in the Civil War.* Boston: Little, Brown, and Co., 1953.

Randall, James G., and David Donald. *The Civil War and Reconstruction.* Lexington, Mass.: D. C. Heath and Co., 1969.

Rousseve, Charles B. *The Negro in Louisiana: Aspects of His History and His Literature*. New Orleans: Xavier University Press, 1937.
_____. *The Negro in New Orleans*. New Orleans: Archives of Negro History, Inc., 1969.
Shugg, Roger W. *Origins of Class Struggle in Louisiana*. Baton Rouge: Louisiana State University, 1939.
Simmons, William J. *Men of Mark: Eminent, Progressive, and Rising*. Cleveland: Geo. M. Rewell and Co., 1887.
Smith, Samuel D. *The Negro in Congress, 1870–1901*. Chapel Hill: University of North Carolina Press, 1940.
Stampp, Kenneth M. *The Era of Reconstruction, 1865–1877*. New York: Alfred Knopf, 1965.
Stover, John F. *The Railroads of the South, 1865–1900. A Study in Finance and Control*. Chapel Hill: University of North Carolina Press, 1955.
Taylor, Joe Gray. *Louisiana Reconstructed, 1863–1877*. Baton Rouge: Louisiana State University Press, 1974.
Tinker, Edward L. *Creole City: Its Past and Its People*. New York: Longmans, Green and Co., 1953.
West, Jr., Richard S. *Lincoln's Scapegoat General: A Life of Benjamin F. Butler, 1818–1893*. Boston: Houghton Mifflin Co., 1965.
Wharton, Vernon L. *The Negro in Mississippi 1865–1890*. Chapel Hill: University of North Carolina Press, 1947.
White, Howard A. *The Freedmen's Bureau in Louisiana*. Baton Rouge: Louisiana State University Press, 1970.
Wiley, Bell I. *Southern Negroes, 1861–1865*. New Haven: Yale University Press, 1938.
Winter, John D. *Civil War in Louisiana*. Baton Rouge: Louisiana State University Press, 1963.
Williams, T. Harry. *Romance and Realism in Southern Politics*. Baton Rouge: Louisiana State University Press, 1966.
Woodward, C. Vann. *Reunion and Reaction: The Compromise of 1877 and the End of Reconstruction*. Boston: Little, Brown and Co., 1951.

Articles

Abbott, Martin, ed. "Reconstruction in Louisiana: Three Letters." *Louisiana History*, I (Spring, 1960), 153–57.

Alwes, Berthold C. "The History of the Louisiana State Lottery Company." *Louisiana Historical Quarterly*, XXVII (October, 1944), 964–1118.

Berry, Mary F. "Negro Troops in Blue and Gray: The Louisiana Native Guards, 1861–1863." *Louisiana History*, VIII (Spring, 1967), 165–90.

Binning, F. Wayne. "Carpetbaggers' Triumph: The Louisiana State Election of 1868." *Louisiana History*, XIV (Winter, 1973), 21–39.

Blassingame, John W. "The Selection of Officers and Non-Commissioned Officers of Negro Troops in the Union Army, 1863–1865," *Negro History Bulletin*, XXX (January, 1967), 8–11.

———. "The Union Army as an Educational Institution for Negroes, 1862–1865." *Journal of Negro Education*, XXXIV (Spring, 1965), 152–59.

Bone, Fanny Z. Lovell. "Louisiana in the Disputed Election of 1876." *Louisiana Historical Quarterly*, XIV (October, 1931), 549–66; XV (January, 1932), 93–116; XV (April, 1932), 234–65.

Calhoun, Robert D. "A History of Concordia Parish, Louisiana." *Louisiana and Historical Quarterly*, XVI (October, 1933), 598–607.

Carleton, Mark T. "The Politics of the Convict Lease System in Louisiana, 1868–1901." *Louisiana History*, VIII (Winter, 1967), 5–25.

Christian, Marcus B. "The Theory of the Poisoning of Oscar James Dunn." *Phylon*, VI (Third Quarter, 1945), 254–66.

Copeland, Fayette. "The New Orleans Press and Reconstruction." *Louisiana Historical Quarterly*, XXX (January, 1947), 149–387.

Cox, John and LaWanda, "General O. O. Howard and the 'Misrepresented Bureau.'" *The Journal of Southern History*, XIX (November, 1953), 427–56.

Davis, Donald W. "Ratification of the Constitution of 1868—Record of Votes." *Louisiana History*, VI (Summer, 1965), 301–305.

Dufour, Charles. "The Age of Warmoth." *Louisiana History*, VI (Fall, 1965), 335–64.

Dunbar-Nelson, Alice, "People of Color in Louisiana, Part II." *Journal of Negro History*, II (January, 1917), 54–78.

Everett, Donald E. "Ben Butler and the Louisiana Native Guards, 1861–1862." *Journal of Southern History*, XXIV (May, 1958), 202–17.

———. "Demand of the New Orleans Free Colored Population for Political Equality, 1862–1865." *Louisiana Historical Quarterly*, XXXVIII (April, 1955), 43–64.

Fischer, Roger A. "A Pioneer Protest: The New Orleans Street Car Controversy of 1867." *Journal of Negro History*, LIII (July, 1968), 227–32.

———. "Racial Segregation in Ante-Bellum New Orleans." *American Historical Review*, LXXXIV (February, 1969), 926–37.

Gonzales, John E. "William Pitt Kellogg, Reconstruction Governor of Louisiana." *Louisiana Historical Quarterly*, XXIX (April, 1946), 394–495.

Grosz, Agnes S. "The Political Career of Pickney Benton Stewart Pinchback." *Louisiana Historical Quarterly*, XXVII (April, 1944), 1–88.

Harris, Frances B. "Henry Clay Warmoth, Reconstruction Governor of Louisiana." *Louisiana Historical Quarterly*, XXX (April, 1947), 523–653.

Johnson, Manie W. "The Colfax Riot of April, 1873." *Louisiana Historical Quarterly*, XII (July, 1930), 391–427.

Johnson, Howard Palmer. "New Orleans Under General Butler." *Louisiana Historical Quarterly*, XXIV (April, 1941), 434–536.

Kunkel, Paul A. "Modifications in Louisiana Negro Legal Status under Louisiana Constitutions 1812–1957." *Journal of Negro History*, XLIV (January, 1959), 1–25.

Leach, Marguerite T. "The Aftermath of Reconstruction in Louisiana." *Louisiana Historical Quarterly*, XXXII (July, 1949), 631–717.

Lestage, Oscar H. "The White League in Louisiana and Its Participation in Reconstruction Riots." *Louisiana Historical Quarterly*, XVIII (July, 1935), 617–95.

Lewis, Elsie M. "The Political Mind of the Negro, 1865–1900." *Journal of Southern History*, XXI (May, 1955), 189–202.

Lowrey, Walter M. "The Political Career of James Madison Wells." *Louisiana Historical Quarterly*, XXXI (October, 1948), 995–1123.

May, J. Thomas. "The Freedmen's Bureau at the Local Level: A Study of a Louisiana Agent." *Louisiana History*, IX (Winter, 1968), 5–19.

Meier, August. "Negroes in the First and Second Reconstruction of the South." *Civil War History*, XIII (June, 1967), 114–30.

Menard, Edith. "John Willis Menard: First Negro Elected to the United States Congress, First Negro to speak in the U. S. Congress, a Documentary." *Negro History Bulletin*, XXVIII (December, 1964), 52–54.

Otten, James. "The Wheeler Adjustment in Louisiana: National Republicans Begin to Reappraise Their Reconstruction Policy." *Louisiana History*, XIII (Fall, 1972), 349–67.

Perkins, A. E. "Oscar James Dunn." *Phylon*, IV (Second Quarter, 1943), 105–21.

_____. "Some Negro Officers and Legislators in Louisiana." *Journal of Negro History*, XIV (October, 1929), 523–28.

_____. "J. Henri Burch and Oscar J. Dunn in Louisiana." *Journal of Negro History*, XXII (July, 1937), 321–34.

Pitre, Althea D. "Collapse of the Warmoth Regime, 1870–72." *Louisiana History*, VI (Spring, 1965), 161–87.

Porter, Betty. "Negro Education in Louisiana." *Louisiana Historical Quarterly*, XXV (July, 1942), 778–821.

Porter, George F., ed. "Documents." *Journal of Negro History*, VIII (January, 1923), 84–87.

Prichard, Walter, ed. "The Origins and Activities of the White League in New Orleans (Reminiscences of a Participant in the Movement)." *Louisiana Historical Quarterly*, XXIII (April, 1940), 525–43.

Rankin, David C. "The Origins of Black Leadership in New Orleans During Reconstruction." *Journal of Southern History*, XL (August, 1974), 417–40.

"Rebuilding the Waste Places After the War." *The Negro History Bulletin*, I (April, 1938), 3–4.

Renolds, Donald E. "The New Orleans Riot of 1866, Reconsidered." *Louisiana History*, V (Winter, 1964), 5–27.

Russ, William A., Jr. "Disfranchisement in Louisiana (1862–70)." *Louisiana Historical Quarterly*, XVIII (July, 1935), 557–80.

_____. "Registration and Disfranchisement Under Radical Reconstruction." *Mississippi Valley Historical Review*, XXI (September, 1934), 163–80.

Sewell, George. "Hon. P.B.S. Pinchback: Louisiana's Black Governor." *The Black Collegian*, IV (May–June, 1974), 8–10, 58.

Shewmaker, Kenneth E., and Andrew K. Prinz, eds. "A Yankee in

Louisiana: Selections from the Diary and Correspondence of Henry R. Gardner, 1862–1866." *Louisiana History*, V (Summer, 1964), 174–95.

Simpson, Amos E., and Vaughan Baker. "Michael Hahn: Steady Patriot." *Louisiana History*, XIII (Summer, 1972), 229–52.

Taylor, Joe Gray. "Slavery in Louisiana During the Civil War." *Louisiana History*, VIII (Winter, 1967), 27–33.

Tunnell, T. B., Jr. "The Negro, the Republican Party, and the Election of 1876 in Louisiana." *Louisiana History*, VII (Spring, 1966), 101–16.

Uzee, Philip. "The Beginning of the Louisiana Republican Party." *Louisiana History*, XII (Summer, 1971), 197–211.

Vincent, Charles. "Negro Leadership and Programs in the Louisiana Constitutional Convention of 1868." *Louisiana History*, X (Fall, 1969), 339–51.

––––––. "Louisiana's Black Legislators and Their Efforts to Pass a Blue Law During Reconstruction." *Journal of Black Studies*, VI (1976), forthcoming.

Weisberger, Bernard A. "The Carpetbagger: A Tale of Reconstruction." *American Heritage*, XXV (December, 1973), 70–77.

Webb, Allie B. W. "Organization and Activities of the Knights of the White Camellia in Louisiana, 1867–1869." *The Proceedings of the Louisiana Academy of Science*, XVII (March, 1954), 110–18.

Wesley, Charles. "The Employment of Negroes as Soldiers in the Confederate Army." *Journal of Negro History*, IV (July, 1919), 239–53.

Williams, Jr., E. Russ. "Louisiana's Public and Private Immigration Endeavors: 1866–1893." *Louisiana History*, XV (Spring, 1974), 153–73.

Williams, T. Harry. "An Analysis of Some Reconstruction Attitudes." *Journal of Southern History*, XII (November, 1946), 469–86.

––––––. "The Louisiana Unification Movement of 1873." *Journal of Southern History*, XI (August, 1945), 349–69.

––––––. "General Banks and the Radical Republicans in the Civil War." *New England Quarterly*, XII (June, 1939), 268–80.

Willey, Nathan. "Education of the Colored Population of Louisiana." *Harper's New Monthly Magazine*, XLIII (1866), 244–50.

Unpublished Theses and Dissertations

Beasley, Leon O. "A History of Education in Louisiana During the Reconstruction Period, 1862–1877." Ph.D. dissertation, Louisiana State University, 1957.

Binning, F. Wayne. "Henry Clay Warmoth and Louisiana Reconstruction." Ph.D. dissertation, University of North Carolina, 1969.

Blassingame, John. "A Social and Economic Study of the Negro in New Orleans, 1860–1880." Ph.D. dissertation, Yale University, 1971.

Campbell, Clara L. "The Political Life of Louisiana Negroes, 1865–1890." Ph.D. dissertation, Tulane University, 1971.

Everett, Donald C. "Free People of Color in New Orleans, 1803–1865." Ph.D. dissertation, Tulane University, 1952.

Fischer, Roger. "The Segregation Struggle in Louisiana, 1850–1890." Ph.D. dissertation, Tulane University, 1967.

Gertis, Louis Saxton. "From Contraband to Freedom: Federal Policy Toward Southern Blacks, 1861–1865." Ph.D. dissertation, University of Wisconsin, 1969.

Highsmith, William, "Louisiana During Reconstruction." Ph.D. dissertation, Louisiana State University, 1953.

Holt, Thomas. "The Emergence of Negro Political Leadership in South Carolina During Reconstruction." Ph.D. dissertation, Yale University, 1973.

Kohler, Hilda A. "A History of Public Education in Louisiana During Reconstruction." M. A. thesis, Louisiana State University, 1933.

Leavens, Patrick F. "*L'Union* and the New Orleans *Tribune* and Louisiana Reconstruction." M. A. thesis, Louisiana State University, 1966.

Luke, Josephine. "From Slavery to Freedom in Louisiana, 1862–1865." M.A. thesis, Tulane University, 1939.

McCrary, James P. "Moderation in a Revolutionary World: Lincoln and the Failure of Reconstruction in Louisiana." Ph.D. dissertation, Princeton University, 1972.

Marsala, Vincent J. C. "The Louisiana Unification Movement of 1873." M. A. thesis, Louisiana State University, 1962.

Mills, Wynona G. "James Govan Taliaferro (1798–1876): Louisiana

Unionist Scalawag." M. A. thesis, Louisiana State University, 1968.

Reed, Germaine. "David Boyd: Southern Educator." Ph.D. dissertation, Louisiana State University, 1970.

Tunnell, Teddy B., Jr. "Henry Clay Warmoth and the Politics of Coalition." M. A. thesis, North Texas State University, 1966.

Uzee, Philip D. "Republican Politics in Louisiana, 1877–1900." Ph.D. dissertation, Louisiana State University, 1950.

Vincent, Charles. "Negro Political Leadership in Louisiana, 1862–1870." M. A. thesis, Louisiana State University, 1968.

Webb, Allie B. "A History of Negro Voting in Louisiana, 1877–1906." Ph.D. dissertation, Louisiana State University, 1962.

Williams, Ernest Russ, Jr. "The Florida Parish Ellises and Louisiana Politics, 1820–1918." Ph.D. dissertation, University of Southern Mississippi, 1969.

Windham, Allie B. "Methods and Mechanisms Used to Restore White Supremacy in Louisiana, 1872–1876." M. A. thesis, Louisiana State University, 1948.

Interviews

A. P. Tureaud. Summer, 1970, New Orleans.

C. C. Dejoie, Jr. February 23, 1973, August 27, 1974, New Orleans.

Lillian B. Dunn, November 2, December 7, 1972, February 23, 1973, August 8, 1974, New Orleans.

Index

Adolphe, Curron, 72, 83, 119
African-French, 52, 72
Africans, 11, 102
Alcorn, James L., 166
Alexander, Frank, 72, 86, 107
Alexandria, La., 11, 57, 67, 74, 127, 130, 131, 183, 192
Algiers, La., 200, 203
Allain, Theophile T.: background of, 143, 144; committee assignments of, 155; and taxpayer relief bill, 159, 193, 198; mentioned, 148, 167, 170, 177, 194, 201, 204, 207, 209, 210
Anderson, Thomas C., 215
Anthony, Henry B., 166
Antoine, Arthur, 148, 173
Antoine, C. C.: and Convention of Colored Men of Louisiana, 33, 34, 49, 50, and *n*, 51, 61; committee assignments of, 85; educational efforts of, 92; mentioned, xiii, 7, 14*n*, 36*n*, 72, 110, 117, 139, 145, 150, 185, 214, 216
Antoine, Felix C., xiii, 14*n*, 83, 119, 123, 124, 125, 126, 129*n*, 135*n*, 186*n*
Appropriation, 158, 160, 172, 179, 197
Arkansas, 57, 119, 131, 217
Armistead, J. W., 147
Arroyo, Oscar, 215*n*
Ascension Parish, 74, 100, 111, 144, 148, 197
Assumption Parish, 56, 75, 98, 100, 111, 121, 132, 190, 191, 198, 200, 217
Asylum for the Deaf and Blind, 179

Banks, Nathaniel P.: replaces Butler, 10; inaugurates education system, 11, 12, 13; dismisses black officers, 13, 14, 14*n*, 17; campaigns against Confederates, 19; receives petition from blacks, 21; at the gubernatorial election of 1864, 22; permits segregated streetcars, 23; is criticized at Economy Hall, 35, 36 and *n*; replaced by General Hurlbut, 37; educational system of, 88, 89
Barber, A. E.: early life of, 132; committee assignments of, 124; urges civil rights bill, 126, 127, 166; mentioned, 32, 33, 34, 42*n*, 121, 130, 149, 154, 157, 159, 160, 164, 170, 173, 181
Barrett, William, xiii, 8, 32, 119, 126
Baton Rouge City Council, 178*n*
Baton Rouge, La., 7, 30, 33, 56, 115, 118, 120, 139, 160, 167, 178, 179, 185, 198, 204, 214
Battalion of Free Men of Color, 1
Bayou Goula, La., 191
Beauregard, P. T. G., 167
Belot, Armand, 119
Belot, Octave, 72, 83, 84, 86, 119, 120*n*
Benjamin, Judah P., 77
Bentley, Emerson, 126*n*
Bernard Parish, 30, 182*n*
Bertonneau, Arnold, 22*n*, 34, 41, 64
Bill of Rights, 61
Blackburn, W. J., 69
Black codes, xiv, 24, 66
Black leaguers, 184
Blacks: as troops, 8, 35; registration of, 40
Blacks, Free: serve in U.S. Army, 5; population of, 16; and former slaves, 17; and franchise, 22; mentioned, 1, 2, 9, 20, 21, 38. *See also* New Orleans *Tribune*
Blandin, Ovide C., 55, 60*n*
Blunt, Raiford: background of, 116; elected to Senate, 149; committee assignments of, 154, 207; legislative ac-

255